MW01717472

Growing Sustainable Communities

A Development Guide for Southeast Asia

Linda Brennan, Lukas Parker, Torgeir Aleti Watne, John Fien, Duong Trong Hue and Mai Anh Doan
Editors

Growing Sustainable Communities: A Development Guide for Southeast Asia
First edition, Second printing

Editors
Linda Brennan, Lukas Parker, Torgeir Aleti Watne, John Fien, Duong Trong Hue and Mai Anh Doan

Cover designer
Christopher Besley, Besley Design.

ISBN: 978-0-7346-1081-2 (print)
ISBN: 978-0-7346-2058-3 (ePDF)

Published by:
Tilde Publishing and Distribution
PO Box 72
Prahran VIC 3181 Australia
www.tilde.com.au

TUP-GrowingSustainableCommunities-Brennan-1e2p

Contents

Preface

All of Southeast Asia can benefit from this practical, resourceful, and inspirational approach to influencing sustainable behaviors. It is practical as it provides specific and concrete actions that benefit the individual, the community and the environment. It is resourceful as it includes a variety of success stories that illustrate "what works and what doesn't". And it is inspirational as it recognizes that "people are the nexus of the sustainability 'problem' and the catalyst for the solution".

Nancy Lee (MBA)
Founder and President
Social Marketing Services, Inc

About the editors

Professor Linda Brennan

Professor Linda Brennan is from the School of Media and Communication at RMIT University in Melbourne. Her research interests are social and government marketing and, especially, the influence of marketing communications and advertising on behaviour.

Dr Lukas Parker

Dr Lukas Parker is Assistant Professor in the Centre of Commerce & Management at RMIT University Vietnam. He lectures in communication and advertising to undergraduate students, and supervises postgraduate research students. His research interests are in social marketing and marketing communications.

Dr Torgeir Aleti Watne

Dr Torgeir Aleti Watne is a lecturer in Marketing at Victoria University in Melbourne, Australia. Torgeir teaches marketing subjects to postgraduate and undergraduate students, and supervises postgraduate research students. His research interests are consumer socialisation, with a specific focus on how consumers learn new behaviour and pass it on to others.

Professor John Fien

Professor John Fien is Executive Director of Swinburne Leadership Institute at Swinburne University of Technology, Melbourne. His research interests include strategies for enhancing personal and community resilience and adaptive capacity in the face of natural hazards and climate change, especially in the Asia-pacific region.

Duong Trong Hue

Duong Trong Hue is a lecturer in the Centre of Communication and Design at RMIT University Vietnam. He teaches communication and contextual courses to undergraduate students. His research interests are in health communication and communication strategies in the non-profit sector.

Mai Anh Doan

Mai Anh Doan is a senior lecturer in the Centre of Communication and Design at RMIT University Vietnam. She lectures in public relations and managing communication businesses, and facilitates industry engagement. Her research interests are in public relations and financial communication.

About the contributors

Dr Iftekhar Ahmed

Dr Iftekhar Ahmed [BArch (Hons), IIT India, MSArchS (MIT), PhD (Oxford)] is a Research Fellow of Sustainable Housing Systems in School of Architecture & Design at RMIT University Melbourne, Australia. Dr Ahmed's research focuses on post-disaster housing reconstruction. Some of the key research aspects include sustainable housing systems, humanitarian architecture, disaster risk reduction, and climate change adaptive built environments.

Ruth Bottomley

Ruth Bottomley has a Masters degree in the Anthropology of Development and Social Transformation from the University of Sussex, UK. She has been living in Cambodia and Southeast Asia for the last twenty years, working in community development and landmine action.

Christian Byczek

Christian Byczek holds an MA in Southeast Asian Studies and is working on community-based ecotourism development and sustainability practices in the tourism and hospitality industry in Southeast Asia.

Dr Esther Charlesworth

Dr Esther Charlesworth [BArch (Hons) RMIT, MAUD (Harvard), DPhil (York)] is an Associate Professor in the School of Architecture & Deisgn at RMIT University, Melbourne, Australia and the Founding Director of Architects Without Frontiers. Her interests are in design for communities in need, sustainable development, international development, and remote Indigenous housing.

Alin Chintraruck

Alin Chintraruck is a doctoral candidate at the School of Management, Shinawatra University. She is also a Planning and Policy Analyst, Head of International Relations Unit, Department of Groundwater Resources, Ministry of Natural Resources and Environment. Alin's research interests are on prospects for integrated water resources management in Thailand.

Dr Jerome Donovan

Dr Jerome Donovan is a lecturer in International Business at Swinburne University of Technology, Melbourne, Australia. His research interests include foreign direct investment, economic development, innovation, and firm internationalization.

Jessie K Fly

Jessie K Fly is an environmental anthropologist with research experience in Vietnam, Uganda, and the Southern Appalachians, concerning the relationship between environmental and social vulnerability. Jessie is Assistant Professor of Anthropology at Eckerd College in St Petersburg, Florida.

Nicholas J Goodwin

Nicholas J Goodwin is the director of Goodwin Collaboration, and a PhD Candidate at the University of Sydney, and Research Scholar at the George Washington University. Nicholas works in communications, marketing, community development, and capacity building with government, private sector, university, non-profit, and multi-lateral organizations throughout the Asia Pacific, the Americas, and Africa.

Patrice Lamballe

Patrice Lamballe is a French Agronomist working for Gret (French NGO), a Research and Technological Exchange Group. Patrice has been working for 22 years in Southeast Asia (Vietnam and Cambodia) in action research for agricultural development (for example civil society organizations, cropping systems, animal husbandry, agroforestry, bamboo value chain).

Dr Áron Perényi

Dr Áron Perényi is a Hungarian lecturer in International Business at Swinburne University of Technology, Melbourne, Australia. Áron's research interests are economic development and small business life-cycles.

Dr Josephine Previte

Dr Jo Previte is a lecturer in Marketing at the University of Queensland in Brisbane, Australia. Her research interests are the area of social marketing and particular the use of social media in social marketing situations. She is currently working on developing a responsible drinking social marketing strategy.

Istvan Rado

Istvan Rado is a member of the 'International Political Ecology' research group and PhD candidate in the Department of Political Science at the University of Vienna, Austria. His main research interests are in alternative development conceptions, including Buddhist Economics, Post-development, and related community-based approaches.

Vorada Savengseuksa

Vorada Savengseuksa is a Masters in Public Administration (MPA) Candidate at the Evans School of Public Affairs in Seattle, Washington. Her current focuses are on NGO management and leadership, capacity building in the public sector, and health disparities in Southeast Asia.

Dr Hong Anh Vu

Dr Hong Anh Vu received her PhD in 2012 from the Department of Anthropology at Syracuse University. Her dissertation research in a coastal province of Vietnam's Mekong Delta focused on the impact of globalization and neoliberal policies on rural livelihoods, particularly as a result of intensified shrimp aquaculture. Her future projects will be exploring the impact of continuing changing land rights on women, poor and marginalized people in the delta and their implications on local climate change adaptation ability.

Dr John Walsh

Dr John Walsh is an Assistant Professor at the School of Management, Shinawatra University, Director of the SIU Research Centre, and Editor of the SIU Journal of Management. John attained his PhD from the University of Oxford in 1997. His research interests focus on social and economic development of the Mekong Region.

Dr Anthony Ware

Dr Anthony Ware is a lecturer in International Development at Deakin University. Anthony was based in Southeast Asia for almost 10 years during the 1990s and 2000s. His research primarily examines the Myanmar socio-political context and its impact on international development assistance policies and approaches. Anthony also works as an adviser to the board and voluntary project manager for Graceworks Myanmar.

Dr Andrew Wells-Dang

Dr Andrew Wells-Dang currently works for Oxfam in Vietnam. He holds a PhD from the University of Birmingham, UK and is the author of *Civil Society Networks in China and Vietnam.*

Giang Wells-Dang

Giang Wells-Dang is a native of Hanoi and director of Action for the City since 2006. She has an MA in Sociology from the Catholic University of America (2002).

Liza Wood

Liza Wood is a graduate from the College of Charleston whose research interests are ecology and food systems. Her research is based on immersion in environmentally vulnerable communities of northeast Thailand.

Acknowledgements

The completion of any book is a task that requires input and talent from many people. We would like to thank the following people without whom this work would not have made it to the publisher.

Firstly, there are the authors who contributed to this book and who persevered though a sometimes arduous review and revision process. Their ability to collaborate across the virtual and physical boundaries that makes an international book has been a model of cooperation.

Secondly are the many anonymous reviewers who understood the importance of providing formative advice to sometimes new authors. In the extensive review process they managed to see their way through some academic flaws to make the practical chapters come to life as theoretically relevant practice. In the process, they helped to create some much needed and practically relevant theory.

Thirdly, there are the people at Tilde University Press who from the very first stage of putting this together understood the need for a regionally relevant and readily available and accessibly priced book. Their supportive encouragement throughout the project has made it what it is.

Finally, there are the many supporters who have helped with various stages of production. The foremost of these is Ms Dang Nguyen who began her life as a scholar on the whirlwind that became this book. We would also like to thank Mr Hau Pham for his cheerful assistance in the final editing process and RMIT University for providing the training for these exceptional professional communicators.

The editorial team:

Linda Brennan
Lukas Parker
Torgeir Aleti Watne
John Fien
Duong Trong Hue
Mai Anh Doan

Introduction

Southeast Asia is undergoing a major transformation both economically and socially. This transformation has been largely through the initiatives of villages, communities and governments grappling with challenges using locally available resources and the best of traditional skills and external advice. International aid and development funding, for example from the Asian Development Bank (ADB), the World Bank, Australian, Japanese and Korean development agencies and many national and international NGOs, is responsible for much of the innovation in sustainable community development in the region. However, such developments are a challenge for the region with some organizations withdrawing from long-term projects because they have reached the point at which further efforts are not required. This is not to say that the role of these organisations is complete, far from it. There is much work to do yet.

In recent times there has been a shift of development efforts towards a more holistic approach combining poverty alleviation, empowerment and environmental actions at a grass roots community level as well as at a more policy driven and macro level. These shifts have yet to leave their legacy of change. The development efforts are building on several long-term projects over many years to establish sustainable practices within the countries that are at the greatest risk from climate change. Climate change brings with it the risks of greater severity and frequency of storms and subsequent flooding, food and water security risks, and hotter or colder weather patterns affecting capacity to continue existing patterns of farming and thereby threatening subsistence in already vulnerable populations. There are commensurate risks to bio-diversity and food-producing systems such as the oceans are being depleted by over fishing and chemical pollution. Deforestation is also an issue with a decreasing capacity to produce oxygen as the Southeast Asian forests are cut down to 'fuel' unsustainable levels of economic growth.

However, this book does not aim to contribute to the doomsayers. While there are a myriad of issues, there are also many sustainable development efforts being channelled across thousands of projects scattered throughout Southeast Asia, this book aims to provide a realistic account of what 'works' and what 'doesn't work' in the Southeast Asian context. We hope that this book will provide a useful resource to bring together existing findings from current and completed projects that can be used as case studies for future projects and to also educate up-and-coming community development practitioners in Southeast Asia.

The purpose of this book is to present a practical, yet academically sound, manual for community development practitioners, NGOs and community groups undertaking projects related to developing sustainable lifestyles in Southeast Asia. The handbook looks at the existing knowledge of what activities have already been undertaken in Southeast Asia, reviewing case studies of successful projects with an aim to summarise these into a set of clear 'key learnings'. In turn, these will be translated into a clearly organised set of guidelines for future projects in Southeast Asia.

The book is organised in four parts: Part I: Challenges and Opportunities for Change; Part II: Strategies for Change; Part III: Praxis – case studies – demonstrated success stories where multi-dimensional sustainability has been achieved by the communities of practice in the Southeast Asian countries; and Part IV: Conclusion: Ways forward for sustainable practice and key learnings from the book.

Part I: Challenges and Opportunities for Change

In Part I, through the contributors' chapters, we outline the importance of understanding society, the environment and economies in Southeast Asia. Southeast Asia consists of sovereign nations with a common economic organisation: the Association of Southeast Asian Nations (ASEAN). Although the size of the landmass is less than half of Europe, the size of the total population is comparable, with more than 600 million people living in the region. Southeast Asian nations have a diverse climate and geography, relatively close relationships to each other, a shared history, and yet they have immensely different languages, customs, religions and cultures. Its diversity is both a challenge and an opportunity for change. There are nations that can be exemplars for economic growth and sustainability, and nations which are aspiring to greater things for themselves at the same time as making headway when it comes to environmental issues.

The region consists of modern nations with growing economies and rapid industrialisation within many of the countries. Rapid economic growth and industrialisation can sometimes pose threats to the environment without a plan for sustainable development. For community development practitioners interested in developing sustainable lifestyles in Southeast Asia, it is therefore important to understand the environmental and economic challenges the region faces as well as understanding the cultural traditions, barriers and facilitators of change. The aim of this section is to provide insight into challenges and opportunities for change in the region as well as advance understanding of the culture and traditions.

Chapter 1, The sustainable communities challenge in Southeast Asia, by John Fien and Linda Brennan, provides an overview of a region where for thousands of years human societies have proved that living sustainably — as healthy and happy individuals, within caring and stable families and communities, and in harmony with the natural world — is possible. This long-term sustainability of economic and cultural systems is the result of indigenous and other local systems of socialization and learning that established a human and natural ecology at one with each other. The hope of this book is that the learnings from the regions' ancient sustainable practices can be known to a wider audience.

Chapter 2, Economic development and sustainability in South-East Asia: Potential for international coordination and the civil society, by Áron Perényi and Jerome Donovan, is a comparative analysis of the ASEAN region presented to identify issues, existing cooperation and potential for civil society contribution to economic development and sustainability. Analysis is conducted using data on the Millennium Development Goals. Existing regional cooperation is reviewed based on relevant ASEAN agreements. It is found that civil society in the region has a potentially diverse role across the different countries.

Chapter 3, Aquaculture and debt: Undermining sustainability in the Mekong Delta, by Jessie K Fly and Hong Anh Vu, looks at shrimp aquaculture. Shrimp aquaculture was introduced in many Southeast Asian countries as an income-diversifying enterprise. Based on data collected using a variety of ethnographic methods and long-term participant observation in the Mekong Delta, Vietnam, the research reveals that the most common outcome of shrimp farming – mounting debt – actually constrains households' options for making a living.

The Vietnamese family is changing and so may be the way they make mid-to-high involvement consumer decisions. Chapter 4, Consumer socialisation agency in Vietnam: Understanding family decisions in relation to sustainable consumption, by Torgeir Aleti Watne, Linda Brennan and Lukas Parker, investigages how traditional three-generational Vietnamese families living in the same household communicate about consumption decisions relating to environmentally friendly household products, including uncovering how family members learn from each other. The findings show that each of the generations may have a role to play in these decisions albeit in different ways.

Part II: Strategies for Change

Part II presents some success stories in terms of strategies that have lead to positive outcomes. Strategies can be broadly understood as the planning of a course of action to meet one's objectives based on their available resources. The formation of strategies is necessary for negotiation, development and implementation of field activities. This process is particularly relevant to non-government organizations (NGOs) due to their organizational missions and institutional nature which require them to maximize the outcomes based on scant mobilized resources. The understanding of Southeast Asia, including its history, culture, modernity and related sustainable development issues, is described in Part II. This section offers a great opportunity for policy makers and development practitioners, notably NGOs, to roll up their sleeves carrying out strategic planning to provide immediate and effective responses to communities in need.

NGOs and INGOs generally occupy an ambiguous position in terms of sustainable development. They are not 'embedded' within the governance and policy structures of the country, nor are they 'empowered' to undertake independent activities. Notwithstanding that, some of the strategies presented in this section offer exciting potential to design sustainable activities across sectors and the region. Along with the public and private sectors, the role of I/NGOs in developing sustainable communities has been influential in developing civil societies that have at the core of their values a respect for community and often display a deep, sometimes spiritual connection with the land.

Furthermore the strategies presented in this section demonstrate the ability to influence sustainable social change and also illustrate some mechanisms used by the authors to help balance policy negotiations among stakeholders in socio-economic areas. Such achievements would be impossible without 'institutional' strategies. This section highlights the development and effective functioning of strategies implemented by different I/NGOs active in Southeast Asia to fulfil their social role by examining a number of sustainable development projects in various social settings. However, the significance of the discussion presented in the following chapters goes beyond the introduction of theoretical models underpinning strategies by offering important implications drawn from experience, both successful and unsuccessful lesson learned, which we believe important to working in the region.

Chapter 5, Integrated water resources management in Thailand and Southeast Asia, by John Walsh and Alin Chintraruck, looks at water-related issues in the region. Water resource management in Thailand is characterized by competition for scarce resources between industry, the tourist sector and public citizens, in a country in which environmental degradation and erratic climatic patterns are making the controlled flow of water increasingly difficult. To overcome this, a new water management approach is emerging which is fraught with pragmatic compromise and the postponement or avoidance of power relations issues. This situation is relevant to other Southeast Asian nations, both in terms of geographical and climatic pressures on water resources and also in terms of competing interests in conditions of constrained democracy.

In a time of rapid change and globalization, the Lao PDR (hereinafter referred to as Laos) stands in a unique position in the world of development. Chapter 6, Developing a framework for improved leadership in the Lao PDR for sustainable development, by Vorada Savengseuksa, examines INGOs as non-state actors in Laos who aim to contribute to the public service sector through a variety of projects. Country directors and program managers from seven INGO entities shared their insights on their thoughts of organizational success, sustainability, and leadership as it relates to working within the political context of Laos. We hope a discussion of these themes will support the development of a strategic framework that supports in-country leadership and capacity building for INGOs.

Chapter 7, Supporting development of local enterprises, bamboo forests, sustainable livelihoods and civil society organizations in the mountainous region of Thanh Hoa province, Vietnam, by Patrice Lamballe, is set in Thanh Hoa in Northwest Vietnam, bordering Laos. The region is a mountainous region and is home to ethnic minorities (90 percent Thai and Muong minorities). The region remains one of the poorest regions in the country. This chapter describes the region's strategies to develop social and environmentally sustainable enterprises and describes efforts to establish a sustainable bamboo industry.

Chapter 8, Sowing sustainability: Rice commodity pathways, NGOs, and farmers' engagement with alternative agriculture in Northeastern Thailand, by Liza Wood, deals with the vital topic of rice. Rice is the cornerstone for much of Thailand's agricultural development. However, moving from subsistence farming to commercial agriculture has greatly altered its role in the country's northeast region. Particularly, the Green Revolution impacted farmers' livelihoods, environment, health, and culture. Farmers in non-governmental organizations base their rice variety choices primarily on factors of price and marketability. This market-based motivation is critical for NGOs to consider, particularly on balance with their larger goals of environmental and cultural sustainability.

Highly participatory and community-led approaches to development have previously been shown to be effective forms of poverty mitigation and community empowerment. Chapter 9, Asset-based community development in Myanmar: Theory, fit and practice, by Anthony Ware, explores the applicability and effectiveness of the most highly participatory and community-led approach to development, Asset Based Community Development (ABCD) in Myanmar both theoretically and in practice.

The process for developing effective partnerships across sectoral boundaries is an important component of many social change programs. Chapter 10, Perspectives on multi-sector social partnerships for social change, by Josephine Previte, overviews the rationale and processes for establishing social partnerships and how they contribute to sustainable communities. The chapter provides a framework for partnership formation and guidelines on managing partnership relationships that consider the balance of power between collaborators and how power imbalances impact social change outcomes in Southeast Asia.

Part III: Praxis (Case Studies)

This part provides examples of sustainable 'good' practice within the Southeast Asian context. The case studies cover a range of activities and contribute examples of approaches that have been demonstrated to be successful. The NGO and INGOs included here have long standing involvement within the region and are therefore contributing significant wisdom to the readers of this book.

The case studies illustrate how the combined challenges of environmental, social and financial sustainability are being met. The cases include a consideration of the conditions that prevail within their respective countries and provide meaningful examples of how to create practices that work in the given context.

Each of the organisations presented in this section have had to develop practices that are cross-sectoral and to develop strategies are, of necessity, stakeholder focussed. Stakeholders in this section range from governments to tiny rural communities. Each of these groups have been dealt with in quite different ways and there are some lessons to be learned in how sustainability can be fostered at a macro, meso and micro level; although probably not all at the same time! Some significant outcomes in terms of both public policy and community practice have been achieved by the people who have contributed to this section.

One of the biggest issues facing Southeast Asia is that of rapidly developing urbanization. Cities are increasingly crowded and pollution of all types is increasing in severity and toxicity. However, the case studies in this section provide some insight into how these challenges are being tackled within the countries and by the contributing organizations. The rapidly developing urban community takes precedence in many Southeast Asian countries but there is still a significant population of rural and regional peoples, often of ethnic minorities. Three of these case studies are based in regional areas and are illustrative of 'grassroots' sustainable practices.

Each of the case studies is unique in terms of what it aims to demonstrate. However, one of the overarching themes is that of collaboration and cooperation between the various stakeholders who contribute, participate in and benefit from the practices. These collaborations between industry, government and non government organizations illustrate the myriad of possibilities that are available.

Chapter 11, Sustainable change marketing: An approach to development and communications programs in Indonesia and beyond, by Nicholas Goodwin, looks at Indonesia's Fantastic Mom health project. The issue is communications and sustainability. The approach uses the Sustainable Change Marketing (SCHEMA) model. Findings include success in changing behaviors but failure to engage authorities, implying participation is vital. The originality is using SCHEMA, providing a management guide as value.

Chapter 12, Sustainable Lifestyles in Vietnamese Cities, by Giang Wells-Dang and Andrew Wells-Dang, looks at urbanization. Rapid urbanization in Vietnam poses multiple risks to environmentally sustainable development. The innovative Green Living program of Action for the City, a Hanoi-based NGO, seeks to change environmental behaviors at the neighborhood and ward levels. Their experiences demonstrate the possibility of citizen action to find cooperative solutions to urban problems.

Chapter 13, Sustainable community development in Northeastern Thailand: The Inpaeng, by Istvan Rado, discusses the activities of Inpaeng, a farmers' network in Northeastern Thailand committed to empower farming households through a mix of homegrown strengths and acquired know-how. Based on on-site findings as well as secondary data the chapter demonstrates innovative strategies to maintain economic, social, and environmental sustainability in the region. The example of Inpaeng moreover shows that the initiative of farmers themselves and their engagement in an ongoing learning process are crucial factors for the long-term success of community development projects.

Chapter 14, Disaster risk reduction for sustainable development: The case study of Development Workshop France (DWF), Vietnam, by Iftekhar Ahmed and Esther Charlesworth, is about Development Workshop France's (DWF) work in disaster-prone central Vietnam. Local interviews allowed understanding DWF's efforts for building resilient housing with key stakeholders, highlighting that communities cannot be sustainable without safe housing. Generalisable lessons for agencies in

Southeast Asia are thereby offered about building sustainable communities by reducing disaster risk.

Oxfam Australia has worked in Cambodian villages for almost 20 years, delivering integrated community development that aimed to meet basic livelihood needs while encouraging community ownership and self-reliance. In the face of rapid economic development, this work could be undermined as communities are negatively impacted by economic concessions or major infrastructure projects. Chapter 15, Capacity, sustainability and accountability in the face of modern development: Lessons from Oxfam Australia's development model in Cambodia, by Ruth Bottomley, is based on qualitative research in two villages. It considers how well the Oxfam Australia approach has assisted villagers to become engaged as citizens in shaping and defining their own development and demanding accountability from government officials.

Tourism development has created substantial sustainability challenges for Bali in Indonesia. Chapter 16, Cultural traditions, sustainable livelihoods and community-based ecotourism: Alternative development paths for tourism on Bali, by Christian Byczek, shows that community-based ecotourism initiative, Jaringan Ekowisata Desa, promoting traditional ecological knowledge and resource management practices can empower local communities with the ability to help mitigate effects of a rapid shift from an agriculture-based economy to a service-based economy.

Chapter 17, Personal hygiene, environmental sanitation: A case of social marketing in the Mekong Delta, by Lukas Parker, presents a case of using social marketing to improve personal hygiene and environmental sanitation within schools throughout the Mekong Delta in southern Vietnam. The campaign incorporated appeals to the social benefits of good hygiene behaviour alongside a conventional health education campaign. The Cuu Long Rural Water Supply and Sanitation Project was demonstrably successful in improving these behaviours, which can lead to a reduction in incidences of waterborne disease. Recommendations are made for how to ensure sustainable outcomes for similar projects.

Part I

Challenges and Opportunities for Change

Chapter 1

The sustainable communities challenge in Southeast Asia

JOHN FIEN AND LINDA BRENNAN

ABSTRACT

This chapter provides an overview of a region where for thousands of years human societies have proved that living sustainably — as healthy and happy individuals, within caring and stable families and communities, and in harmony with the natural world — is possible. This long-term sustainability of economic and cultural systems is the result of indigenous and other local systems of socialization and learning that established a human and natural ecology at one with each other. The hope of this book is that the learnings from the regions' ancient sustainable practices can be known to a wider audience.

Background

For thousands of years human societies have proved that living sustainably — as healthy and happy individuals, within caring and stable families and communities, and in harmony with the natural world — is possible. This long-term sustainability of economic and cultural systems is the result of indigenous and other local systems of socialization and learning that established a human and natural ecology at one with each other. Unfortunately, local knowledge and wisdom have been undermined by the experience of colonisation, industrialisation and globalisation. By and large, local priorities and systems of social ecology have been supplanted by the somewhat narrow view that the environment and culture are valuable only in so far as they are economically productive. The consequent disregard for the land and culture has meant that knowledge, values and skills for living sustainability have been underplayed in contemporary ways of living.

The wider Asia-Pacific region covers a quarter of the world's total land area and extends from Mongolia in the north to Tonga in the south, Japan in the east to Afghanistan in the west. It contains nearly forty countries, of which seven are in South Asia, five in North-East Asia, fifteen in the Pacific and Oceania, and eleven in Southeast Asia: Brunei Darussalam, Cambodia, Indonesia, Lao People's Democratic Republic, Malaysia, Myanmar, Philippines, Singapore, Thailand, Timor-Leste, and Vietnam. The case studies in this book are drawn from these eleven (see Table 1.1), but the lessons, when appropriately contextualized, are of relevance across the wider region because the socio-economic forces that are driving unsustainable development and the human capacity to live a better life, and to learn and change, are the same worldwide.

The wider Asia-Pacific region is home to more than sixty percent of the world's population but over 40 percent of the region's population is concentrated into five countries: China, India, Pakistan and Bangladesh, and Indonesia in Southeast Asia. The economy and the livelihoods of most people in the region are predominantly rural but urbanisation has been so rapid in recent years that the region also contains fifteen of the twenty-five cities in the world with over 10 million people - and thirteen of the fifteen most polluted cities in the world. Indeed, the movement of people from the countryside to cities is a particularly important challenge across the growing Asian economies, where rapid urbanization is the key driver for economic growth and poverty alleviation. With the peri-urban areas of these cities rapidly expanding, Asia is now home to almost half of all urbanites on Earth and its urban population is more than three times that of Europe, the world region with the second largest urban population (Asian Development Bank 2012: xxxvii).

Asia-Pacific is a region of great cultural, economic and environmental diversity. This is reflected in the description of the region in UNESCO's 50th anniversary commemoration publication on the region which described it in the following way:

Table 1.1a Environmental overview

Factor	Brunei	Myanmar	Cambodia	Indonesia	Laos	Malaysia
Population (000s)	406	61,000	14,953	249,000	6,587	29,180
Population growth rate (%)	1.70	1.07	1.69	1.03	1.66	1.54
Arable land proportion (%)	2.80	14.92	20.44	11.03	4.01	5.46
Government	Sultanate	Parliamentary government	Multiparty democracy with constitutional monarchy	Republic	Socialist republic	Federation of constitutional sultanates
Primary source of external income	Natural resource extraction	Agriculture, gems	Textiles, forestry	Natural resource extraction, forestry, textiles, appliance manufacturing	Natural resource extraction, forestry,	Natural resource extraction, forestry, textiles, appliance manufacturing, chemical, palm oil
GDP growth rate percentage (2012)	2.70	6.20	6.50	6.00	8.30	4.40
GDP per capita (PPP) ($US)	$50,000	$1,400	$2,400	$5,000	$3,000	$16,900
Literacy levels (%)	92	89.9	73.6	90.4	73	88.7
Proportion of population in tertiary education (%)	20	15	14	23	18	40
Proportion with access to sanitation (%)	Not available	81	29	52	53	96
Quality of air and pollution (CO2 omissions per capita)	23.6	0.3	0.4	1.8	0.3	7.6
Rate of deforestation	-0.47	-0.95	-1.22	-0.71	-0.49	-0.42

Table 1.1b Environmental overview

Factor	Philippines	Singapore	Timor Leste	Thailand	Vietnam
Population (000s)	103,775	5,354	1,444	67,091	91,520
Population growth rate (%)	1.90	1.99	2.50	0.54	1.05
Arable land proportion (%)	19.00	1.47	8.20	27.54	20.14
Government	Republic	Republic	Republic	Constitutional monarchy	Socialist republic
Primary source of external income	Electronic equipment, textiles, coconut oil, fruit, petroleum	Machinery, banking, shipping and transport	Oil, coffee, sandalwood	Textiles & footwear, fishery products, rice, rubber,	Agriculture, industry, garments & textiles
GDP growth rate percentage (2012)	4.80	2.10	10.00	5.60	5.10
GDP per capita (PPP) ($US)	$4,300	$60,900	$9,500	$10,000	$3,500
Literacy levels (%)	92.6	92.5	58.6	92.6	94
Proportion of population in tertiary education (%)	28	n/a	17	48	22
Proportion with access to sanitation (%)	76.00	100.00	50.00	96.00	75.00
Quality of air and pollution (CO2 omissions per capita)	0.8	6.39	0.2	4.2	1.65
Rate of deforestation	0.73	0	-1.44	0.08	1.08

> *From the world's highest city, Lhasa ... to the world deepest lake...; from the highest mountain to the deepest seas; from the driest deserts to the dampest forests; the Asia-Pacific region covers an outstanding array of geography and culture.*
>
> *The region is one of sharp contrasts. It has two of the world's most populous countries, China and India, and some of the world's smallest countries, Nauru in the Pacific and the Maldives in the Indian Ocean. It has one of the world's richest countries, Japan, and [some of] the world's poorest, Cambodia and Bangladesh.*
>
> *With over 700 languages in Papua New Guinea alone, the region's ethnic and linguistic diversity is greater than anywhere else in the world. Great cultures have left legacies such as the Great Wall of China - 2350 kilometres long - ... and the legendary temples of Borobudur in Indonesia. A wealth of religions crisscross the region, ranging from Buddhism, Hinduism, Christianity, Islam and Sikhism, to other faiths such as Confucianism, Jainism and Taoism (UNESCO-PROAP, 1996).*

The countries of Southeast Asia are a microcosm of both this geographic and cultural, social and economic diversity – and sadly too, of deteriorating socio-ecological conditions.

The state of the planet and the lives of the people who call it home have been exhaustively documented by such bodies as the United Nations Development Programme, the United Nations Environment Program, the World Bank, the World Resources Institute, and the World Wide Fund for Nature. A synthesis of these reports was recently prepared by the Stockholm Environment Institute, whose researchers identified nine planetary boundaries, which they argue delineate a safe living or operating space for humanity. According to their analysis, three boundaries - climate change, disruption of global cycles and, most notably, loss of biodiversity, have already been crossed.

This is not news to people in Asia, where state of the environment reports paint a generally bleak picture of a descending spiral of unsustainable development. For example, a WWF-ADB report, *Ecological Footprint and Investment in Natural Capital in Asia and the Pacific* (2012), reported that:

> *In the past two decades, the state of ecosystems in Asia and the Pacific has been declining. Conversion of primary forests to agricultural land or monoculture plantations has resulted in a marked decrease in so called "old growth" forests that are more biologically diverse. Old growth forests and other types of ecosystems provide essential services such as carbon storage and clean water. Extensive coastal development and unsustainable exploitation of marine resources have resulted in the destruction of many major coastal habitats, including corals, mangroves, seagrasses, wetlands and salt marshes. Freshwater ecosystems have been converted for agricultural use and polluted with agricultural and urban waste, and their natural flow has been disrupted by water storage for agriculture, domestic use and hydropower. This has resulted in lower agricultural yields, declining*

> *freshwater fish stocks, and reduced access to clean drinking water (pp. 10, 12).*

The social and economic costs of environmental degradation in the region are very high, with the descending spiral of environmental decline and lost social and economic opportunities reflected in the diverse patterns of living conditions, health and well-being. Despite being home to some of the world's largest and fastest growing economies, the region is also one of great poverty. The acute impacts of the 1997 and 2008 economic crises in the region are evidence of the precarious nature of the last three decades of development efforts. Thus, the region is home to over two-thirds of the world's poor and an equal percentage lack basic literacy. Population numbers have doubled over the past forty years and are still on the increase, and the environmental and social effects of such numbers are taking their toll. By 2040, the population of the Asia-Pacific region is expected to have more than doubled to four billion people for whom food requirements will have doubled and the need for water and sanitation quadrupled. The consumption of energy and manufactured goods will increase fivefold, while pollution may increase up to tenfold (Asian Development Bank 2012).

The situation in Southeast Asia is particularly acute, with major problems of biodiversity loss in forest and wetland systems, the over-fishing of river and marine systems, air and water pollution, disrupted river flows brought about by big dams and hydroelectric projects, and the increasing intensity and frequency of floods, typhoons, and heat stress from climate change (ASEAN 2002, p. 28). Summing up the inter-relatedness of these issues, the Asian Development Bank notes that:

- Southeast Asia is one of the world's most vulnerable regions to the impact of climate change because of its long coastlines and tropical climate.
- Despite being one of the world's fastest growing regions, it faces the challenges of poverty - with the poor the most vulnerable to climate change impacts.
- Agriculture provides nearly half of all employment but the increasing demand for food and other crops has intensified agricultural production and competition for land and water resources, generating considerable environmental pressure.
- Much of the region's growth is dependent on natural resources, particularly forestry, mining and fishing, which puts considerable pressure on the environment and ecosystems.
- Urbanization rates in Southeast Asia are among the fastest in the world and mostly in coastal areas—with about 80 percent of the population living within 100 kilometers of the coast—leading to an over-concentration of economic activity and livelihoods in coastal megacities, where they are most prone to coastal typhoons and flooding.

(Asian Development Bank, 2009)

Such extensive problems are the result of the changed patterns of economic activities in the region, especially the widening and intensifying of commercialisation of agriculture, forestry and fishing, urbanisation and the movement of low-cost, highly polluting manufacturing plants into the region from OECD countries. The resultant demographic and cultural changes - coupled with less than ideal governance and policy frameworks - have led to a lack of capacity to use natural resources sustainably.

Given the scale of these problems and their roots in economic modernization, it is not surprising that improving environmental quality and redressing poverty are often seen as technical problems to be managed by professional economists, engineers, planners and other experts. However, when the forces of unsustainable development are catalysed by the same experts, it is similarly not surprising that scientific and economic expertise is not the whole answer to the problem. Thus, there have been numerous calls for a democratisation of the process of working towards local sustainability through a wide range of community development, education and capacity building programs. For example, Clover, Jayme, Follen and Hall (2012) argue that 'The production and distribution of ecological knowledge and the learning of new skills and methods … [are now] crucial to the survival of the planet' (p.7). The participatory, community-based approaches they recommend reflect the root causes of environmental decline in unsustainable social, economic and political priorities and that these root causes can only be effectively addressed through social and cultural change. Accordingly, they have identified eight features of effective community sustainability projects, such as those represented in this book:

1. They address the root causes of problems not their outward manifestations or symptoms.
2. They make links between environmental issues and social concerns.
3. They often recognise the power of nature as a setting for learning and action and for stimulating deep appreciations of home and place.
4. They begin from people's experiences, feelings and contexts.
5. They draw on people's own potential to find solutions to their own problems.
6. They emphasise an analysis of power relations.
7. They promote skills in taking concrete actions.
8. They encourage reflection and personal and collective evaluation.

(Clover, Jayme, Follen & Hall, 2012, p. 2)

The case studies in this book illustrate the many different ways in these principles are being applied in Southeast Asia. To clarify and give life to these principles, the next section of this chapter provides a brief case study of the experiences of the residents of a Tambon Administrative Organisation (TAO), or local government district council, in Thailand in applying these principles to some of the problems they face as a community.[1]

The case study focuses on a two-day workshop in which community members identified these problems and then developed agreed action plans for addressing them. Another, and longer term, aim of the workshop was to enhance the processes of local governance in the TAO by developing knowledge and skills for local environmental protection. The case study is presented in three sections. An analysis of the local and national contexts that influence life in the community is provided in the first. This is followed by a description of the workshop processes and outcomes. The final section analyses how the principles of sustainable community problem-solving that were used in the workshop contributed to its success.

Participatory community problem-solving in rural Thailand

A TAO is a local government district of ten to fifteen thousand people in rural Thailand. A TAO usually contains six to twelve *muban* or villages and the farm and forest lands between them. The TAO is a relatively new level of governance in Thailand and, until their formation in 1994, all administrative decisions were made at the national and provincial level. Thus, the establishment of TAOs is a reflection of the increasing democratisation of Thai society. This is not only a timely development for political rights; it is also timely in terms of environmental and health issues. The breakdown in traditional muban leadership that has followed economic modernization, together with the increased mobility of the population, has also caused a breakdown of the traditional systems of mutual obligation and community work through which appropriate strategies for hygiene, waste management, flood control and water and food security were ensured. The resultant demand for an enhanced approach to local governance and environmental management was made all the more urgent by the increases in traffic, industrial pollution, waste levels and demand for water brought by modernization over recent decades.

These issues are faced by all TAOs in some form or another. This case study took place in La-Ngu TAO in the far southwest of peninsula Thailand on the Andaman Sea. In close proximity to the Malaysian border, over 80 percent of the population is Muslim. The people live on small holdings, little more than a few hectares in size, growing kitchen supplies of vegetables, fruit, herbs, spices and eggs, and cash crops of fruit, coconuts, palm and/or rubber. A large number also make a living by fishing from two to three person open boats. However, fish stocks are being so badly depleted by commercial drift net trawlers, mostly owned by families and companies in Bangkok, that three protest blockades of local ports have been mounted in the region in the previous year. National and provincial governments have provided a social infrastructure of telecommunications and

[1] The case study is summarised from a report by one of the authors (Fien *et al.*, 2002).

major and minor roads. Indeed, mobile phones, motorcycles and small pick-up trucks abound. Clinics and schools are provided for all at minimal cost, and there are district hospitals and a provincial university in the city of Hat Yai, which is two hours distance by road. A rainforest and marine national park, called Mu Ko Phetra, is located within the borders of the TAO. This is controlled by the National Royal Ministry of Forests which officially also owns much of the surrounding land on which the fishing and farming families live. As a result, land title is often insecure and the possibility of being dispossessed for an expansion of the national park or sale of local land to an agribusiness or industrial concern is a strong disincentive to sustainable agriculture and participation in local governance.

It was a recognition of problems such as these that led the La-Ngu TAO to establish a participatory planning process. This followed attendance at a regional training course on environmental management by a small number of TAO representatives. This course was organised by the Faculty of Environmental Science at Prince of Songkla University. Many participants at this course requested the assistance of university staff to initiate environmental management projects in their TAOs. The La-Ngu workshop was the result of one of these requests.

The workshop was facilitated by university staff and held over two days in an open-sided traditional-style meeting place built on stilts above the waters on the shore of the national park. Just over fifty people from the TAO attended, including elected representatives from each muban, teachers, religious leaders, and some headquarters staff of the forest fire service. About a quarter were women. A wide range of participatory techniques were used, including group discussion, brain storming, nominal group technique, flip chart summaries, problem-solving and a visit to a nearby waste dumping site (when it emerged that this was one of the issues of greatest concern).

The workshop progressed through a number of phases:

- short, but formal introductory speeches;
- personal and muban introductions;
- brainstorming a list of problems in the TAO - with 'problem' being defined as 'something that could be changed to make life better';
- identification of concrete examples of these problems - where? how serious?;
- categorization of problems into three groups: physical problems, social context problems, and problems that exist because of a breakdown of management or enforcement systems;
- clarification and prioritization of problems in these three groups (see Table 1.2);
- small group and plenary discussion of the top one or two problems in each group;
- selection of one problem for detailed analysis, and development of possible solutions;

- discussion and evaluation of proposed solutions; and
- making an action plan to address the problem.

Table 1.2 Groupings and rankings of major problems in La-Ngu TAO after using the nominal group technique

Problem category	Problems	Points
Physical problems	1. Waste	23
	2. Water supply for drinking, using and agriculture	14
	3. Landscape and air pollution	11
	4. Transportation, road	8
	5. Encroachment of public properties	6
	6. Flood	4
	7. Coastal erosion/corrosion	3
	Total	**69**
Social/surrounding problems	1. Drugs	32
	2. Disco operation among the local leaders	15
	3. Rights for using land	11
	4. Lack of taking care of the culture	7
	5. Lack of act by religious rule	3
	Total	**68**
Management problems	1. Lack of environmental awareness education	17
	2. Religious conflict	15
	3. Forest damage	14
	4. Environmental health	13
	5. Database information error	4
	6. Noise pollution	3
	7. Agricultural price decrease	1
	Total	**67**

The major problems that were identified included: a recent increase in drug taking, waste management, security of water supplies for drinking and agricultural purposes, and a lack of education for environmental awareness. The problem that the workshop participants chose to address in detail was waste management, especially in relation to a rubbish tip that was so ill-managed that toxins from domestic, hospital and industrial waste were infiltrating the water table and making their way from there into canals and the river upon which the TAO depends. Of particular concern was the fact that the tip was for rubbish from a neighbouring TAO. The outcome of the workshop was the beginning of a TAO-agreed plan for rehabilitating the site, seeking a provincial grant to buy back the site, regular water quality testing, and so on.

The relative success of the workshop - as seen in the enthusiastic participation, the spirit of cooperation and good will, and the fact that so much was achieved in only two days - was a reflection of the practice of a number of principles of sustainable community development. These relate to aspects of: (i) the preparation for the workshop, (ii) the holistic view of environment that was taken, (iii) the setting, (iv) the facilitation style, (v) the experiential learning model that was followed, (vi) respect for local knowledge, and (vii) the action orientation.

Preparation for the workshop

The workshop arose from needs in the TAO community and was actively sought by them. Thus, it was not imposed by local leaders, a higher level of government, the university staff, or the project staff, all factors that would have undermined local ownership and responsibility for the workshop outcomes and the participatory process itself. The university staff involved adopted the view that they were facilitators of a process. Their preparation consisted of negotiating the process with TAO leaders, familiarising themselves with local issues, and preparing flip charts and writing materials to support the group work.

A holistic view of environment

The wide ranging membership or multi-sectoral nature of the workshop group meant that a diverse range of social, economic, cultural, political and biophysical issues was discussed. This ensured that a holistic view of environment and sustainability (although the word was rarely used) was taken. Indeed, such holism is characteristic of Thai Buddhist and Muslim society. Thus, issues of environment and health, nutrition, local culture, family livelihoods, economic changes, and human rights and political reforms were seen as inextricably related. This view of the environment meant that root causes and not just symptoms of problems were analysed and addressed, and the participants could feel empowered by being able to 'name' the causes of their concerns, have their often unvoiced suspicions vindicated, and act collectively to find a lasting solution.

The setting

One of the key elements of sustainable community development is contact with nature. This is often lost in urban communities where people live at a remove from Earth, and is especially so in the North where common reductionist ways of thinking compartmentalise nature and culture, facts and values, and so on. In La-Ngu TAO, people live close to the land and the sea, both economically and spiritually, and this aspect of their society was a dominant aspect of the workshop due to the setting that was chosen. The workshop was held in a small meeting place set on stilts above the water on the edge of the marine national park. Thus, the meeting was held in a familiar local location. This gave the participants a sense of ownership of the proceedings and the honour of hosting guests from the outside. The design of the meeting place reflected local architectural and building traditions with the roof constructed of woven leaves, only waist-high side walls, and no (glass) windows between the walls and the roof. This enabled the workshop to be held 'in nature' with all senses engaged through the view of the sea on three sides and the rainforest on the fourth, the smell and taste of the sea and salty air, the sound of water beneath the floor, and the feel of sea breezes on the skin - and the darkening sky and wind-blown rain as early monsoon showers arrived (and drenched flip-charts) providing reminders, as if they were needed, of the cycles of the earth, the sea and the sky.

Thai traditions were practised, e.g. all shoes were removed before stepping onto the floor of the meeting place, and the meeting was opened quite formally by a representative from the national government. Muslim traditions were also followed with many women wearing long dresses and head scarves and sitting separately for the men for the formal opening. A two hour lunch break was provided on the first day of the workshop as it was a Friday, and religious duties needed to be observed by many participants.

The facilitation style

The facilitators were steeped in the traditions of community development and public participation. Their approach was based on questioning not telling, setting group tasks, facilitating group reporting and debriefing activities, summarising almost every point that was said on flip charts, and relaying questions from participants back to the group before giving their own answers. It was a team effort with three facilitators rotating sessions and moving around groups during group activities. An air of openness to suggestions, procedural flexibility and lots of humour ensured that they had the support and confidence of the participants.

An experiential learning model

The sequence of workshop activities was structured to reflect the four phases of the experiential learning cycle (experience, reflection, generalisation and application) at both the macro-level of the two day workshop process and the micro level of individual activities. For example, at the macro-level, the workshop activities were structured as follows:

Experience	▪ Brainstorming issues of concern in the TAO
Reflecting on experience	▪ Clarifying the nature of the problems ▪ Discussing their impacts
Generalising from experience	▪ Categorising and prioritising the problems ▪ Assessing their root causes
Application	▪ Agreeing on one key problem to work on ▪ Developing an action

Many of the activities that were part of the overall programme were structured to follow these four phases of experiential learning. An overview of the activity that was used to prioritise the problems illustrates this. The concrete experience was the use of the nominal group technique to develop a consensus view of the most significant problems in the TAO. The reflection phase that followed involved small group and plenary accounts of the concrete ways the participants experienced the major problems and how they felt about the way their individual and family lives were affected. Generalization from these experiences involved mini-lectures (3-5 minutes each) and flip-chart summaries by university facilitators in which they outlined the regional, national and, sometimes, global nature and manifestations of the problems. During the application phase of this activity, the facilitators asked questions to explore how the participants felt about learning that their problems are shared by many other communities and that their causes often go beyond local influences. They also discussed what this meant about the type of problems they can address at the local level from their own resources compared to problems that require wider coalitions of action to resolve. This process helped to maintain a focus on action throughout the two days even though action planning was not undertaken until the second afternoon.

Respect for local knowledge

The academic expertise of the facilitators allowed them to provide case studies to clarify and exemplify the problems being discussed by the workshop participants and to help place these problems in their regional and national economic and political contexts. As university professors they had access to knowledge that the TAO members, many of whom had only a few years of elementary education, could not have. However, the facilitators were judicious in the timing and depth of the information inputs they provided and always did so only after issues and questions were raised by the group. Thus, while the workshop was an educational one, and the participants seemed to learn many things, it could not be said that they were 'taught' these things or that they 'gained new' knowledge. Rather, the workshop process showed intense respect for the knowledge that the participants collectively owned and that was endemic to life in the TAO. Thus, instead of knowledge being 'taught', the process of knowledge production and distribution in the workshop meant that knowledge was 'shared', 'respected', 'collected', 'clarified', 'contextualized', 'extended', 'organised', 'evaluated' and 'applied'. This respect for, and encouragement of, local knowledge provided the foundation for community empowerment. Thus, the opportunity to give voice to tacit, intuitive and experiential knowledge helped build self- and group-esteem, confidence, and a sense that 'we' can solve many of our own problems, and that the resources to do so reside in local, but often now neglected, traditions and collective resources.

An action orientation

The purpose of the workshop was to develop an action plan to address key local problems. Thus, there was an action orientation at all times. As explained in the earlier account of the nominal group activity, the application phase of the experiential learning cycle that was used in all the workshop activities created a focus on action even before the action planning began. This focus was also supported by the processes of empowerment that resulted from local knowledge.

Local skills for problem identification, scoping and clarification were enhanced in the two days of the workshop. However, two days were not sufficient for a detailed action plan to be developed. Instead, only ideas for action were developed. However, being local farmers and fishers, the workshop participants had families, boats and fields to tend to, and being quite poor, even giving two days to the workshop was a significant financial sacrifice. Thus, the workshop ended with a plan for three TAO leaders to meet the university staff the following week in order to obtain technical information on waste management and water testing and to develop strategies for getting provincial government support and resources to close, relocate and rehabilitate the rubbish tip site.

This book

The participatory workshop in La-Ngu TAO illustrates the value of sustainable community planning as a strategy for building civic capacity for local governance and sustainability in rural Thailand. It is possible that it may be applicable in urban areas of Thailand and in other national settings. And it is only one strategy for facilitating local sustainability. This book provides examples of many more of these. But, in common, all demonstrate a focus on the principles of sustainable community planning used in La-Ngu TAO.

Thus, as you read the chapters that follow, please reflect on the ways in which the following principles are used:

1. Addressing the root causes of problems not their outward manifestations or symptoms.
2. Making links between environmental issues and social concerns.
3. Recognizing the power of nature as a setting for learning and action and for stimulating deep appreciations of home and place.
4. Beginning from people's experiences, feelings and contexts.
5. Drawing on people's own potential to find solutions to their own problems.
6. Emphasising an analysis of power relations.
7. Promoting skills in taking concrete actions.
8. Encouraging reflection and personal and collective evaluation.

References

ASEAN (2002) *ASEAN Report to the World Summit on Sustainable Development*. Jakarta: ASEAN.

Asian Development Bank (ADB) (2009) *The Economics of Climate Change in Southeast Asia: A Regional Review*. Manila: ADB.

Asian Development Bank (ADB) (2012) *Key Indicators for Asia and the Pacific 2012*. Manila: ADB.

Asian Development Bank and World Wide Fund for Nature (2012) *Ecological Footprint and Investment in Natural Capital in Asia and the Pacific*. Manila: ADB.

Clover, D., Jayme, O., Follen, S. & Hall, B. (2012) *The Nature of Transformation: Environmental Adult Education*, 3rd edition, Sense Publishers, Rotterdam.

Fien, J., Chatchai, R., Umaporn, M. & Rapeepun,S. (2002) Participatory planning as environmental adult education for enhancing local governance at the Tambon Administrative Organisation level in Thailand. *Journal of Applied Environmental Education and Communication*, 1(4), 255-262.

Rockström, J. and 29 others. (2009) A safe operating space for humanity. *Nature*, 461, 472–475.

UNESCO-PROAP (1996) *Celebrating Diversity, Cultivating Development, Creating Our Future Together: UNESCO in Asia and the Pacific.* Bangkok: UNESCO.

Chapter 2

Economic development and sustainability in Southeast Asia

Potential for international coordination and the civil society

Áron Perényi & Jerome Donovan

Abstract

A comparative analysis of the ASEAN region is presented to identify issues, existing cooperation and potential for civil society contribution to economic development and sustainability. Analysis is conducted using data on the Millennium Development Goals. Existing regional cooperation is reviewed based on relevant ASEAN agreements. It is found that civil society in the region has a potentially diverse role across the different countries.

Introduction

Sustainability for emerging economies is an important item on the agenda of global economic development. The Bruntland Report of the United Nations (World Commission on Environment and Development, 1987) already emphasised the essential nature of sustainability several decades ago. The development divide highlighted between the rich and the poor has remained a crucial issue, and with the 2015 target rapidly approaching for achieving the Millennium Development Goals (MDG), the international community is confronted by a range of challenges for how to accelerate development in the poorest countries around the world. This is particularly the case of Southeast Asia, where a distinct development divide is evident between rapidly industrialising economies and least developed countries (LDC, including Laos, Myanmar, Vietnam and Cambodia). As progress is increasingly being made towards the 2015 and 2020 targets of regional economic integration, the development gap between these countries is becoming even more visible. Civil society has the potential to play a substantive role in establishing the framework for facilitating this process.

Concepts and issues of economic development and sustainability

Three broad areas of sustainability were re-iterated at the World Summit on Sustainable Development held in Johannesburg in 2002 – economic, social and environmental dimensions (von Schirnding, 2005). These areas are closely interlinked aspects of the same phenomenon, and there is a scholarly consensus on the holistic and inclusive identification of factors in relation to sustainability and development (Grabowski, Self & Shields, 2006; Griffin, 1999; Nafziger, 2012; Roy, Blomqvist & Clark, 2012; Todaro & Smith, 2009). A range of different development factors have been identified across the environmental (pollution, biodiversity, urbanisation and urban congestion), societal (health, education and skills, poverty, welfare, governance, transparency, democracy, corruption, legal systems and property rights) and economic (bottlenecks in development such as technology, savings and investment, or the 'dual economy', economic openness, economic growth, population growth, resource access) dimensions. Questions remain as to the best model for achieving sustainable development, due to the breadth of issues to consider.

Industrialisation in Western countries was aided by social and ideological change (such as protestant ethics, enlightenment and liberalism) which laid the ground rules for modern capitalism. However, there have been several other successful developmental models, such as the ones implemented in Japan, South Korea and Taiwan. Moreover, the development models of economic giants such as the previous Soviet Union, or India and China cannot be disregarded (Nafziger, 2012). These models contextualise development within the region, not only the accounting for their geographical proximity, but also a shared cultural and historical heritage.

Japan's case was the first successful example of state-led economic development in the broader (Asia Pacific) region. Japan embarked on a centralised effort of modernisation in 1868, called the Meiji reforms. The government assisted entrepreneurs, fostered the development of education and emphasised openness to the world looking to rapidly industrialise following western oriented models of industrial transformation (Nafziger, 2012). The success stories of South Korea and Taiwan, on the other hand, are that of systematic government intervention, combined with gradual economic openness and liberalisation. In both countries the government aggressively developed infrastructure and increased exports through autonomously managed state owned enterprises, while also providing directed tax-incentives for private businesses (Nafziger, 2012). In South Korea, this development program was facilitated by the government-Chaebol cooperation (Todaro & Smith, 2009). Taiwan had its policies focussing on science and technology, and the dissemination of knowledge in the economy (Nafziger, 2012). Under the nurturing guidance of government policies, a healthy and merit based private sector evolved.

India and China – following the development philosophy of the previous Soviet Union – emphasised the development of the heavy industries. In India, under the leadership of Nehru and Mahalanobis, the objective was a fixed proportion of investment to go into capital goods. This approach, however, resulted in progress far below expectations. For similar reasons, China also abandoned the Soviet development model of overly focussing on heavy industries, and found a much more effective way of fostering development by balancing between sectors, capital and consumer goods (Nafziger, 2012). However, China's relative success was not only due to finding a controlled balance, but also the intensive effort of developing its human capital with education programmes and investment into the next generations (Todaro & Smith, 2009).

These examples highlight the broader implications of development models and agendas. *Social development* needs to progress hand-in-hand with economic development. In fact, economic and social developments mutually reinforce each other, because human capital accumulation has been proven to be significantly linked with *economic development*. Institutions facilitating social and economic development are thus essential to progress. Political freedom and liberties, transparency and good governance, a strong and well-functioning legal framework and lack of corruption all contribute to development. Security of property rights, the situation of political elites and history of western political domination have also been demonstrated to have a far-reaching impact on development (Nafziger, 2012). Indeed, extant literature has pointed to how having a colonial heritage can have a strong negative effect on countries' development in Latin America (Bruhn & Gallego, 2012) and Africa (Lumumba-Kasongo, 2011; Mkandawire, 2011) and with the substantive colonial heritage of Southeast Asian countries, this can also be expected to be the case. Whitfield (2012) also emphasises the role of a holistic view of understanding economic development, and in particular the pivotal role of agriculture in the development of Southeast Asian countries. These observations are underpinned by empirical evidence from several countries of the region, such as Malaysia (Ibrahim, Basir & Rahman, 2011), Laos (Phimphanthavong, 2012), Thailand, Vietnam (Whitfield, 2012) and Singapore (Roy, Blomqvist & Clark, 2012).

The third – *environmental* – aspect of sustainability in development is also emphasised, although in somewhat different contexts (Rangarajan *et al.*, 2012). For example, environmentally sustainable rural development is suggested as the path to follow in Sri Lanka (Daskon & McGregor, 2012), but also mentioned in relation to agriculture, economic development and reform in Laos (Phimphanthavong, 2012).

These dimensions of sustainability in development highlight the various areas in which action needs to be taken to foster and support economic development in the countries of Southeast Asia. The review of experiences shows that developmental models in the region, impacted upon by their (British, Dutch, French) colonial heritage, should be approached in the context of continuous social and economic reform, as well as economic, social and environmental aspects of development. Hence it can be argued, that – like China, South Korea and Taiwan – these countries are also still searching for a development model that suits their heritage and needs. This provides a wide potential space for NGOs and other alternate facilitators of sustainable development.

A road map for a sustainable future

In order to be able to design development models for the countries of Southeast Asia, targets need to be considered. This section aims to estimate, develop and quantify such developmental targets, based on objectives currently laid out by international organisations (such as the United Nations Millennium Development goals), global thinkers (e.g. scholars, such as Professor Hans Rosling), and other global benchmarks displayed (such as 'the World average' or the 'developed West').

Text box 1

Professor Hans Rosling – Is Southeast Asia really stuck below the 'airline' for the next 40 years?

As the popular public lecture of Professor Rosling shows in his speech titled 'The magic washing machine'[1], mankind currently has two major dividing lines: the 'wash line' and the 'airline'. The 'wash line' isolates the poorest living on less than $40 a day suggesting they cannot even access what the rest of the world would consider as basic necessities. Those of them living at less than $2 a day have no access to any of industrialisations' wonders, and live in poverty (the poverty line). About half the amount of people live above the 'airline' (approximately $80 a day) suggesting that their lifestyle is truly at a global standard, and can even choose their locations freely (in other words can fly wherever they want to). As human development indicators suggest, much of Southeast Asia's fast growing population is still under the wash line, a substantial amount of them below the poverty line. In forty years' time, substantial population growth is expected below the poverty line, while the rest of mankind will be pre-occupied with improving their lifestyles crossing the wash line and the airline, moving up. Hence it is of paramount importance to address both major global changes, and ensure availability of a modern, clean, healthy and productive life of all mankind in a way, that utilises Earth's limited resources in an efficient and sustainable way.

[1] *See www.ted.com/talks/hans_rosling_and_the_magic_washing_machine.html.*

It can be argued that the complex nature of sustainable economic development requires a multidimensional view for identifying areas of improvement. Such a view composed for particularly reflecting the developmental needs of the least developed countries is shown by the Millennium Development Goals (UNDP 2011). Many of the indicators in this model are related to the very basics of human development, and are highly relevant to the least developed and developing countries of Southeast Asia. It is through this complex, multidimensional lens, that the development gap of Southeast Asian countries is analysed.

Explanation of the development gap for Southeast Asia

We seek to more thoroughly examine the sustainable development context within the region, with a specific focus on comparing the development divide evident between the industrialised, more highly developed countries and the developing

Text box 2

Professor Hans Rosling – Is Southeast Asia really stuck below the 'airline' for the next 40 years?

As the popular public lecture of Professor Rosling shows in his speech titled 'The magic washing machine'[1], mankind currently has two major dividing wash line and the airline, moving up. Hence it is of paramount importance to address both major global changes, and ensure availability of a modern, clean, healthy and productive life of all mankind in a way, that utilises Earth's limited resources in an efficient and sustainable way.

"We can end poverty in our lifetime..." – it is the thought that drives many of the world's politicians, societal activists and community groups. The five simple objectives declared by the United Nations 2000 (UN, 2000) are: peace, development, poverty eradication, environment protection, human rights, democracy and protecting the vulnerable. These have been later transformed into the eight Millennium Development Goals, which are meant to track economic, social and environmental development of disadvantaged communities around the world. Particular regions' performances are regularly monitored and reported upon along these indicators in the Millennium Development Reports (UNDP, 2012). The United Nations has set objectives around these dimensions to be achieved by 2015. In order to facilitate achievement of these objectives, the UNDP (2010) recommends:

1. supporting country-led development and effective governance;
2. fostering inclusive and pro-poor economic growth;
3. increasing public investments in education, health, water, sanitation and infrastructure;
4. scaling up targeted interventions, including social protection and employment programmes;
5. investing in expanded opportunities for women and girls and advancing their economic, legal and political empowerment;
6. enhancing access to energy and promoting low-carbon development;
7. accelerating domestic resource mobilization to finance the MDGs;
8. ensuring the global partnership creates an enabling environment for the MDGs, particularly delivering on ODA commitments.

(UNDP, 2010, p. vi.)

countries of the region. This is contextualised using seven of the key Millennium Development Goals. These Millennium Development Goals provide a cross-section of important development related indices that relate most broadly to the sustainable development dimensions identified in the discussion above. This section now turns to examining the performance of the countries within Southeast Asia, identifying the developmental issues evident across these three dimensions.

Poverty eradication and employment

The eradication of extreme hunger and poverty remains a central objective within the Millennium Development Goals. And while impressive achievements are evident internationally, with the number of people in extreme poverty reducing by over 100 million in a matter of three years between 2005 and 2008 (UNDP, 2012), poverty levels remain significant within the least developed countries of Southeast Asia. Looking more closely, a disjuncture is noticeable between the more developed countries - Brunei, Singapore and Malaysia - and the less developed or developing countries - ranging from Thailand to Laos (see Table 2.1). These figures represent a significant challenge for the region, particularly as it moves towards the ASEAN Economic Community. Furthermore, the increasing connectedness between the countries within the region will potentially open new opportunities for poverty stricken populations to move to more prosperous positions.

Table 2.1 Poverty, unemployment rates and GDP per capita purchasing power parity (PPP) for ASEAN

Country	Proportion of population below $1 (PPP) per day (2008)	Unemployment (2011)	GDP per capita (PPP) (2011)
Brunei Darussalam	0	2.7% (2010)	$49,500
Singapore	0	2%	$59,700
Malaysia	0	3.10%	$16,200
Thailand	0.4	0.70%	$9,400
Vietnam	16.9	3.60%	$3,400
The Philippines	18.4 (2009)	7%	$4,100
Indonesia	22.6	6.60%	$4,700
Cambodia	22.8	3.5% (2007)	$2,200
Myanmar	32.7 (2007)	5.50%	$1,300
Laos	33.9	2.5% (2009)	$2,800

Source: ADB (2012); World Bank Group (2012b); CIA (2012).

An examination of the unemployment rates illustrates the ongoing struggle some of the larger developing countries have within the region. In particular, the Philippines, Indonesia and Myanmar all have unemployment rates over five percent. Beyond the poverty rates and unemployment across the region, it is evident when examining GDP per capita purchasing power parity (PPP), just what a challenge the region has in accelerating development progress of the poorer nations, and bridging the development divide evident. With the vast majority of the region, including the majority of the most populace countries on less than $5,000 GDP per capita (PPP), and a substantial gap with the more wealthy countries of Singapore and Brunei, the region clearly needs to focus on accelerating employment opportunities for many of the poorer workers residing within the least developed countries.

Achieve universal primary education

Access to primary education is the second key Millennium Development Goal. This includes both enrolment, as well as completion of primary schooling (UNDP, 2012). Internationally, the objective of having both boys and girls complete their entire primary education has encountered many issues, particularly in the post-2004 period, whereby progress has slowed dramatically. In Southeast Asia, overall enrolment figures have seen some dramatic increases from their levels in 1990 (see Table 2.2). This has particularly been in the case with some of the least developed countries, including Cambodia and Laos, which have both seen increases of approximately 30 percent in overall enrolment for primary education. However, there have also been some decreases in the overall level of primary education for

Myanmar and the Philippines. The Philippines in particular has seen a decrease of almost ten percent.

Table 2.2 School enrolment and completion for ASEAN

Country	School enrolment, net primary, total		Pupils starting Grade 1 who reach last grade of primary (%)
	1990	2010	2008
Brunei Darussalam	89.7	96.9 (2009)	96.2 (2007)
Cambodia	66.6	95.9	54.5 (2007)
Indonesia	96.7	99.1	80 (2007)
Laos	62.6	96.8	67 (2007)
Malaysia	93.7	94.1 (2008)	97.7
Myanmar	97.8	95.5 (2000)	69.6
The Philippines	96.5	88.7 (2009)	75.8
Singapore	96.4	96.4 (1990)	98.7
Thailand	75.9	89.7 (2009)	94.1 (1998)
Vietnam	90.5	98.1	92.1 (2005)

Source: UNESCO (2012); World Bank Group (2012b); ADB (2012).

More importantly, an examination of the translation of these enrolment figures into completion rates paints a different picture. An examination of the completion rates (as indicated by those students that reach the last grade of primary education) show the substantive increases in enrolment has not necessarily translated into more students completing primary education. This is particularly the case with Cambodia, Laos, and Myanmar, which experience much lower rates of completion. This clearly impacts upon the overall effect of increases in enrolment on increasing the overall educational levels of these countries. This indicates short run benefits from the education for these countries, with much fewer students actually taking advantage of increasing access to educational opportunities.

Promote gender equality and empower women

The third key Millennium Development Goal aims to increase gender equality and increase the level of women in top-level jobs. One of the key targets for gender equality is the involvement of women in parliament. Current targets aim to increase the involvement of women in parliamentary roles to 30 percent (UNDP, 2012). An examination of the involvement of women in parliament throughout Southeast Asia show that while progress has been made since 1990 in the majority of countries, there is still substantial progress needed to reach the 30 percent target. This is particularly noticeable in Myanmar and Malaysia, which appear to lag behind the rest of the countries in the region. This is somewhat surprisingly when examining Malaysia, which is considered one of the more developed countries of the region. Nevertheless, the majority of the countries in the region are making some good progress (see Table 2.3) towards greater gender engagement in parliaments.

Table 2.3 Seats held by women in parliament within ASEAN

Country	Seats held by women in national parliament, %		
	1990	2000	2012
Brunei Darussalam	0	8.2	20.3
Cambodia	12.4	*	18.2
Indonesia	6.3	21.2	25
Laos	5.1	10.4 (2001)	10.4
Malaysia	0	0	3.5
Myanmar	9.1	12.4	22.9
The Philippines	4.9	4.3	22.2
Singapore	2.8	5.6	15.8
Thailand	17.7	26	24.4
Viet Nam	0	8.2	20.3

* *Data not available.*

Source: UNESCO (2012); World Bank Group (2012b); ADB (2012).

Improve maternal health

Three of the Millennium Development goals are targeted at health related issues, including maternal health. In terms of improving maternal health, one of the key indicators that has been utilised is the maternal mortality ratio – the risk of death associated with pregnancy (UNDP, 2012). Targets set aimed to reduce by three quarters the level of the maternal mortality ratio. While many of the countries within the region did not reach this level of reduction, significant improvement has been seen. This is particularly the case within the least developed countries of the region. Having said this, the comparative performance of developing and least developed countries in the region is still significantly behind that of the high income, developed countries. When comparing Singapore, Brunei and Malaysia with the other countries in the region, there are clear, and very significant gaps (see Table 2.4).

Arguably, the considerable gap between the developed and developing countries in the region could be reduced through better access to health care professionals during pregnancy. This is particularly the case with Laos – which has one of the highest maternal mortality rates – only have approximately 20 percent of births attended by a health care professional. Clearly an area requiring redress within the region is the overall access to greater health care options, if these countries are expected to narrow the gaps in mortality rates.

Table 2.4 Maternal mortality and attendance of health personnel in ASEAN

Country	Mortality, maternal, per 100,000 live births			Births attended by skilled health personnel
	1990	2000	2010	% per year
Brunei Darussalam	29	24	24	99 (1999)
Cambodia	830	510	250	43.8 (2005)
Indonesia	600	340	220	79.4 (2007)
Laos	1600	870	470	20.3 (2006)
Malaysia	53	39	29	98 (2005)
Myanmar	520	300	200	57 (2001)
The Philippines	170	120	99	61.8 (2008)
Singapore	6	15	3	100 (1998)
Thailand	54	66	48	97.3 (2006)
Viet Nam	240	100	59	87.7 (2006)

Source: WHO (2012); UNICEF (2012).

Reduce child mortality

The next health related MDG relates to reducing overall levels of child mortality. An ambitious target was set to reduce the overall level of mortality in the under-five age bracket by two-thirds. An examination of the recent data suggests that the majority of the countries in the region are progressing towards this 2015 target. Some of the outlying countries have made substantial progress (see Table 2.5).

Table 2.5 Child mortality rates in ASEAN

Country	Mortality, under-five, per 1000 live births			Mortality, infant (0-1), per 1000 live births		
	1990	2000	2010	1990	2000	2010
Brunei Darussalam	12	9	7	9	7	6
Cambodia	121	103	51	87	77	43
Indonesia	85	54	35	56	38	27
Laos	145	88	54	100	64	42
Malaysia	18	11	6	15	9	5
Myanmar	112	87	66	79	64	50
The Philippines	59	40	29	42	30	23
Singapore	8	4	3	6	3	2
Thailand	32	18	13	26	15	11
Viet Nam	51	35	23	37	27	19

Source: UNICEF (2012).

This is particularly the case with Cambodia, Indonesia, Laos and Myanmar, all of which have had very high incidence of child mortality. The highest rate within the region is in Laos. However, considerable progress has been made with a two-third reduction. This is also the case when examining infant mortality rates, with wholesale reductions across all the countries in the region. Nevertheless, a distinct divide remains between the overall figures in the developed versus developing country brackets.

Combat HIV/AIDS, malaria and other diseases

The final health related MDG is related to infectious diseases within the region. Perhaps most importantly has been the targeted halt and reverse in the spread of HIV/AIDs within many parts of the region. While in many cases, data have not been available for detailing the spread and scope of the HIV prevalence within the region, there has been an increased level of infection in Malaysia and Viet Nam (see Table 2.6). Other countries which had received substantial increases throughout the 1990s – such as Thailand, Myanmar and Cambodia – have seen the numbers stabilise and begin to be reversed.

Table 2.6 HIV prevalence rates and malaria incidence in ASEAN

Country	HIV prevalence among population aged 15-49 years			Malaria incidence: notified cases per 100,000 population	
	1990	2000	2010	2003	2008
Brunei Darussalam	12	*	0.1	*	*
Cambodia	121	1.3	0.5	536.3	1798
Indonesia	85	*	0.2	104.1 (2002)	1645
Laos	145	*	0.2	349.8	327
Malaysia	18	0.4	0.5	25.3	75
Myanmar	112	0.8	0.6	1345.4	7943
The Philippines	59	*	*	53.3	96
Singapore	8	0.1	0.1	0	0
Thailand	32	1.8	1.3	58.7	322
Viet Nam	51	*	0.1	*	*

* *Data not available.*

Source: UNAIDS (2012); ADB (2012); WHO (2012).

The other health related indicator here is related to Malaria rates, which can have not only a deadly outcome, but also cripple sufferers and incur significant expenses for the countries within the region. An examination of the rates between 2003 and 2008 demonstrates a dramatic increase in reported cases across Cambodia, Indonesia and Myanmar. These figures potentially point to the importance of preventative actions by the governments.

Ensure environmental sustainability

One of the final key MDGs is related to environmental sustainability. This goal has sought to increase the integration of sustainable development principles into the countries across the region, and to slow or halt the loss of key environmental resources. In particular, de-forestation has been flagged as a key issue within several of the developing and least developed countries within the region, which look to this as a resource to help in accelerating their income generation and economic growth. While some countries, such as Viet Nam and the Philippines appear to have managed to reverse the trend within their country, a number of countries have continued to experience reductions in their land covered by forests (see Table 2.7). Cambodia, Indonesia, Laos and Myanmar - four of the poorer countries within the region - have continued to see declines in the forested areas of their countries.

Table 2.7 De-forestation, carbon emissions and CFC consumption in ASEAN

Country	Land area covered by forest (%)			Carbon dioxide emissions (thousand metric tons)			Ozone-depleting CFCs consumption (ODP Tons)		
	1990	2000	2009	1990	2000	2009	1990	2000	2009
Brunei Darussalam	78.4	75.3	72.1	6421	6527	9281	*	47.8	6.9
Cambodia	73.3	65.4	57.2	451	2255	4613	*	97	12.8
Indonesia	65.4	54.9	52.1	149566	263419	451782	*	5451.2	433
Laos	75	71.6	68.2	235	972	1811	0	45.2	2.5
Malaysia	68.1	65.7	62.3	56593	126603	198348	4193.7	2435	542.8
Myanmar	59.6	53	48.3	4276	8889	11093	*	26.6	4.5
The Philippines	22	23.9	25.7	41763	67660	68551	3477.2	3064.3	222
Singapore	2.9	2.9	2.9	46941	47623	31896	4855.2	168	207
Thailand	38.3	37.2	37.1	95833	201549	271721	6984.2	5104.6	1088.8
Viet Nam	30.2	37.8	44.5	21408	53142	142258	*	369.4	311.7

Source: FAO (2012), ADB (2012); CDIAC (2012); UNEP Ozone Secretariat (2012).

Looking further at carbon emissions, and perhaps reflective of the ongoing drive towards further industrialisation and development, most countries across the region have seen dramatic increases in the level of carbon emissions. It is likely that this trend will continue, as further development takes place, and access to disposable income result in greater consumption – particularly in the context of personal transportation and energy consumption. However, this appears to be an issue for the entire region to address, rather than evidence of a distinct gap between approaches of developed and developing countries.

Strategies to close the development divide in the region

The previous sections have highlighted the various aspects of the development divide in Southeast Asia, particularly from the perspective of the three aspects of sustainability. There is a wide range of actors in the institutional framework addressing this divide. They are found at the government level, above (supra-national bodies) and below (NGOs, companies).

The inter-governmental response

The ASEAN Economic Community Blueprint (ASEAN, 2007) – a major strategic developmental document of Southeast Asia – has specifically declared addressing aspects of this development divide, with a particular reference to accelerating the integration of Cambodia, Laos, Myanmar and Viet Nam. Further policy initiatives of the ASEAN include the Political-Security Community Blueprint (ASEAN, 2009a) and the Socio-Cultural Community Blueprint (ASEAN, 2009b), which address various, non-economic aspects of the development gap. Using the data presented on the development gaps in Southeast Asia (see Tables 2.1 to 2.7), outstanding countries with low or high levels of various indicators in relation to the MDGs in comparison to others have been highlighted. In this summary, the nature and country-specific identification of the development gaps highlighted by these indicators are displayed in Table 2.8.

The ASEAN strategy for closing the development gaps is envisaged through integration of the member countries into a common market, ensuring the free movement of goods, services, capital and people, fostering development with social and environmental sustainability in mind. In fact, this developmental agenda supersedes the individual, nation state level development agendas. One could thus argue that the developmental models warranting success in the broader region have gradually shifted from Japan's state driven development through Taiwan and South Korea's market infused, export and innovation driven development models into a liberal, open, internationalised development framework of the ASEAN. Strengths of this framework include increased integration of the countries into the global economy, thus enabling technology transfer, foreign investment and through these factors, productivity increase. The achievement of MDGs is an essential enabler to this strategy. Shortcomings of this approach include developmental gaps between the countries in the ASEAN community, and the question where resources – fostering closing the development gap – are meant to come from. Hence the key to the development of the region in an economically sustainable fashion seems to be resource access, and the challenge is to harvest the winds of globalisation to fuel the development needs of these courtiers through trade, foreign investment and aid.

Table 2.8 Millennium Development Goals performance gaps and strategic initiatives

MDG performance gaps	MDG performance gaps	ASEAN strategic initiatives
MDG 1 Poverty eradication and employment	▪ Substantial unemployment (rate over 5 per cent): the Philippines, Indonesia, Myanmar ▪ High levels of poverty remaining: Viet Nam, the Philippines, Indonesia, Cambodia, Myanmar, Laos	ASEAN Economic Community Blueprint (2007)
MDG 2 Achieve universal primary education	▪ Decreasing primary education enrolment: Myanmar, the Philippines ▪ Low primary education completion rates: Cambodia, Laos, Myanmar ▪ Moderately low primary education completion rates: the Philippines, Indonesia	ASEAN Socio-Cultural Community Blueprint (2009b)
MDG 3 Promote gender equality and empower women	▪ Female political representation very low: Malaysia, Myanmar ▪ Female political representation at moderately low levels: Indonesia, Thailand	ASEAN Political-Security Community Blueprint (2009a)
MDG 4 Improve maternal health	▪ Professional attendance very low at childbirths: Laos; and moderately low: Myanmar, the Philippines, Cambodia ▪ High maternal mortality: Cambodia, Indonesia, Laos, Myanmar	ASEAN Economic Community Blueprint (2007) ASEAN Socio-Cultural Community Blueprint (2009b)
MDG 5 Reduce child mortality	▪ High infant and child mortality rates: Cambodia, Indonesia, Laos, Myanmar	ASEAN Economic Community Blueprint (2007)
MDG 6 Combat HIV/AIDS, malaria and other diseases	▪ HIV prevalence high: Thailand; and moderately high: Cambodia, Malaysia, Myanmar, Viet Nam ▪ Malaria incidences very high: Myanmar; and high: Indonesia, Cambodia	ASEAN Socio-Cultural Community Blueprint (2009b)
MDG 7 Ensure environmental sustainability	▪ Deforestation substantial: Cambodia, Indonesia, Laos, Myanmar ▪ Top CO2 emitters: Indonesia, Malaysia, Thailand ▪ Top CFC consumers: Malaysia, Thailand, Viet Nam	ASEAN Economic Community Blueprint (2007)

Potential of civil society

Chandra (2009) highlights the versatile nature of the civil sector in the ASEAN countries, and emphasises the role of NGOs in establishing alternative regionalism. Views on regionalism in the ASEAN countries range from *mainstream* to *progressive*. Mainstream regionalism subscribes to the neo-liberal ideology fostering a spontaneous process of opening and integration of the nation states. Progressive regionalism is ideologically closer to the political left, and is modelled in Latin America. As an alternative perspective on regionalism, the emphasis on the role and importance of civil society has emerged in Southeast Asia.

In fact, both at the community level (alternative ASEAN regionalism) and at the level of the individual societies (NGOs - non-government organisations - and CBOs - community based organisations), ever wider community groups are engaged with addressing a range of developmental issues (Aviel 1999).

As discussed with regards to MDGs earlier, the opportunities presenting themselves for the civil society (NGOs and CBOs) are highlighted across the majority of ASEAN (see Table 2.9). A weaker performance on the MDGs respectively (see Table 2.8) indicates a strong potential, a very poor performance (or poor performance in more than one aspect of the goals) suggests a very strong potential for civil society contribution in the various countries, as well as at the regional level. There are particularly strong opportunities for civil society in Cambodia, Laos, and Myanmar. In these countries, there is a potential to address a wide range of development gap issues. In countries, such as the Philippines or Thailand, deficiencies are only present in a few, isolated areas.

Table 2.9 Millennium development goals and potential for civil society in the ASEAN

Country	MDG 1	MDG 2	MDG 3	MDG 4	MDG 5	MDG 6	MDG 7
Brunei Darussalam							
Cambodia	+	++		+	++	++	+
Indonesia	++	+	+	+	++	+	++
Laos	+	++		++	++		+
Malaysia			++				++
Myanmar	++	++	++	+	++	++	+
The Philippines	++	++					
Singapore							
Thailand			+			++	++
Viet Nam	+					+	+

\+ *Strong potential for civil society impact;*
++ *Very strong potential for civil society impact.*

It is clearly demonstrated that there is potential for civil society involvement in several areas and NGOs can be recommended to address these niche areas in the different countries. Cross-country cooperation can also be fostered not only at the governmental level, but also at the level of civil society, to contribute to the ASEAN integration.

Countries, such as Cambodia, Indonesia, Myanmar and Laos are facing many gaps. Other countries such as Malaysia, the Philippines, Thailand and Viet Nam have more specific issue areas. The comparatively wealthier states (Brunei and Singapore) appear to have already dealt with most of these development goals. Potentially civil society cooperation could be useful between low performers in specific areas to combine efforts and resources; or between low and high performers to exchange experiences in eliminating the specific issues.

References

ADB (2012). Statistics for Dynamic Policy Making. Retrieved 20 November, 2012, from https://sdbs.adb.org/sdbs/index.jsp.

ASEAN (2007). *ASEAN Economic Community Blueprint*. Jakarta: ASEAN Secretariat.

ASEAN (2009a). *ASEAN Political-Security Community Blueprint*. Jakarta: ASEAN Secretariat.

ASEAN (2009b). *ASEAN Socio-Cultural Community Blueprint*. Jakarta: ASEAN Secretariat.

Aviel, J. F. (1999). The growing role of NGOs in ASEAN. *Asia-Pacific Review, 6* (2), 78-92.

Bruhn, M. & Gallego, F. A. (2012). Good, Bad, and Ugly Colonial Activities: Do They Matter for Economic Development? *Review of Economics and Statistics, 94* (2), 433-461.

CDIAC (2012). CDIAC Mercury Metadata Clearinghouse. Retrieved 20 November, 2012, from http://mercury.ornl.gov/cdiacnew/.

CIA (2012). World Factbook. Retrieved 20 November, 2012, from www.cia.gov/library/publications/the-world-factbook/.

Chandra, A. C. (2009). Civil Society in Search of an Alternative Regionalism in ASEAN. *Hosei Kenkyu Journal of Law and Politics, 75* (4), 47-69.

Daskon, C. & McGregor, A. (2012). Cultural Capital and Sustainable Livelihoods in Sri Lanka's Rural Villages: Towards Culturally Aware Development. *Journal of Development Studies, 48* (4), 549-563.

FAO (2012). FAOSTAT. Retrieved 20 November, 2012, from http://faostat3.fao.org/home/index.html.

Grabowski, R., Self, S. & Shields, M. P. (2006). *Economic Development A Regional, Institutional, and Historical Approach*. Armonk: M.E. Sharpe Inc.

Griffin, K. (1999). *Alternative Strategies for Economic Development* (2nd ed.). Basingstoke: Palgrave Macmillan.

Ibrahim, P., Basir, S. A. & Rahman, A. A. (2011). Sustainable Economic Development: Concept, Principles and Management from Islamic Perspective. *European Journal of Social Science, 24*(3), 330-338.

Lumumba-Kasongo, T. (2011). The National Project as a Public Administration Concept: The Problematic of State Building in the Search for New Development Paradigms in Africa. *Africa Development, XXXVI*(2), 63-96.

Mkandawire, T. (2011). Running While Others Walk: Knowledge and the Challenge of Africa's Development. *Africa Development, XXXVI*(2), 1-36.

Nafziger, E. (2012). *Economic Development*. Cambridge: Cambridge University Press.

Phimphanthavong, H. (2012). Economic Reform and Regional Development of Laos. *Modern Economy, 3*(2), 179-186.

Rangarajan, K., Long, S., Ziemer, N. & Lewis, N. (2012). An evaluative economic development typology for sustainable rural economic development. *Community Development, 43*(3), 320-332.

Roy, K. C., Blomqvist, H. C. & Clark, C. (2012). *Economic Development in China, India and East Asia Managing Change in the Twenty First Century*. Cheltenham: Edward Elgar Publishing.

Todaro, M. P. & Smith, S. C. (2009). *Economic development*. Boston: Pearson Addison Wesley.

UN (2000). United Nations Millennium Declaration (A/RES/55/2). Retrieved 20 November, 2012, from http://www.un.org/millennium/declaration/ares552e.pdf.

UNAIDS (2012). Data and analysis. Retrieved 20 November, 2012, from http://www.unaids.org/en/dataanalysis/.

UNDP. (2010). What will it take to achieve the Millennium Development Goals? An international assessment Retrieved 20 November, 2012, from www.undp.org/content/dam/aplaws/publication/en/publications/MDG/international-assessment---english-full-version/IA_English.pdf.

UNDP (2011). *Human development report 2011: Sustainability and equity: a better future for all*. New York: United Nations Development Programme.

UNDP (2012). *The Millennium Development Goals Report 2012*. New York: United Nations Development Programme.

UNEP Ozone Secretariat. (2012). Data Access Centre. Retrieved 20 November, 2012, from http://ozone.unep.org/new_site/en/ozone_data_tools_access.php.

UNESCO (2012). World Data on Education. VII. Retrieved 20 November 2012, 2012, from http://www.ibe.unesco.org/en/services/online-materials/world-data-on-education.html.

UNICEF (2012). Statistics and Monitoring. Retrieved 20 November, 2012, from http://www.unicef.org/statistics/index_step1.php.

United Nations Department of Economic and Social Affairs. (2012). *World economic and social survey 2012: In search of new development finance*. New York: United Nations.

United Nations Development Programme. (2012). *The Millennium Development Goals Report 2012*. New York: UNDP.

von Schirnding, Y. (2005). The World Summit on Sustainable Development: reaffirming the centrality of health. *Global Health, 1*(8), 8-14.

Whitfield, L. (2012). How Countries Become Rich and Reduce Poverty: A Review of Heterodox Explanations of Economic Development. *Development Policy Review, 30*(3), 239-260.

WHO (2012). Global Health Observatory Data Repository. Retrieved 20 November, 2012, from http://apps.who.int/gho/data/.

World Bank Group. (2012a). GINI index. Retrieved 20 November, 2012, from http://data.worldbank.org/indicator/SI.POV.GINI.

World Bank Group. (2012b). World Development Indicators. Retrieved 20 November, 2012, from http://data.worldbank.org/indicator.

World Commission on Environment and Development. (1987). *Our Common Future*. Oxford; New York: Oxford University Press.

Chapter 3

Aquaculture and debt

Undermining sustainability in the Mekong Delta

JESSIE K FLY AND HONG ANH VU

ABSTRACT

Shrimp aquaculture was introduced in many Southeast Asian countries as an income-diversifying enterprise. Based on data collected using a variety of ethnographic methods, including long-term participant observation in the Mekong Delta, Vietnam, our research reveals that the most common outcome of shrimp farming – mounting debt – actually constrains households' options for making a living.

Introduction

'It is a miserable life, being in debt', a 65-year-old man lamented as he drank green tea in his two-room thatch house, surrounded by shrimp aquaculture ponds and patchy mangrove forest. He moved to Đông Hải Commune, a small village on the eastern edge of the Mekong Delta, Vietnam, in 1992, from a rice-producing district further inland. He was 'encouraged' to move to the coast by local government officials, promising large tracts of available land, lucrative shrimp farming, and low-interest loans to get started. He bought 50,000 m^2 of land, dug a 30,000 m^2 pond out of the mud, and hauled in disappointing harvests year after year. At the time of this interview in February 2008, when he said he was 'too old to catch fish or work hired labour', he was 140 million VND (US$8,750) in debt to the Vietnam Bank for Agriculture and Rural Development (VBARD). Sixteen years after his hopeful migration to the coast, his wife and six children continued to live inland, as he was never able to build a suitable home for them in Đông Hải, and his two adult sons had ended their formal education early in order to help their father pay off his debts. The man feared he would soon lose his sons to Vietnam's urban areas because so many other adult children had already out-migrated in search of better economic opportunities.

Livelihood sustainability, both at the community and household levels, is an important goal of development initiatives, as these initiatives focus on increasing the 'capitals and capabilities' of the poor (Bebbington, 1999; Carney, 2002; Moser, 1998). In line with this focus, microcredit has become an extremely popular development strategy, offering small subsidized or collateral-free loans to the poor in an effort to jumpstart self-employment, agricultural intensification, etc., and to promote further and sustainable income generation (Weber, 2002). Microcredit programs aim to promote livelihood diversification and/or improve the income-generating capacity of activities the household already pursues through the enhancement of different kinds of assets, particularly financial and physical capital.

This model of development has proven very popular in Southeast Asia. In 2003, Indonesia, Thailand, Vietnam, and Cambodia were among the six countries demonstrating the highest microfinance institution penetration rates (borrowing clients as a percentage of the population), with VBARD considered 'among the giants of the microfinance industry' (Henley & Goenka, 2010, p. 7). During the era of economic reform in Vietnam, the expansion of microcredit lending has carried the promise of not only reducing poverty in the country but also catalysing the expansion of shrimp aquaculture and hastening rural market integration. In 2006 through 2008, we collected stories from households struggling to construct and maintain sustainable livelihoods in several villages in the marginal, coastal region of Trà Vinh Province. We argue that, rather than promoting livelihood sustainability, the accumulation of formal debt has undermined rural households' ability to achieve and maintain sustainable livelihoods, with particularly undesirable consequences for women and the elderly. why?

Aquaculture and debt during Đổi Mới

Soon after the Government of Vietnam's announcement of the beginning of *Đổi Mới* in 1986, the decentralization of the country's economy and integration into the world market proceeded rapidly. To encourage these trends, the state significantly increased rural households' access to formal lines of credit. VBARD, a new state bank, was established in 1988 for directed lending to the agricultural and rural sector, while the Vietnam Bank for the Poor (VBP; now, the Vietnam Bank for Social Policies) was created in 1995 to provide credit to very low-income households. By 2000, those two institutions, along with the People's Credit Funds (PCFs) created with the assistance of foreign NGOs, provided almost half of all rural credit (Henley & Goenka, 2010). This was a dramatic change, as less than ten years earlier, three-quarters of rural loans came from informal sources, such as private moneylenders and relatives (Conroy, 2003).

As a consequence of these and other reform-era policy changes, Vietnam's coastline underwent an economic and environmental transformation. Once covered by dense mangrove forest, the southern coast was quickly transformed in the mid-1990s to support aquaculture production, particularly tiger shrimp (*Penaeus monodon*) cultivation. In the Mekong Delta, the surface area of shrimp ponds grew from 90,000 ha in 1991 to 430,000 ha in 2003 (Joffre & Bosma, 2009). A study of land use change in northern Vietnam, using remote sensing data, shows that 63 percent of 1986 mangrove forest areas were partially or entirely replaced by aquaculture in 2001 (Beland *et al.*, 2006). With financial successes around the world since the 1970s, aquaculture was a promising way to increase seafood production for export, to transform unproductive coastal land into a site for lucrative industry, and to boost economic development and poverty alleviation in marginalized areas.

Our research concerns several communities in Duyên Hải District, Trà Vinh Province, that experienced this dramatic transformation. According to interviews with provincial- and district-level Forest Department officials and local residents of the area, the coast was very sparsely populated before the 1990s. The few inhabitants of the mangrove forest there were primarily fishers in the South China Sea (or the East Sea as it is known in Vietnam), grew cassava in forest clearings, collected wild plants for food and medicine, and hunted now locally-extinct animals. These households provided for their members, met their goals, and coped with crises within this subsistence and local cash economy. This changed, however, as the Vietnamese government aimed policy changes at converting the unproductive coastline to profitable land. Inland populations were encouraged to migrate to the coast, uproot the mangrove forest, and construct shrimp ponds. Among the incentives for migrating were offers of low-interest loans from the state bank.

Communes that contained only a few households in the 1970s had population booms. Đông Hải Commune's population, for instance, increased to 5000 people in 2007, about two-thirds of whom were shrimp farmers. According to the manager of the Long Thanh Industrial Zone, 70 percent of the population of

Duyên Hải District was made up of relatively recent immigrants from other districts and provinces in 2006. This mass in-migration to the coastal district began in 1995, around the time the first incentives were offered to promote coastal conversion to shrimp aquaculture. In addition to the other changes brought about by this transition, formal debt became a significant part of the lives and livelihoods of the majority of households in these communes. Consequently, the ways in which households provide for themselves, meet their goals, and cope with crises have also changed. The remainder of this chapter will explain how this high prevalence of debt threatens the sustainability of these households and communities in the Mekong Delta.

Figure 3.1 A shrimp aquaculture farm in Đông Hải Commune, Trà Vinh Province, Vietnam (2008)

Photo credit: Jessie Fly.

What is a sustainable livelihood?

definition [A sustainable livelihood is one that is composed of a particular combination of income producing, subsistence, and coping strategies that generates an adequate standard of living and fulfils other household goals without compromising these functions of the livelihood in the future.] Allison and Horemans (2006) write that livelihoods are sustainable 'if people are able to maintain or improve their standard of living related to well-being and income or other human development goals, reduce their vulnerability to external shocks and trends, and ensure their activities are compatible with maintaining the natural resource base' (p. 759). A household must have access to different types of capital (financial, natural, physical, human, social) to support the portfolio of activities that produces these desirable outcomes (Bebbington, 1999; Ellis, 2000; Igoe, 2006). Microcredit services aim to increase poor households' access to financial capital to improve market integration and diversification within the livelihood portfolio.

Unfortunately, when the various components of a household's livelihood portfolio, particularly the activities supported by microloans, are unstable or unreliable, debt payments (interest and principle) become yet another household expense to be juggled along with all the others. Furthermore, the continuous need to produce cash to make loan payments under legal and social pressure transforms debt into a livelihood stress with which a household must cope. Many researchers have demonstrated that individuals and/or households resort to coping strategies in a predictable order once exposed to livelihood stress and it is the severity of the strategies used that allows for assessment of livelihood sustainability (Bukusuba *et al.*, 2007; Corbett, 1988; Hadley *et al.*, 2007). Early strategies ('non-erosive') in the sequence can be resorted to again and again without damaging the household's ability to cope with the next stress or shock. However, if the household is forced by the type, severity, or duration of the stress to resort to more severe or erosive strategies, then the household may deplete its resources necessary for fully recovering from the shock or coping with the next one (Chambers, 1989). The use of unsustainable coping methods puts households at risk of failing to maintain standards of living and other household goals – undesirable livelihood outcomes. In the next section, we provide evidence from Hiệp Thạnh and Đông Hải Communes that household debt resulting from government microloans has disproportionately increased the vulnerability of two important sectors of the population, women and the elderly.

Case studies

The extent of formal debt

A brief history of loan extension in the study area illustrates well the industrial shrimp aquaculture development initiative, in the case of Hiệp Thạnh Commune, and the reliance on small loan extension for poverty alleviation, in the case of Đông Hải. In Hiệp Thạnh Commune, industrial shrimp farms were actively promoted through state-subsidized loans. Owners of two-hectare aquaculture farms could obtain a loan of 100 million VND (US$6,250), three times higher than the largest loans they could receive for agriculture. Households eligible for these large loans also received a 10 million VND (US$625) bonus, which households often used for purchasing water pumps. These incentives were the first of their kind in the Mekong Delta and attracted thousands of farmers to move to the area and apply for these loans. In some cases, siblings combined their farms to obtain several loans simultaneously. By 2006, the majority of borrowers had fallen into the category of 'bad debts'. According to representatives of the Duyên Hải branch of VBARD, the size of outstanding loans grew from 184 billion VND (US$11.5 million) in 2002 to 325 million VND (US$20.3 million) in 2005. Ninety percent of those outstanding loans were earmarked for intensive shrimp aquaculture.

Of 117 research participants in Đông Hải, where loan extension was more often aimed explicitly at poverty alleviation, 87 (74 percent) were in debt in 2007 to either VBARD or VBP. Eighteen percent of these research participants had outstanding loans with informal moneylenders only - shopkeepers, neighbours, relatives - and only eight percent of the sample had no debt at all. The average year that households first borrowed money from a formal lending institution was 2003. There was a first wave in 1997, when the government first offered small individual loans after destruction caused by Typhoon Linda. There was a second wave around 2001 as fishing households, displaced by the Coastal Wetlands Protection and Development Program, were moved from their homes on the beach, 'encouraged' to farm shrimp, and given priority lending. There was a third wave around 2007 when other fishing households were encouraged to participate in a clam-raising project, which involved borrowing money from VBARD. Participants' debt ranged from 2 million VND (US$125) to 300 million VND (US$18,750), with a median of 15 million VND (US$938). Furthermore, the interest that each household paid on its bank loans in 2007 ranged from 0 VND (some households could not afford to make interest payments and so did not) to 40 million VND (US$2,500), with a median payment of 1.5 million VND (US$94). The percentage of a household's reported annual income spent on interest ranged from zero percent to 300 percent, with an average of nearly 30 percent of the household's income.

Đảo Nợ - The cycle of debt

In these small communities in the Mekong Delta, debt mounted quickly due to unproductive shrimp farms, declines in income from other subsistence sources, the falling price of *cây thuốc cá* (a major cash crop in the region), and accumulating interest. Under these circumstances, households had to cope not only with cyclical and stochastic livelihood stressors but also with a constant need for cash to service their debts. Described below, households were forced to rely on different coping strategies, reprioritize household needs and goals, and make sacrifices of well-being. At least one third of the participating households in Đông Hải were caught in a cycle of debt (*đảo nợ*), a commonly reported consequence of microcredit projects (Cons & Paprocki, 2010; Rahman, 1999; Turvey & Kong, 2010). This cycle is a complex social and economic phenomenon that involves borrowing from private moneylenders to pay off the bank and then taking out more bank loans to pay off the moneylenders and on and on. For many households, microloans were less an enhancement of financial capital and more a problem to be solved by a reapportionment of resources.

Women in Hiệp Thạnh

Despite their exclusion from production of relatively new commercial cash crops, such as intensively-farmed tiger shrimp, women usually controlled the household's finances. Women were responsible for the 'behind-the-scenes' work of ensuring the supply of food, medicine, and other chemicals for the shrimp ponds, sending children to school, and feeding the family. Women were also responsible for coping with debt. This coping involved *đảo nợ*, the complex social and economic phenomenon that involves both the formal and informal financial sectors.

Although women were often seen as the cause of 'bad luck' and shrimp investment failures (Vu, 2012) and had difficulties accessing bank loans because household registration and land titles often only carried the husbands' names (Tran, 2001; Tinker & Summerfield, 1999), women were primarily charged with servicing and settling government microloans. Even though *dảo nợ* was at the heart of a masculine enterprise (commercial shrimp farming), it was an activity that men shied away from because it required 'begging and borrowing' (*nài nỉ, quy lụy*). Interaction with bank staff, cadastral officers, and informal moneylenders required patience and humility that women, not men, were perceived to possess. Therefore, men pushed the task of loan rotation onto their wives. A local moneylender said, 'Here, the women go to the bank because the men are not fond of begging and showing subordination by waiting and begging.'

Figure 3.2 A woman counting her money outside the Mekong Delta Housing Bank in Duyên Hải District, Trà Vinh Province, Vietnam (2008)

Photo credit: Hong Anh Vu.

Additionally, women's roles in the informal credit sector, both as borrowers and lenders, contrasted sharply with their marginal position in the formal sector. Women in the Mekong Delta controlled the diverse networks of rotating local credit groups (*hụi*), which have long played an important economic function in the region (Sansom, 1970). Under the umbrella of the Women's Union, one of Vietnam's mass organizations, women formed these local credit groups to help one another in times of need. In Hiệp Thạnh, women formed over a dozen credit groups with 10 to 30 members each. Members made small monthly contributions according to ability and these contributions were combined to help two or three members every month. This small source of credit was valuable for smoothing consumption during times of economic stress. Along with *hụi*, the majority of private moneylenders were also women. These two informal credit networks were the main sources of funding for economic activities that did not fall under formal development policies and programs and that women accessed for the purposes of loan rotation.

Women's resourcefulness and efforts to constantly juggle the needs of all household members was the most important buffer for farming households (Meinzen-Dick, 2003; Quisumbing *et al.*, 2004). However, and more so since the introduction of microloans, women were forced to sacrifice their own well-being and make other difficult decisions about the diversion of resources in order to cope. To maintain household food security and subsistence, women employed a number of strategies. They relied on their social networks. They purchased rice, oil, kerosene, and other daily consumables on credit from local traders. They repaid the traders with the proceeds from selling their next harvest of wild-caught fish, shrimp, and other marine species. Women with land grew vegetables in the poor, salty soil, raised cattle, or fished in common waterways or family ponds. Other women wove leaf panels for thatch housing or engaged in petty trading. Many women contributed substantially to the household's income by renting their labour. In Vĩnh Châu and Sóc Trăng Provinces, 65 percent of women earned income by working as hired labourers (Martinelli, 2000). In these ways, women struggled to ensure desirable livelihood outcomes for their families, the definition of which varied from household to household but included basic food security, an adequate cash income, education for their children, or merely preventing their families from falling into the most abject poverty.

Figure 3.3 A meeting of a local women's rotating credit group in Hiệp Thạnh Commune, Trà Vinh Province, Vietnam (2008)

Photo credit: Hong Anh Vu.

Cutting expenses was one of the most common strategies women employed to cope with economic stress. When cash was difficult to earn and the majority of it was diverted to loan payments, the cash available for food, health care, and education disappeared. Except for a few wealthy households, the members of most participating households in Hiệp Thạnh and Đông Hải consumed only two meals per day to minimize food expenditures. Yet, no matter how strapped for cash, women made sure that men had breakfast before leaving for the field, pond, or ocean in the morning. Priority was also given to small children. Thus, when trimming expenditures to channel scarce resources into debt and shrimp ponds, women often first reduced their own food intake and spending on other necessities, such as clothing. Under economic stress, women even compromised their own health to make ends meet – they skipped meals, watered down rice, and endured pains to save on medical expenses. One woman worked extra hours to supplement her household's income following a massive loss of investment in shrimp farming. She said that indebtedness had forced her to work harder in hopes of making up for the loss.

> *If I work, I do not rest. If I rest, I do not work. I am always eager for more work (tham công tiếc việc), I am always greedy to work to the extent of compromising my own health. But I am not greedy for myself. Everyone has something to be greedy about. Like myself, I think that I work for my children and my family. When the children were small, I worked so that they are not materially deprived as compared with others. Then I want the family to fare better, to have a brick house, to send the children to college. Dreams never end (Interview in Cây Đa).*

Coping with change

This self-denial of wives and mothers is a fairly common coping strategy. Consumption modification (e.g. maternal buffering, collecting edible wild plants, eating less-preferred foods) is often the first strategy employed in a sequence of household coping strategies because, in response to low-severity/short-duration stress, these strategies are relatively sustainable. Resorting to these activities does not reduce the resources the household has to cope with the next stress or shock. With the advent of market integration and microcredit programs growing in size and reach in the coastal region of southern Vietnam, however, these initial strategies became insufficient to cope simultaneously with debt and other economic stress. An elderly woman, who had lived in Đông Hải all her life, commented, 'In the past, even during the war, when we had hard times, we would just go to the ocean and fish or collect some plants to eat. Now, we must always have money, even when we are hungry.' To cope with debt, many women must scrimp and save to their own detriment, but even this was often not sufficient and more resource-depleting strategies were required.

Illustrative of this trend, in 2007 and 2008, when one of the researchers attempted to elicit sequences of coping strategies from participants in Đông Hải by asking what they did when they did not have enough money to buy rice, participants did not respond with lists that were in accordance with the coping literature – these lists did not proceed from most sustainable to least sustainable strategy. These responses also differed from older people's recollections of coping in the past. In response to these inquiries about coping with food insecurity, about one-third of participants listed only one strategy, rather than a sequence. Of those who listed only one strategy, the majority of strategies involved credit and borrowing (e.g. borrowing money from the bank, moneylenders, or family members) and the other strategies involved the intensification of cash-generating enterprises. Of the participants who listed more than one strategy, about two-thirds listed a first strategy that involved credit and borrowing. Because this kind of coping strategy is generally unsustainable and increases the household's vulnerability by depleting resources, the results of this coping strategy elicitation exercise illuminated the changes in dealing with stress since the proliferation of aquaculture and debt.

The elderly in Đông Hải

In addition to the increased vulnerability of women because of severe consumption modification, a relatively new type of household was created, in part, by these changes in coping – elderly-only households. Households moved through their sequences of coping strategies faster and out of order as they contended with interest payments in addition to the 'normal' stresses and strains, and many older people in Đông Hải said they had no choice but to send their adult children away to urban or other rural areas to search for work. Furthermore, many of these elderly parents felt they had reached the end of the line in terms of coping, and that sending their children away was a strategy of last resort. Our research indicates that the creation of these vulnerable elderly-only households, some containing young grandchildren as well, resulted in additional undesirable livelihood outcomes.

A Vietnamese proverb states, 'Có con nhờ con, có của nhờ của. If you have wealth, you depend on your wealth in times of need; if you have children, you depend on your children in times of need.' As elderly people's productive capacity diminished, due to decreased stamina and increased ailments, their adult children traditionally lived with and supported them. Thus, until recent years, the typical Vietnamese household cycled through a multigenerational phase, when older people, their adult children (usually a son and daughter-in-law), and their grandchildren lived together (Hirschmann & Vu, 1994). If the elderly became incapacitated, the able-bodied adults would generate income and provide food for the household. Older people in Vietnam were rarely left to fend for themselves. Due to changing coping strategies, an unstable local economy, and the relaxation of governmental restrictions on population movement, however, this situation was changing. Of 117 participating households in Đông Hải, about 20 percent were elderly-only households.

Research in Đông Hải showed that elderly parents did not change their livelihood activities when their children out-migrated; their households simply became less productive upon the loss of human capital (extra hands, physical strength, and oftentimes more education). Elderly-only households, then, depended on their neighbours for support, particularly during times of illness or other economic stress. For example, when first asked how they fed themselves and the other members of their households, these research participants (a widower living alone, an elderly couple, an old woman caring for her young grandson) often replied, 'My neighbours love me. My neighbours take care of me so carefully.' There was a sense of responsibility for elderly neighbours in the village. However, when times were hard for the community in general, these neighbouring households often had to cope by cutting off support to the elderly. Thus, this support dried up, according to the elderly respondents, around 2008, when the World Food Crisis caused the price of food items, gasoline, and agricultural inputs to spike. When asked about food procurement and consumption after that event, elderly participants chuckled sadly and replied, 'Rice is too expensive to share now' or 'My neighbours can't even give me vegetables because food is too expensive to share.' This vulnerability in the livelihood portfolios of elderly-only households – reduced productivity and unreliable coping strategies – resulted in undesirable livelihood outcomes, compared to other household types in the community.

According to quantitative research conducted in Đông Hải Commune, elderly-only households (22 percent of the sample) experienced more undesirable livelihood outcomes than nuclear (37 percent) or multigenerational (41 percent) households, in terms of household income, use of coping strategies, and food security. Elderly-only households had a significantly lower median income in 2007 than multigenerational and nuclear households (10 million VND compared to 16 million VND for the other two household types; $X^2 = 9.650$, $p < .01$). During a weekly Food Frequency Survey carried out for 35 weeks from January to September 2008, research participants from elderly-only households reported instances of eating just one meal in a day to conserve food more often than members of multigenerational and nuclear households. This coping strategy was reported during 17.7 percent of the weekly survey visits with elderly-only households and during 4.4 percent and 0.8 percent of the weekly visits with the other two household types, respectively ($X^2 = 67.6397$, $p < .001$). Finally, the researcher computed an average dietary diversity score (DDS) for each participant based on scores collected weekly. Dietary diversity is a common measure of food security and a good proxy for dietary quality (Arimond & Ruel, 2004; Hatloy *et al.*, 1998; Mishra & Ray, 2009; Moursi *et al.*, 2008; Ogle *et al.*, 2001). In this case, the score ranged from 0 to 8. The median DDS for members of elderly-only households (4) was significantly lower than the median DDS for members of multigenerational (5) and nuclear (6) households, signifying greater food insecurity and poorer dietary quality among elderly people living alone ($X^2 = 77.732$, $p < .001$).

Elderly-only households, once rare in Vietnam, are, in part, a product of the unsustainability of economic development along the southern coastline. As shrimp aquaculture fails many families and debt rises, the careful balancing act represented by livelihood portfolios and most often juggled by women is disrupted. Families are forced to rely on coping strategies more often and in different sequences than before they had to service debts from microloans. Certain family members become more vulnerable as a result and some families disintegrate altogether as young adults out-migrate to find work to cope with these debts. The result is the most vulnerable household type of all, elderly people living alone or with young grandchildren. With lower cash incomes and lower food security, these households are particularly at risk of ever-increasing vulnerability as their resources available for maintaining a standard of living and coping with stresses and shocks diminish.

Recommendations

'In the past we were poor, now we are indebted,' a shrimp farmer from Mỹ Quý explained the conundrum of coastal communities in Vietnam. Likewise, a man in Đông Hải Commune, new to shrimp farming after his ocean fishing community was displaced by a forest conservation/economic development project, expressed his ambivalence: 'I have a more solid house and some land now. Aquaculture is an easier job than fishing. But I used to have money in my pocket. Now everything extra goes to pay the interest on my debt.'

As part of the attempt to promote economic development in rural areas of Vietnam, microcredit loans – seen as a fundamental driver of growth – were introduced to aid income-generating activities. However, more often than not, loans have helped few to fare better while increasing the debt burden of the vast majority of borrowers. The pathways from loans to bad debts may vary, but the end result is that households have to extract every bit of income from other sources to service their debts. As demonstrated above, debts eat into households' subsistence resources, and it is women, children, and the elderly who suffer the most by reducing their expenses on food, health, and education.

Navajas *et al.* (2000) write, 'The question ... is not whether microfinance is better than nothing for its users. The question is whether microfinance is better than some other development project for the poor as a whole' (p. 334). Likewise, this paper does not aim to suggest the elimination of microcredit. Recognizing its pervasiveness and its prominent, if fraught, position in people's lives, we suggest that these loans have to be arranged in such a way that they best support household livelihoods in order to ameliorate economic situations like that in Duyên Hải District and to build sustainable communities. In other words, microcredit loans must be transformed from a stressor with which households must cope to a tool families can use to cope with other stressors.

If microcredit is to be used to truly help households and communities, its place within the intricately interconnected web of sustainable livelihoods must be considered. As evidenced by our case studies, the role of women in Vietnamese households is of key importance to the construction and maintenance of sustainable livelihoods. Women are the bookkeepers and consumption smoothers of the household. They beg and borrow and scrimp and save and juggle the family's resources to continuously meet the short- and long-term goals of the household. In order to help transform the role of loans from stressor to coping tool, all local people, but specifically women, must feel they have gained control of the credit system.

We recommend direct and indirect approaches for this capacity building among women. Directly, both male and female household head signatures should be required on formal loan applications, acknowledging the agreement of adult household members on the appropriate financial strategy for the household. Additionally, while aquaculture extension services, when offered, are often geared toward men, household finance education should be offered and targeted at women. Indirectly, recognizing the strategies many women in Duyên Hải use to cope with debt and balance resources, we recommend more formal microsavings in addition to microlending services. These suggestions are in line with many of the 'credit-plus' programs that are having success in other parts of the world (e.g. Ahmed, 2009; Caldas *et al.*, 2010).

We also recommend better coordination among the state-run banks, VBARD and VBP, and Vietnam's mass organizations (e.g. Women's Union, Elderly People's Association). Mass organization local leaders should be encouraged to take a more active leadership role in local savings and credit associations. In many parts of the world, these associations effectively place control of savings and credit within the local community (Stoffle *et al.*, 2009; Eroglu, 2010). Rather than one stop in the cycle of debt, with better coordination, informal credit associations have the potential to aid in purposeful asset diversification for Vietnam's women. We feel strongly that the inclusion of women in the control of household debt will strengthen household resilience, promote sustainable communities, and curb the creation of more vulnerable families.

References

Ahmed, S.M. (2009). Capability development among the ultra-poor in Bangladesh: A case study. *Journal of Health, Population, and Nutrition 27*(4), 528-535.

Allison, E.H. & Horemans B. (2006). Putting the principles of the Sustainable Livelihoods Approach into fisheries development policy and practice. *Marine Policy 30*(6), 757-766.

Arimond, M. & Ruel, M.T. (2004). Dietary diversity is associated with child nutritional status: Evidence from 11 demographic and health surveys. *The Journal of Nutrition 134*(10), 2579-2585.

Bebbington, A. (1999). Capitals and capabilities: A framework for analyzing peasant viability, rural livelihoods, and poverty. *World Development 27*(12), 2021-2044.

Beland, M., Goita, K., Bonn, F. & Pham, T.T.H. (2006). Assessment of land-cover changes related to shrimp aquaculture using remote sensing data: A case study of the Giao Thuy District, Vietnam. *International Journal of Remote Sensing 27*(8), 1491-1510.

Bukusuba, J., Kikafunda, J.K. & Whitehead, R.G. (2007). Food security status of people living with HIV/AIDS (PLWHA) in a Ugandan urban setting. *British Journal of Nutrition 98*, 211-217.

Caldas, A., Arteaga, F., Munoz, M., Zeladita, J., Albujar, M., Bayona, J. & Shin, S. (2010). Microfinance: A general overview and implications for impoverished individuals living with HIV/AIDS. *Journal of Health Care for the Poor and Underserved 21*, 986-1005.

Carney, D. (2002). *Sustainable livelihoods approaches: Progress and possibilities for changes.* London: Department for International Development.

Chambers, R. (1989). Vulnerability, coping and policy. *IDS Bulletin 20*, 1-7.

Conroy, J.D. (2003). *The challenges of micro financing in Southeast Asia*. Singapore: Institute of Southeast Asian Studies.

Cons, J. & Paprocki, K. (2010). Contested credit landscapes: Microcredit, self-help and self determination in rural Bangladesh. *Third World Quarterly 31*(4), 637-654.

Corbett, J. (1988). Famine and household coping strategies. *World Development 16*(9), 1099-1112.

Ellis, F. (2000). A framework for livelihood analysis. In F. Ellis (Ed.), *Rural livelihoods and diversity in developing countries* (pp. 28-51). Oxford: Oxford University Press.

Eroglu, S. (2010). Informal finance and the urban poor: An investigation of rotating savings and credit associations in Turkey. *Journal of Social Policy 39*(3), 461-481.

Hadley, C., Borgerhoff Mulder, M. & Fitzherbert, E. (2007). Seasonal food insecurity and perceived social support in rural Tanzania. *Public Health Nutrition 10*(6), 544-551.

Hatloy, A., Hallund, J., Diarra, M.M. & Oshaug, A. (2000). Food variety, socioeconomic status and nutritional status in urban and rural areas in Koutiala (Mali). *Public Health Nutrition 3*, 57-65.

Henley, D. & Goenka, A. (2010). Introduction: From moneylenders to microfinance in Southeast Asia. In A. Goenka & D. Henley (Eds.), *Southeast Asia's Credit Revolution: From moneylenders to microfinance* (pp. 1-17). London: Routledge.

Hirschmann, C. & Vu, M.L. (1994). Family and household structure in Vietnam: Some glimpses from a recent survey. Working Paper No. 94-3. Seattle: University of Washington.

Igoe, J. (2006). Measuring the costs and benefits of conservation to local communities. *Journal of Ecological Anthropology 10*, 72-77.

Joffre, O.M. & Bosma, R.H. (2009). Typology of shrimp farming in Bac Lieu Province, Mekong Delta, using multivariate statistics. *Agriculture, Ecosystems and Environment 132*, 153-159.

Martinelli, A. (2000). *Finding a balance between riches and ruin: An assessment of the shrimp industry in the Mekong River Delta of Vietnam and prospects for sustainable poverty alleviation*. Hong Kong: Oxfam.

Meinzen-Dick, R. (2003). *25 years young: Reflecting on achievements and planning for the future*. World Agroforestry Centre.

Mishra, V. & Ray, R. (2009). Dietary diversity, food security and undernourishment: The Vietnamese evidence. *Asian Economic Journal 23*(2), 225-247.

Moser, C.O.N. (1998). The asset vulnerability framework: Reassessing urban poverty strategies. *World Development, 26*(1), 1-19.

Moursi, M.M., Arimond, M., Dewey, K.G., Treche, S., Ruel, M.T. & Delpeuch F. (2008). Dietary diversity is a good predictor of the micronutrient density of the diet of 6- to 23-month-old children in Madagascar. *The Journal of Nutrition 138*(12), 2448-2453.

Navajas, S., Schreiner, M., Meyer, R.L., Gonzalez-Vega, C. & Rodriguez-Meza, J. (2000). Microcredit and the poorest of the poor: Theory and evidence from Bolivia. *World Development 28*(2), 333-346.

Ogle, B.M., Pham, H.H. & Ho, T.T. (2001). Significance of wild vegetables in micronutrient intakes of women in Vietnam: An analysis of food variety. *Asia Pacific Journal of Clinical Nutrition 10*(1):21-30.

Quisumbing, A.R., Brown, L.R., Feldstein, H.S., Haddad, L. & Pena, C. (2004). *Women: The key to food security*. Washington, DC: IFPRI.

Rahman, A. (1999). Micro-credit initiatives for equitable and sustainable development: Who pays? *World Development 27*(1):67-82.

Sansom, R.L. (1970). *The economics of insurgency in the Mekong Delta of Vietnam*. Cambridge, MA: The MIT Press.

Stoffle, B.W., Purcell, T., Stoffle, R.W., Van Vlack, K., Arnett, K. & Minnis, J. (2009). Credit, identity, and resilience in the Bahamas and Barbados. *Ethnology 48*(1), 71-84.

Tinker, I. & Summerfield, G. (1999). *Women's rights to house and land: China, Laos, Vietnam*. Boulder, CO: Lynne Reinner.

Tran, T.Q. (2001). *Land reform and women's property rights in Vietnam*. Center for Gender, Environment, and Sustainable Development. Hanoi: Vietnam.

Turvey, C.G. & Kong, R. (2010). Informal lending amongst friends and relatives: Can microcredit compete in rural China? *China Economic Review 21*(4), 544-556.

Vu, H.A. (2012). Gender and sustainability: Negotiating risk strategies among shrimp farming households in Vietnam's Mekong Delta. In M. Cruz-Torres & P. McElwee (Eds.), *Gender, natural resources and sustainability: Critical case studies from the Americas and Asia* (pp. 165-186). Tucson: Arizona University Press.

Weber, H. (2002). Global governance and poverty reduction: The case of micro credit. In R. Wilkinson & S. Hughes (Eds.), *Global governance: Critical perspectives* (pp. 13151). London: Routledge.

Chapter 4

Consumer socialisation agency in Vietnam

Understanding family decisions in relation to sustainable consumption

TORGEIR WATNE, LINDA BRENNAN AND LUKAS PARKER[2]

ABSTRACT

The Vietnamese family is changing and so may be the way they make mid-to-high involvement consumer decisions. We investigate how traditional three-generational Vietnamese families living in the same household communicate about consumption decisions relating to environmentally friendly household products, including uncovering how family members learn from each other. The findings show that each of the generations may have a role to play in these decisions, albeit in different ways.

[2] We would like to acknowledge Dang Nguyen, Mai-Anh Doan, and Duong Trong Hue for their considerable involvement in survey translation and data collection for this project.

Summary

A dynamic economy, rising standards of living and an increasingly consumption-oriented society are changing the way families in Vietnam interact, especially about consumption. Such changes will of course also impact family decisions regarding the purchase and usage of sustainable household products and adoption of other environmentally sustainable behaviours. The traditional belief that the big decisions are always made by the paternal head of family is no longer the norm. In some cases the household head is switching from the eldest male to the main salary earner. With increasing education levels of younger generations and changing family dynamics, modern Vietnamese families are likely to involve the younger generations in the purchase decisions the family makes. As such, communicating with younger people about family consumptions may be more effective to change behaviour towards more sustainable patterns of consumption.

We investigate how traditional three-generational Vietnamese families living in the same household communicate about consumption decisions of environmentally sustainble products to assist INGOs and NGOs working to promote sustainable households and communities. The aim was to find out how decisions are made in these close-knit families with regards to purchases of sustainable household products in order to tailor effective communication to families. Thus, we looked at what role various family members are likely to have in the purchase decision process. We investigated which family member is most likely to purchase various sustainable household products, how the family find information about such products, when they last made a purchase, and how interested they are in products that are environmentally friendly. Finally, we investigated who are most likely to be the decision maker in the family and who are likely to function as 'socialisation agents' or influencers.

Introduction

The two most populous cities in Vietnam, Ha Noi and Ho Chi Minh City, are facing environmental problems typical to that of most major cities in developing countries in Southeast Asia. In addition to infrastructure and developmental pressures, there is the pressure of a rapidly growing number of middle class families (General Statistics Office, 2010). The newly arising middle class in Vietnam is both large and relatively wealthy (Penz & Kirchler, 2012). Middle classes are often characterised by accelerated consumption patterns (Hanser, 2010), search for social status, prestige and an appearance of 'taste' (Hughes & Woldekidan, 1994; Singh, 2005). Consumption focused to status and appearances reflects the importance of 'others' with regards to what the individual consumes and is indicative of 'collectivism', which is typical cultural traits of the region (Schütte & Ciarlante, 1998). Vietnam is widely considered to be collectivistic society (Jamieson, 1995; McCann, Cargile, Giles, & Bui, 2004; P.-M. Nguyen, Terlouw, & Pilot, 2005).

In collectivistic societies, purchase decisions are not made alone; they are made in agreement with significant others around each individual. In collectivist societies, individuals consider themselves to be a part of a greater entity (Hirschman & Minh, 2002); they consult others before making purchases for themselves. For example, people in collectivistic societies are much more likely to discuss with their networks in social media before making a purchase decision for themselves (Goodrich & de Mooij, 2013). Moreover, collectivism includes a view of the family as the central and basic decision-making unit, with individual members rarely considering themselves as individual and autonomous units. Thus, it is important to understand how families make decisions in order to effectively promote environmentally friendly alternatives in cultures with collectivistic traditions.

The evolving family unit

The Vietnamese family is often seen in a Confucian light (Whitmore, 1984). That is, families possess a structure of great rigidity and it is one that is patrilineal[3], patrilocal[4], and patriarchal[5] (Hirschman & Loi, 1996; Hirschman & Minh, 2002; Hoang, 2011). However, as a Southeast Asian country, Vietnam tends to be more flexible in terms of family structure and is partly due to the social 'superstructure' borrowed from other Eastern or Western countries overlaid on top of the Confucian influence (Brown, 1976). Vietnam has been a pathway to and from Asia for centuries, resulting in a diverse range of cultural practices based in Buddhist and later Confucian traditions.

According to the 2009 Vietnamese population and housing census the average household size is 3.8 persons (3.7 in urban areas and 3.9 in rural areas) (General Statistics Office, 2010). This represents an overall reduction in the average household size of 0.8 (17.4% decline) persons since the year 2000. As the fertility rate has declined, while life expectancy continues to increase, Vietnam's population is beginning to age. This is combined with rapidly declining dependency ratios. Therefore there are fewer people aged under 15 and over 65 in comparison to those of working age. Concurrently the prevalence of traditional multi-generation households has reduced (Ruggles & Heggeness, 2008), but the prevalence of patrilocality has largely remained unchanged. However, the co-residence is more likely to be for a shorter duration (Hirschman & Nguyen, 2002). Regardless of patrilocality, co-resident and non-co-resident elders are generally supported by those in the family of working age (Knodel, Friedman, Truong & Bui, 2000). Whilst patrilocality is still commonplace, patrilineality is becoming less strong; whereas in the past, wealth, property and power were concentrated in the hands of the oldest male, in many families this is shifting to the younger working generations (Ruggles & Heggeness, 2008). This may have implications of who plays what role in the family decision-making process.

---

3 Tracing descent through the paternal line.

4 Located at or centred around the residence of the of the husband's family or tribe.

5 Characteristic of a society which puts men into a higher rank and more likely to receive benefits of male inheritance.

The relationship between parents and children

Although the reliance on educational institutions and services is increasing for child support and development, people in both urban and rural areas agree that the relationship between parents and children should be harmonious. Children should be obedient, listen and pay respect to their parents and grandparents (UNICEF, Ministry of Culture, General Statistics Office & Family and Gender Institute, 2008) and parents, in turn, will invest time and financial resources in the children (Le, 2008). When growing older, children are expected to take care of their parents. Hirschman and Nguyen (2002) and Knodel *et al.* (2000) noted that the majority of elderly parents receive money, durable items or daily living items from both the live-in and non co-resident children. The live-in child is often the main income earner for the family (Hirschman and Nguyen, 2002). In addition, Vietnamese parents, especially in urban areas, are actively engaged with their children's education and the children's choice of friends. In a nuclear family, the task of educating children falls on the mother and is co-ordinated between mother and father. In an extended family, this role expands to the grandparents as well, although grandparents are not engaged in educating children to the same extent as the parents (C. D. Nguyen, 2006).

In Vietnamese families, there is a strong correlation between the perceived role of the father and the number of children in a family: the more children there are in a family, the more influential is the role of the father (Vu, 2002). The perceived responsibility of the father with his children compared to the mother is also different. For example, while the three main responsibilities of a father are helping children study, attending meetings with the children's schools, making decisions regarding punishment and rewards, the responsibilities of the mother are feeding, taking care of hygiene, and entertainment of the children. On the other hand, Nguyen (2009) found that more Vietnamese high school students aged 16 to 18 want to assert themselves in their family. They want to make their own choice when it comes to use of time and study method, clothes, appearance, and making friends. They are, however, less assertive in deciding about their own physical and entertainment needs. Students at this age also want to take on a bigger role in the family by participating in household tasks although they may be assigned to tasks such as cooking and dishwashing.

Importantly, there are also many intergenerational families in Vietnam, despite there being changes to the family dynamics. Thus, not only are there relationships between parents and children, there are also relationships between grandparents and grandchildren to consider. In this study, we will focus on these traditional families with three generations living under the same roof. We look at how such families make decisions related to purchases of environmentally friendly household products. In particular, we investigate how family members socialise each other with regards to consumption decisions.

Consumer socialisation

Consumer socialisation is known as the process of developing knowledge, beliefs and attitudes that are relevant to functioning in the marketplace (John, 1999). Consumer socialisation (like all forms of socialisation) is a lifelong process as consumers continue to learn throughout their lifetime (Ekström, 2006). Most consumer socialisation takes place in the family (Moschis, 1987), and learning though the family may continue throughout a person's lifetime (Mathur, 1999). Our investigation builds on previous studies of Australian families relating to 'reciprocal consumer socialisation' (Watne, 2010; Watne & Brennan, 2011; Watne, Lobo & Brennan, 2011). Reciprocal consumer socialisation have been found to be particularly common in families with young adults above 18 years living at home have over their parents. Reciprocity with regards to consumer socialisation reflects the idea that children and parents may equally influence and educate each other, in this case with regards to consumption decisions. Reciprocal consumer socialisation has been found to be particularly common in families with young adults above 18 years of age living at home with their parents. Education and learning may flow in any direction, based on whom the family considers to be the expert within a given product category. The expert is often recognised as the socialisation agent, as opposed to the learner.

In consumer socialisation processes, socialisation agents are specific sources from which norms, attitudes, motivations, and behaviours are transmitted to consumers (Chan & McNeal, 2006). Socialisation agents transmit norms, attitudes, and values to the learner by actively or passively communicating certain expectations and behavioural patterns (Moschis, 1987). The intercession or mediation a learner receives from a socialisation agent is known as 'consumer socialisation agency' (CSA). CSA exists where there is an acceptance of an agent's influence from another party (the learner) with regard to consumption. This can be reciprocal socialisation: agent<>learner<>agent, whereby each party learns from the other. CSA is the act of influencing another about consumption within the social context. Key components of this conceptualisation are that learners and agents, through interactions over time, influence each other about consumption. Further, these interactions are not based in the sender>receiver model of communication; they are conceived as gift>acceptance. That is, consumption knowledge is offered as a gift to the learner, and the learner accepts the gift from the agent. For example, if a child educates their parent to use energy saving light bulbs in the house or teach them how to recycle the household waste, the child provides consumer socialisation agency for the parent. Since family decision-making in Vietnam is known to be complex, we do not assume a direction of socialisation, but acknowledge that parents, children or grandparents may be agents or learners, or both.

In determining who are more likely to be the agent or the learner within a consumer socialisation framework, Watne and colleagues (2011) suggested that the interest and knowledge of the parties involved have an impact on the degree of consumer socialisation agency (CSA). When consumers perceive someone to hold 'social expert power' (French & Raven, 1959) in a given product category, CSA is likely to be communicated. This means that adult consumers (e.g. parents) learn from others (e.g. their children) when they perceive them to be knowledgeable in the product category. For example, if children learn about recycling at school and demonstrate knowledge on the topic to their parents, parents may change their behaviour accordingly. However, when it comes to environmentally friendly household products, Watne and Brennan (2011) found that most of the Australian families did not see their adolescent children as more knowledgeable than the parents. However, the level of knowledge the family perceives the child to have was strongly related to how much influence the child then had over the parent. The level of perceived 'expertness' the family attribute to the child was strongly related to CSA from children to parents.

Research approach and questions

The main aim for this study was to investigate how traditional three-generational patrilocal Vietnamese families make decisions about environmentally friendly household products. In particular, we wanted to know how decisions are made, who purchase the products and who influence the purchase. We assumed that children, parents or grandparents might be both socialisation agents and learners when it comes to environmentally sustainable household products. As such, we looked at agent and learner properties in Vietnamese family triads with children aged above 18 living together with their parents and grandparents. This approach allowed us to find out how education and decision-making is done within these families. The particular questions we sought to answer were as follows:

RQ 1. Who are the main purchasers of environmentally friendly household products within patrilocal Vietnamese families?

RQ 2. What are the main sources of influence behind such purchases?

RQ 3. How often do various family members purchase these products?

RQ 4. What are the perception of interest, knowledge and consumer socialisation agency between children, parents and grandparents?

RQ 5. What impact does interest and knowledge have on consumer socialisation agency?

To approach these questions, we used a dyadic design (Kenny, Kashy & Cook, 2006). This means distributing surveys to children, parents and grandparents and analyse the relationship and levels of agreement (nonindependence) within the families. We asked the families who the main purchasers were for various environmentally friendly household products, what the main sources of information were, and how often each individual family member would purchase such products.

The families were also asked questions about consumer socialisation agency (CSA) within the family as learners and agents. CSA was measured on the scale developed by Watne (2010), based on the classical primary components of an attitude, i.e. cognitive, affective-evaluative, and conative factors (e.g. Jacoby, 1971;

Quester & Lim, 2003). The CSA scale contained items relating to learners and agents such as 'I get useful information from my child about environmentally sustainable products' and 'I influence my parent to buy the right environmentally sustainable products'. In addition, we looked as the family members' interest and knowledge in each of these categories. To measure interest and knowledge, we used well know marketing measures; Interest was measured with Laurent and Kapferer's (1985) consumer involvement scale, while Bloch, Ridgway and Sherell's (1989) was used for product category knowledge.

Data collection and analysis

The data for this study was collected between November 2012 and January 2013. The sample size consisted of 102 parent/child/grandparent triads, surveyed in Ha Noi and Ho Chi Minh City. The 'children' in the survey were above 18 years old and were living in the same household as their parents and grandparents. 52.9 percent of the sample was collected in Ha Noi (through RMIT University Vietnam, Ha Noi), the rest was collected in Ho Chi Minh City (through RMIT University Vietnam, Saigon South and Vietnam National University Ho Chi Minh City: International University). Table 4.1 shows the demographic profiles of these households.

Table 4.1 Sample profile

	Children	Parents	Grandparents
Mean age	20.57	49.20	75.93
Female	77.6%	66.0%	64.6%
Male	22.4%	44.0%	35.4%
Level of education			
Did not go to school			8.3%
Did not finish primary school		1.0%	10.4%
Finished junior high school	1.0%	2.0%	12.5%
Finished high school	21.9%	18.0%	31.3%
University diploma	14.6%	10.0%	11.5%
Bachelor degree	61.5%	52.0%	18.8%
Postgraduate degree	1.0%	17.0%	7.3%

When analysing the data, families were used as the unit of analysis. Simple aggregate statistics (means) and t-tests were used to determine whether the differences in mean ratings were statistically different. Correlation analysis was used to determine the relationship between CSA and interest and knowledge for parents, grandparents and children within each family. Reliability was tested in terms of internal consistencies for the scales used with Cronbach's Alpha (Cronbach, 1951). The Cronbach's Alpha values for all items ranged between .69

and .98 which is considered as being reliable (Churchill & Iacobucci, 2005; Hair, Black, Babin & Anderson, 2010).

Results

The families were asked to indicate on a 7-point scale which environmental products were purchased for the household by which person, anchored in 'hardly ever' and 'most of the time'. All generations indicated that the parent would be the purchaser for these products most of the time (see Table 4.2). Both children and grandparents would fall closer to the 'hardly ever' end of the scale. This indicated that although children and grandparents may influence the purchases, they do not seem to be the final decision-makers when it comes to environmentally friendly household products. The t-test indicates that parents are significantly more likely to be the main purchaser of all these products, while the likelihood of children and grandparents being the purchaser are the same for three of the seven products. The results indicated that the parents are perceived as being the head of the household when it comes to making purchases (RQ1). This may be related to the fact that they are the breadwinners, and as such responsible for most of the consumer related decisions in the household.

Table 4.2 Main purchasers of environmental products for the household

	Children	Parents	Grandparents	Paired samples t-test*
Recycled papers	3.81	4.40	3.29	.00/.00/.01
Energy saving light bulbs	3.78	5.52	3.56	.00/.00/.26
Recycled glassware	3.40	3.98	3.03	.00/.00/.02
Personal care products	3.85	4.69	3.27	.00/.00/.00
Biodegradable/paper/ cloth bags	4.27	4.66	3.41	.01/.00/.00
Products operating on green energy (solar, wind tidal, hydro energy) – e.g. solar energy water heater	2.51	4.36	2.44	.00/.00/.62
Environmentally friendly washing machines	2.34	4.13	2.44	.00/.00/.41

* *Paired samples t-tests were conducted between children-parents, parents-grandparents, and children-grandparents. The results of the t-test are presented in that order.*

Although Table 4.2 seems to indicate that children and grandparents may have equal likelihood of purchasing many types of environmental products for the family (perhaps in the absence of the parent), they do not seem to have the same level of influence over the purchase decision. When asked to rank various sources of information based on importance of finding information about environmentally friendly products, grandparents were regarded as the least important source

(RQ2). Again, the families seemed to rely on the parents for information. In addition, non-personal commercial sources were popular. As such, it seems that 'standard' media such as radio and TV would be a favourable way of reaching Vietnamese consumers with regards to sustainable consumption.

Table 4.3 shows the mean rank of the sources for the families. A lower rank means that the source of information is more likely to be used (respondents ranked the sources 1-9). T-test were used to test what sources of information were more or less important than children, parents and grandparents. The results indicate that not all sources of information were significantly more or less important to each other. What is clear, though, is that parents are significantly more important as an information source than children, and children are significantly more important than grandparents. Compared with other sources, parents, children and grandparents are of high, medium and low importance respectively.

Table 4.3 Sources of information for environmental products

	Mean	t-test children	t-test parents	t-test grandparents
1. Radio & TV	4.21	.00	.70	.00
2. Parents	4.28	.00	1.00	.00
3. Magazines & newspapers	4.36	.00	.60	.00
4. Internet	4.74	.41	.00	.00
5. Children	4.86	1.00	.00	.00
6. Friends	5.15	.06	.00	.00
7. Sales people	5.51	.00	.00	.04
8. Other family members	5.89	.00	.00	.87
9. Grandparents	5.91	.00	.00	1.00

The frequency of purchase also seems to indicate that grandparents are the least frequent shopper when it comes to sustainable products (RQ3). Grandparents are the most likely to never have purchased an environmentally friendly product (see Table 4.4). Parents and children seem to have very similar frequency of making such purchases. There is no statistical difference in the frequency of purchase between parents and children. However, (judging from Table 4.2), the children may either purchases these products for themselves (and not the household), or they may be referring to smaller and less expensive purchases (e.g. biodegradable/paper/cloth bags). Nevertheless, this may indicate that children are more involved in the families purchases that the grandparents, when it comes to environmentally friendly products.

We also investigated the level of interest and knowledge in sustainable products, as well as the family members' likelihood of functioning as socialisation agents for each other (RQ4). The results in Table 4.5 indicate that grandparents may be the least interested and knowledgeable in this product category. However, grandparent's interest and knowledge is not statistically different from the children. The results also indicate that the grandparents are the significantly least important socialisation agents for the parents or children, possibly because of the low interest and knowledge. Nevertheless, the parents seem to be making an effort to educate the grandparents about environmentally friendly products. This means that the family perceive (and perhaps expect) the parent generation to inform and educate their elderly parents. As far as patriarchy goes, this may reflect a need for the parent generation to educate and socialise the family regarding important issues within their society. Interestingly, the perception of CSA between children and parents were much stronger for Vietnamese families compared with Watne and Brennan's (2011) study of Australian families. This may be related to the collectivistic culture and higher importance placed on family communication. It also reflects the importance of considering the family and not just individuals in collectivistic societies.

Table 4.4 When did you last purchase an environmentally friendly product for the household?

	Children	Parents	Grandparents	Paired sample t-test*
Mean (1-5)	2.16	1.94	2.80	.16/.00/.00
1: (1-4 weeks ago)	45%	46%	35%	
2: (1-6 months ago)	29%	34%	17%	
3: (7-12 months ago)	5%	6%	8%	
4: (More than a year ago)	7%	8%	14%	
5: (Never bought)	14%	6%	26%	

* *Paired samples t-tests were conducted between children-parents, parents-grandparents, and children-grandparents. The results of the t-test are presented in that order.*

Table 4.5 Interest, knowledge and CSA for sustainable products

	Mean	Paired samples t-test*
Child knowledge	4.33	
Parent knowledge	4.53	.07/.00/.13
Grandparent knowledge	4.10	
Child interest	4.35	
Parent interest	4.73	.00/.00/.22
Grandparent interest	4.17	
CSA from children	4.24	
CSA from parents	4.64	.00/.00/.00
CSA from grandparents	3.39	

* *Paired samples t-tests were conducted between children-parents, parents-grandparents, and children-grandparents. The results of the t-test are presented in that order.*

Our final analysis (RQ5) looked at the relationships between interest, knowledge and CSA (see Table 4.6). The results suggest that the families perceived any family member that is interested and knowledgeable about environmentally friendly products to be an important socialisation agent. However, the strong correlations above 0.64 between CSA from grandparents to both parents and children, and grandparents' knowledge and interest, may be related to the grandparents' lack of knowledge in the product category. Finally, the correlation between CSA towards children from both parents and grandparents are weakly or insignificantly related to interest and knowledge in the child. This indicates that parents and grandparents attempt to educate their children, regardless of the interest and knowledge of the child, reflecting a society with respect for their elders.

Table 4.6 Correlations between interest, knowledge and CSA for sustainable products

	Children's knowledge/ interest	Parents' knowledge/ interest	Grandparents' knowledge/ interest
Children to parents	0.41**/0.43**	0.36**/0.33**	-
Parents to children	0.24*/0.25*	0.39**/0.41**	-
Parents to grandparents	-	0.41**/0.38**	0.43**/0.49**
Grandparents to parents	-	0.40**/0.32**	0.64**/0.69**
Grandparents to children	0.07/0.10	-	0.65**/0.73**
Children to grandparents	0.37**/0.29**	-	0.30**/0.30**

** Correlation is significant at the 0.05 level (2-tailed).*
*** Correlation is significant at the 0.01 level (2-tailed).*

Perhaps somewhat surprisingly, the results indicated no differences between gender, age and education level between children, parents or grandparents. None of the demographic variables had an impact on the participant's level of knowledge, interest or capacity to be a socialisation agent or learner for the other family members (the results are not presented here because they were insignificant). The only exemption was that grandparents with a university degree were more likely to be a socialisation agent for the parents and children than those who did not have a university degree. Table 4.1 indicates that the grandparents generally are much less educated that the parents and children, and this may be one of the reasons why they are not perceived to be important as socialisation agents. As such, the family dynamics with regards to consumer socialisation within Vietnamese families are likely to change over the next generation as education is becoming more available to the middle class.

Implications of findings to INGOs and NGOs

Many campaigns aiming at changing attitudes and behaviour, such as promoting sustainable lifestyles, are targeted at individuals (see for example Donovan, 2011; Lefebvre, 2011; Wymer, 2011). However, as our results indicate, such individual-centred strategies may not work as well in Vietnam since intergenerational families are making collective decisions. This is evident due to the high level of CSA between the family members; they are actively educating each other. As such, families need to be convinced of the benefits for the collective group before purchasing pro-environmental products. Collectivist traditions are active in decision-making, and this makes a difference to campaigns designed around individual free choice environments. Harmony seeking within the family unit may also lead to a faster integration of communication strategies about environmental issues. That is, once one family member is made aware, the family are more likely to agree that the issue is family matter, not individual. The results of the use of media sources (Table 4.3) indicate that Vietnamese families rely on 'traditional media' such as TV, radio and newspapers to find information about sustainable behaviour. As such, using these sources of media will likely reach the target audience.

For INGOs and NGOs engaged in promoting more sustainable lifestyles, our insights into Vietnamese families show that the parent generation is the main purchaser of environmentally friendly household products. This is possibly because they are the breadwinners as previous research has suggested. In addition, parents are one of the main sources of information for the family when purchasing such products as well as the most likely to have made such purchases in the last week. Parents are also the most interested and knowledgeable about pro-environmental alternatives in the family, and are also the most likely to educate the other family members. This last point is important; parents do take care to educate both children and grandparents. As such, effective communication with Vietnamese families about environmentally friendly household products may be targeted at parents but should also include suggestions of how such consumer behaviour is important for the whole family.

Whilst there is evidence of a shift in household power in purchase decisions from paternal head of family to the main income earner (Ruggles & Heggeness, 2008), influence is also likely to come from younger generations who have greater exposure to information, and therefore are mediators of social influence. Even if parents seem to dominate the decision-making, it is unlikely that there is a fixed decision-maker in any given situation *per se* in Vietnamese families. Instead, the decision-maker arises out of a contested and ever-changing arena of power and control within the family. Vietnamese children are just as likely as their parents to purchase environmentally friendly products for the family. The family also perceived the children as an important source of information as well as socialisation agents. As such, the younger generation may also be targeted with campaigns aimed at changing consumer behaviour in the family. Such approaches are likely to be particularly successful when the older generations, who are the decision-makers, are interested and knowledgeable about the products.

For the youngest generation, the need for social status, prestige and an appearance of 'taste' may be particularly strong, as previous research has indicated. Conspicuous consumption is also a trend in the increasingly better-off middle class in the region. Such consumption patterns may be linked to Asian cultural values such as collectivism, combined with an 'indiscreet' adoption of

Western consumption values. The widespread adoption of Western consumerism is a serious concern throughout Asia, primarily because of the potential impact on the environment (Bardhan, 2006; Sheth, 2011; Sheth, Sethia & Srinivas, 2011). However, it may not be a bad thing in itself. Environmentally sustainable products in Vietnam are a still relatively new concept. Thus, they are more expensive than 'normal' products and may therefore have the potential to be perceived as both 'Western' and reflect an appearance of taste. For INGOs and NGOs promoting environmentally sustainable household products, it may be effective to design their products to reflect such prestige values.

Finally, grandparents seem to be a less important socialisation agent as well as information source and purchaser for the family with regards to these categories. However, the results show that when they are interested and knowledgeable, they are likely to greatly impact the behaviour of the younger generations. As such, targeting grandparents through mainstream media may still be a successful strategy. This generation have lived through times of war and have seen great changes in their country. Without doubt, they have seen things change for both the better and worse. One of the negative recent changes threatening cities such as Ha Noi and Ho Chi Minh City is increasing air and water pollution levels and problems associated with waste management. As such, nostalgic appeals related to 'how things used to be' and how grass root movements such a purchasing environmentally friendly household products can slow down the threats to the environment could be a good way to increase the interest in the oldest generation.

References

Bloch, P. H., Ridgway, N. M. & Sherell, D. L. (1989). Extending the Concept of Shopping: An Investigation of Browsing Activity. *Journal of the Academy of Marketing Science, 17*(1), 13-21.

Blood, R. O. & Wolfe, D. M. (1960). *Husbands & wives: The dynamics of married living*: Free Press New York.

Brown, D. E. (1976). *Principles of social structure: Southeast Asia*: Duckworth London.

Chan, K. & McNeal, J. U. (2006). Chinese children's understanding of commercial communications: A comparison of cognitive development and social learning models. *Journal of Economic Psychology, 27*(1), 36-56.

Chang, C.-O., Chen, S.-M. & Somerville, T. (2003). Economic and Social Status in Household Decision-making: Evidence Relating to Extended Family Mobility. *Urban Studies, 40*(4), 733-746.

Churchill, G. A. & Iacobucci, D. (2005). *Marketing research: methodological foundations* (9 ed.). Mason, Ohio: Thomson South-Western.

Cronbach, L. J. (1951). Coefficient alpha and the internal structure of tests. *Psychometrika, 16*(3), 297-334.

Donovan, R. (2011). Social marketing's mythunderstandings. *Journal of Social Marketing, 1*(1), 8-16.

Douglas, S. P. (1983). Examining family decision making processes. *Advances in Consumer Research, 10*(1), 451-453.

Ekström, K. M. (2006). Consumer Socialization Revisited. In R. W. Belk (Ed.), *Research in Consumer Behavior* (Vol. 10, pp. 71-98). Oxford: UK: Elsevier Science Ltd.

Foxman, E. R., Tansuhaj, P. S. & Ekström, K. M. (1989). Adolescents' influence in family purchase decisions: A socialization perspective. *Journal of Business Research, 18*(2), 159-172.

French, J. R. P. J. & Raven, B. (1959). The bases of social power. In D. Cartwright (Ed.), *Studies in Social Power* (pp. 150-167). Ann Arbor, Michigan: University of Michigan, Institute for Social Research.

General Statistics Office. (2010). *The 2009 Vietnam Population and Housing Census: Major Findings*. Ha Noi: Central Population and Housing Census Steering Committee, General Statiistics Office.

Hair, J. F., Black, W. C., Babin, B. J. & Anderson, R. E. (2010). *Multivariate data analysis: a global perspective* (7 ed.). Upper Saddle River, N.J.: Pearson Education.

Hempel, D. (1975). Family role structure and housing decisions. *Advances in consumer research, 2*, 70-80.

Hirschman, C. & Loi, V. M. (1996). Family and household structure in Vietnam: Some glimpses from a recent survey. *Pacific Affairs, 69*(2), 229-249.

Hirschman, C. & Minh, N. H. (2002). Tradition and change in Vietnamese family structure in the Red River Delta. *Journal of Marriage and Family, 64*(4), 1063-1079.

Hoang, L. A. (2011). Gendered networks and migration decision-making in Northern Vietnam. *Social & Cultural Geography, 12*(5), 419-434.

Howard, D. R. & Madrigal, R. (1990). Who makes the decision: the parent or the child? The perceived influence of parents and children on the purchase of recreation services. *Journal of Leisure Research, 22*(3), 244-258.

Jacoby, J. (1971). A model of multi-brand loyalty. *Journal of Advertising Research, 11*(3), 25-31.

Jamieson, N. L. (1995). *Understanding Vietnam*: University of California Press.

John, D. R. (1999). Consumer socialization of children: A retrospective look at twenty-five years of research. *Journal of consumer research, 26*(3), 183-213.

Kenny, D. A., Kashy, D. A. & Cook, W. L. (2006). *Dyadic data analysis*. New York: Guilford Press.

Knodel, J., Friedman, J., Truong, A. S. & Bui, T. C. (2000). Intergenerational exchanges in Vietnam: family size, sex composition, and the location of children. *Population studies, 54*(1), 89-104.

Laurent, G. & Kapferer, J.-N. (1985). Measuring Consumer Involvement Profiles. *Journal of Marketing Research, 22*(1), 41-53.

Le, N. V. (2008). Nghiên cứu gia đình trong bối cảnh mới (Family studies in the new context). *Nghien cuu gia dinh va gioi (Vietnamese Journal of Families and Genders), 18*(3), 3-11.

Lefebvre, R. C. (2011). An integrative model for social marketing. *Journal of Social Marketing, 1*(1), 54-72.

Mathur, A. (1999). Adoption of technological innovations by the elderly: a consumer socialization perspective. *Journal of Marketing Management, 9*(3), 21-35.

McCann, R. M., Cargile, A. C., Giles, H. & Bui, C. T. (2004). Communication ambivalence toward elders: Data from North Vietnam, South Vietnam, and the USA. *Journal of cross-cultural gerontology, 19*(4), 275-297.

Moschis, G. P. (1987). *Consumer Socialization: A Life-Cycle Perspective.* Lexington, Massachusetts: Lexington Books.

Nguyen, C. D. (2006). Kiểu loại gia đình và giáo dục trẻ em trong gia đình ở Hà Nội hiện nay (Family types and education of children within the family unit in Hanoi). *Tạp chí Xã hội học (Vietnamese Sociological Review),, 2* (94), 21-27.

Nguyen, M. T. T., Jung, K., Lantz, G. & Loeb, S. G. (2003). An exploratory investigation into impulse buying behavior in a transitional economy: A study of urban consumers in Vietnam. *Journal of International Marketing, 11*(2), 13-35.

Nguyen, P.-M., Terlouw, C. & Pilot, A. (2005). Cooperative learning vs Confucian heritage culture's collectivism: confrontation to reveal some cultural conflicts and mismatch. *Asia Europe Journal, 3*(3), 403-419.

Nguyen, T. M. L. (2009). Định hướng giá trị nhân cách của học sinh Trung học phổ thông thể hiện trong quan hệ gia đình và quan hệ bạn bè (Orientating the characteristics of high school students in their relationships with the family and friends). *Tạp chí Tâm lý học (Vietnamese Journal of Psychology), 8*(125), 19-25.

Quester, P. G. & Lim, A. L. (2003). Product involvement/brand loyalty: is there a link? [Research paper]. *Journal of Product & Brand Management, 12*(1), 22-38.

Ruggles, S. & Heggeness, M. (2008). Intergenerational coresidence in developing countries. *Population and development review, 34*(2), 253-281.

UNICEF, Ministry of Culture, S. a. T., General Statistics Office & Family and Gender Institute. (2008). *Report on the findings of the census on Vietnamese families (shortened version).* Hanoi.

Vo, N. M. (2011). *Saigon: A History*: McFarland Publishing.

Vu, T. H. (2002). The perceived role of fathers in families (Vai trò của người cha trong gia đình). *Tạp chí Xã hội học (Vietnamese Sociological Review)*, 29-39.

Wang, K.-C., Hsieh, A.-T., Yeh, Y.-C. & Tsai, C.-W. (2004). Who is the decision-maker: the parents or the child in group package tours? *Tourism Management, 25*(2), 183-194.

Watne, T. (2010). *Reciprocal Consumer Socialisation.* Unpublished PhD thesis, Swinburne University of Technology, Melbourne.

Watne, T. & Brennan, L. (2011). Behavioral Change Starts in the Family: The Role of Family Communication and Implications for Social Marketing. *Journal of Nonprofit & Public Sector Marketing, 23*(4), 367-386.

Watne, T., Lobo, A. & Brennan, L. (2011). Children as agents of secondary socialisation for their parents. *Young Consumers: Insight and Ideas for Responsible Marketers, 12*(4), 285 - 294.

Whitmore, J. K. (1984). Social organization and Confucian thought in Vietnam. *Journal of Southeast Asian Studies, 15*(02), 296-306.

Wymer Jr, W. W. (2011). Developing more effective social marketing strategies. Journal of Social Marketing, 1(1), 17-31.

Part II

Strategies for Change

Chapter 5

Integrated water resources management in Thailand and Southeast Asia

JOHN WALSH & ALIN CHINTRARUCK

ABSTRACT

Water resource management in Thailand is characterized by competition for scarce resources between industry, the tourist sector and public citizens, in a country in which environmental degradation and erratic climatic patterns are making the controlled flow of water increasingly difficult. To overcome this, a new water management approach is emerging which is fraught with pragmatic compromise and postponement or avoidance of power relations issues. This situation is relevant to other Southeast Asian nations both in terms of geographical and climatic pressures on water resources and also in terms of competing interests in conditions of constrained democracy.

Introduction

Although Southeast Asia is a hugely diversified region, Southeast Asian countries share relatively high levels of rainfalls due to its tropical geographic location, and therefore have used water extensively in agriculture throughout history (Hanks, 1972). Water management has been important in terms of controlling seasonal flows to avoid or at least minimize natural disasters such as floods and drought, while channelling the water into the irrigation systems is used to regulate production of rice or other crops. This was assisted by the rain, which fed jungles and forests and the fruit and vegetables that grow within them, since the tree roots helped stabilize the level of water within sub-surface soil. Water was of course important to premodern societies but its management took place in the context of plenty for all: since there was only weak pressure placed on the supply of water, there was little need for states to formalize laws and rights of ownership of water (Boomgaard, 2006). Further, most communities tended to develop their own water management systems according to their own social and economic conditions and in isolation from the rest of the region.

This situation has changed dramatically in recent decades as rapid industrialization has been happening across the region. Industrialization in itself intensifies the demand for water because industry not only uses large amounts of water itself but also pollutes much of it and so reduces the supply of water for other uses (Vörösmarty *et al.*, 2000). Industrialization has also contributed to processes of urbanization, which has produced small areas of densely packed populations that pose issues of water supply that had not previously existed. Increasing standards of living, for some sectors of the population at least, have also led to elevated demand for water (Jenerette & Larsen, 2006). Finally, a number of countries in the region have promoted tourism as a means of furthering economic development and this has greatly increased demand for water in some locations where freshwater might not be abundant: for example, tourism resorts have been established on small islands (such as Samui or Krabi in southern Thailand) where fresh water is not easy to store (Gössling, 2001).

Clearly, therefore, it has become important for states to develop more sophisticated water management regimes that take account of competing demands for water, the equity issues and public health and security issues. These policies should take account of changing conditions arising from global climate change and environmental degradation. For example, changes to the Mekong River basin in recent years have resulted from:

- construction of dams for purposes of irrigation or hydropower generation;
- withdrawal of water for industrial or domestic use;
- land use changes such as deforestation;
- inter- and intra-basin diversions;
- construction of roads, levees, bank protection works (Johnston and Kummu, 2012).

It is clear that water management is likely to be, therefore, a complex undertaking and one that should take account of changing conditions and competing interests.

Water management systems that have been put into place in Southeast Asia have ranged from the autocratic hydraulic empire to colonial systems to those made possible by the rapid industrialization beginning at the end of the past century. The importance of water management in the past prompted the historian Karl Wittfogel (1957) to write about hydraulic empires as aspects of oriental despotism, which was considered to be a distinctive form of governance system in which the manpower and resources of the state were primarily directed towards the control of water; it was considered that successful provision of water was the primary means by which monarchs could obtain legitimation of their role. These ideas have fallen out of favour but it is clear that water management was an important issue and it is one which was subsequently implemented by incoming European colonial powers with a view to organizing peoples and states as well as facilitating extraction of surplus resources. For example, the French colonists in southern Vietnam had canals dug so as to link internal ports of the Mekong Delta to population centres and other ports to transport items back to France (Biggs 2011:30). The same approach was used, for example, by the British in Burma, thereby bringing about the modern shape and structure of Rangoon (Yangon) (Preecharushh, 2009). In some cases, colonial era water management schemes recreated historical systems. By contrast, states which had not been formally colonized, such as Siam (Thailand), mobilised this new technology to modernise their own internal systems (Ten Brummelhuis 2006).

In the period of rapid industrialization, an increasingly influential voice in making decisions has been that of industry, represented by both domestic and international investors. Both factory and hotel owners have considerable demand for high-quality and low-cost water and, given the importance placed upon aggregate economic growth by most governments and their advisors, water distribution systems have often privileged industry above the residential and agricultural sectors. Given the background of apparently unlimited increases in demand for water on the one hand and, on the other, increasing uncertainty about the future supply of water resulting from global climate change, it is clearly important for states to adopt an appropriately joined-up approach to the management of water resources. This chapter outlines contemporary issues of water management in Southeast Asia and uses the example of Thailand to indicate how they are being tackled at the state level.

The integrated water resources management approach

Attempts have been made over the past 60 years or so to create a system of integrated water resources management (IWRM). IWRM incorporates all the various issues relating to water within a geographical territory: groundwater, coastal and riverine resources, distribution and conservation, weather and rain forecasting, public health and the prioritization of different forms of demand for water. The Global Water Partnership (GWP) has defined it as follows:

IWRM is defined as a process which promotes the coordinated development and management of water, land and related resources, in order to maximize the resultant economic and social welfare in an equitable manner without compromising the sustainability of vital ecosystems (GWP, 2000).

The search for a system of IWRM has been supported not just by researchers and civil society activists but, also, by leading international organizations such as the World Bank and Asian Development Bank because it seems to offer an approach that enables quantitative measurement of progress in management in a paradigm of political economy that does not require systematic change. That is, IWRM can be a managerial approach that seeks pragmatically to maximize the efficiency of the system without giving thought to the possibility of an alternative. However, water management problems are not consistent over time or in different geographical areas (Biswas, 2004).

In this context, sustainability is considered to involve the ability to draw upon a resource without compromising the ability of subsequent generations also to draw upon that resource. Of course, the level of accurate data available on the extent to which those resources may be drawn upon in such circumstances is very limited. It is also true that IWRM remains better respected as a concept than as a rigorously tested and examined theory resting on robust data (Stålnacke and Gooch, 2010).

In Southeast Asia, best practice in IWRM is shown in Singapore. It is characterized by a holistic approach to water resources and their management, with advanced technology used to recondition or recycle used water and resources devoted to researching effective use and conservation of water. The citizens of Singapore are aware of water management methods and prepared to put them into practice because they understand the existential threat to the city-state. Of course, the Singaporean government has a number of important advantages in establishing this regime: the limited size of the city state makes the management feasible for individual departments; a unified bureaucracy and political system helps decisions to be made swiftly and with some transparency; a well-educated and motivated population put government initiatives into practice. The water system in Singapore is not ideal, since it is reliant on importing water from neighbouring Malaysia (Tortajada, 2006) and not all aspects of life in Singapore are ideal. However, as a means of putting IWRM into practice, Singapore stands alone in Southeast Asia.

IWRM in practice

IWRM began to emerge as a systematic and sophisticated approach to natural resource management at about the same time that the new public management (NPM) approach was becoming increasingly influential. NPM was first articulated in certain developed nations and was then transmitted to most of the rest of the world by the medium of the international organizations and funding bodies that also adopted it (Lane, 2000). NPM was a response, informed by neoliberalism, to large bureaucratic structures that were perceived to be unwieldy and obstructive to efficient management (König, 1997). NPM proponents called for the fragmentation of bureaucracies and the restructuring of smaller units as agencies, which would compete with each other and bid for scarce resources in a rational manner that should reduce transaction and financial costs. In terms of water management, this has resulted in government agencies at provincial and regional levels providing and demanding water supplies according to a tariff created in line with locally-specific geographic, climatic, infrastructural and supply and demand factors (Bakker, 2003).

This process of marketization or transformation under NPM has also been referred to as a form of transnational enclosure of the commons, which has been described as:

> *... an increasingly centralized decision-making process which enables the state and commercial interests to gain control of territories that have traditionally been used and cherished by local peoples in the Mekong Basin, transforming these areas into expendable resources for exploitation (Santasombat 2011:8).*

When NPM philosophy has been expressed at the local level, through the means of the IWRM, then it has on some occasions been rejected both because of this apparent capture of the commons and because the marketization of water resources seem to be alien concepts and so unwanted (Barlow 2009). This is in addition to the issue of people actually having to manage without sufficient water because of lack of money. These concepts may also be compared unfavourably with locally-specific knowledge and with traditional religious concepts. The opposition to the capitalist exploitation of nature, including water, has also been opposed as a means of promoting both anti-westernization and pro-Buddhism, in which:

> *Species eradication, economic development, individual acquisitiveness, technological control, and anthropocentrism ascribed to Western values are easily contrasted with Buddhist views of humans as part of nature, non-violence, mental awareness, conscious action, and ego extinction (Falvey, 2000).*

IWRM approaches have, notwithstanding these difficulties, been introduced into most Southeast Asian nations in one form or another and with varied degrees of success. Problems that have been experienced as a result relate to lack of technical capacity and physical infrastructure provided by the state and, also, the nature of water resources.

Transboundary issues

One set of issues relating to IWRM in Southeast Asia is that so many water issues are transboundary in nature: in the Mekong Region, most important rivers cross borders and this means that upstream riparian countries have some measure of physical control over the livelihoods of people downstream (Ratner, 2003). In practice, this means that the Chinese state has control over the flow of rivers, which can be affected by building dams and blasting rapids so as to permit the movement of larger boats to trade up and down the river - some of the commodities that may be traded would cause serious environmental damage if there were to be an accident with any of the boats involved. To date, there have been some difficulties in bringing the Chinese government to discuss comprehensive plans for river management (Hensengerth, 2009).

The water supply between Malaysia and Singapore is also problematic (Long, 2001): the latter has insufficient supplies of water to meet the needs of its almost exclusively urban population and must instead import it from its neighbour. Although relations between the two countries are currently more than cordial, this has not always been the case and the future can never be predicted exactly. The Singaporean government has, therefore, been seeking to diversify its possible sources of water through the application of technology and diplomacy (Tortajada, 2006).

Transboundary pollution and climate change issues also affect the other countries of Southeast Asia. Pollution that occurs in one place may exert its primary effects elsewhere, as the *haze* effects from burning agricultural stubble demonstrate (Murdiyaso *et al.*, 2004).

Scale issues

Since traditional water management systems were primarily community-based, they may conflict with state-level management plans. States will appoint agencies to organize water collection and distribution so as to maximize efficiency overall; however, this may not be congruent with the long-term schemes operated by communities, which often utilize local wisdom (i.e. detailed knowledge about geographically specific conditions) and which may incorporate cultural factors into their arrangements. For example, dam building generally required people from a number of villages or larger settlements to be resettled from the affected areas, even though they may have developed religious attachments to specific features in the area and the conditions in any other place might prove unfamiliar and undesirable (MacLean, 2007).

These factors may be complicated by the fact that governments may not always act at the national level. Indeed, governments are very likely to have devolved some authority over water management in some aspects to provincial or district level agencies. If all levels and functions of government mesh together smoothly, then it would not matter at which level any particular action is taken, although many locally-specific differences will also need to be managed (Malano *et al.*, 2009). However, this is rarely the case and, instead, agencies can compete with each other for resources and replicate actions taken by other agencies. This can happen, as has been argued in the case of Thailand, because of conflicting interpretations of legitimacy (Dressel, 2010).

It is not necessary, that is, for people to behave badly to cause this situation. Instead, it can be a measure of the complexity of the issues involved and the nature of competition in trying to resolve them. For example, the island of Phuket off the southern coast of Thailand has passed through a stage of economic development based primarily on tin mining, largely by migrant Chinese labour (Skinner, 1957), to a new stage of economic development dominated by domestic and international tourism (Henderson, 2007). Island authorities - and Phuket is accorded province-level status - find themselves in a situation in which the island has very limited surface and ground water resources to meet the increasing demands for water for both residents and, in particular, hotels and guesthouses. Rivers in Phuket are short; the longest is Klong Bang Yai at just 15 km. As a result, river basins are also limited in size and the river water discharges rapidly into the sea. There is also the problem that the primary provider of ground and surface water is rainfall and this is not just highly variable on a seasonal basis but that variation is negatively correlated with demand: that is, tourists usually want to visit outside of the monsoon season when the rain is less likely to fall. There is only limited scope to retain water for later use for geographical regions.[6] The strategy that has been adopted, largely on a pragmatic or emergent basis, to deal with this situation includes the following elements:

- Diversification of water supply sources: some water is imported from neighbouring Phang-nga and Krabi provinces, where watershed areas are more plentiful. Much of this water arrives in trucks across the bridge that links Phuket to the mainland or else by boat. This is water purchased at a market rate from the water authority active there. Island authorities also purchase water from private sector providers. Prominent among these are owners of the 113 mine pits across the island, many in the Thalang district, which have been converted to reservoirs to hold water for sale to the public sector. There are also a number of registered and unregistered wells that are in private hands and some of these also sell water to the authorities. The ability of central government to keep track of all of these wells is rather limited and accurate data are not always available. Fees are payable on registered wells.
- Improving capacity: both public and private sector activities are involved in increasing water delivery capacity, through a combination of dams, detention basins and water salination plants. Each of these projects has its own calculus of rate of return, payback period and so forth and this will make price calculations continue to be complex.
- Promoting awareness of the importance of water conservation: hotels and businesses are encouraged to display signs pointing out the importance and scarcity of water and the need, therefore, to restrict its use wherever possible. It is not clear to what extent this may be said to be successful in actually reducing water use.

There is a particular problem with respect to promoting the necessary social solidarity required for campaigns that significantly change people's behaviour and that is that most of the people involved are not natives or long-term residents of the island. This is evidently true of tourists who, by definition, have made a

[6] This section relies on findings from doctoral level research conducted by Ms. Alin Chintraruck at the School of Management, Shinawatra University.

comparatively short-scale visit to Phuket but it is also true of the workers in the service sector, the majority of whom are migrants from other parts of Thailand, where average wages are lower.

The example of Phuket indicates a number of the problems attached with the IWRM system in practice. The complexities of mobilizing multiple current and future sources of water and distributing them according to a more or less rational basis are such that little meaningful attention can be given, in the circumstances of limited technical capacity and resources, to long-term issues of sustainability or equity. In some cases, it would be beneficial if cross-border agreements could be reached which united upstream and downstream regions, as well as areas of supply and demand, on a reasonable basis. However, such agreements have not been reached to date and, given the uncertainties represented by global climate change, it is not likely that such agreements will be easily reached in the future. Perhaps the best to be hoped for is that, as time passes, the processes and policies that have been introduced to involved IWRM in local economies will become more deeply embedded and, as a result, local conditions may be used to formulate solutions for any particular problems encountered.

Implications for the field

It is well-established that obtaining community engagement and support is central to achieving the success of development projects, broadly defined. Since water resources and their management are essential elements for life, it is inevitable that people will be occupying areas where water exists and will be making use of them, whether this is for drinking, fishing, irrigation or industry of a different sort. Throughout history, people in Southeast Asia have become accustomed to receiving water services for free and, as mentioned above, for ideological or religious reasons, people and communities generally may feel that they should continue to receive water for free. This desire is contradicted by the various institutions of marketization and that leads to some conflict. As a result, the success of a contemporary IWRM approach is only likely to be achieved when people can be persuaded that they should pay for what they have previously taken for granted and that it is right that they should do so. Moving to a market-based system will inevitably lead to some people being unable to pay for water, unless the water is provided at an unfeasibly low rate or else there is widespread theft. It would benefit from the use of the media, religious figures and celebrities to help persuade people of the benefits of market-based systems. It will also be important to build social solidarity by ensuring that leading figures and organizations are seen to be paying their way in terms of water provision.

In practical terms, the divergences in scale tend to lead to mismatches between the interests and desires of different sets of people affected by the distribution of water resources. For example, in Davao City in the Philippines, 98 percent of the water supply is provided from groundwater sources, which have come under pressure from people who do not have access to potable water of their own and, therefore, have no incentives to try to manage the water sustainably. This represented a serious problem for the responsible agency, Davao City Water District (DCWD). The response needed to be a long-term one, involving a five-year partnership with the central funding agency for water, the Local Water Utilities Administration (LWUA). After initial funding by the DCWD, it became clear that there could be engagement with the affected local people, who could be drawn into the community-based organization and, eventually, the Adopt-a-site campaign. Once the engagement of the people had been obtained, the rehabilitation of the affected area took place much more efficiently (GWP, 2008a).

A slightly different approach has been taken in Vietnam, in part due to the different nature of the relationship state and people. An example of how this took place is in Tien Giang province of Vietnam, where UNICEF had launched a project to dig wells for various communities who were living in areas where much of the available water resources had been negatively affected by animal and human excreta, salinity and other types of pollution. After the campaign had begun other communities tried to follow suit of their own volition but without appropriate levels of engineering knowledge, dug wells that were too shallow and badly positioned to be of any use and, indeed, drew water that was dangerous to use. As a result, the Vietnamese government instituted a national plan for National Rural Water Supply and Sanitation (RWSS) that involved the creation of a coordinated plan for providing the people affected with appropriate degrees of technical assistance and a means of enacting information, education and communication (IEC) activities. Although cooperation was received from the local people and their quality of life and health improved, this was done through complying with the government level plans rather than creating and enacting schemes of their own (GWP, 2008b). The benefit of this has been that a properly integrated approach has been taken into account and the various aspects and tasks have all been included within the overall plan. RWSS has been used as a starting place for campaigns of poverty reduction or eradication and it certainly does have a role to play in forming a baseline for development subsequently.

Conclusion

It seems hard to imagine that a successful IWRM approach can successfully be implemented in Southeast Asia at the state level in any country much larger than Singapore. The messy democracies of the region give too much power to patronage networks and regional power sources and too little effective power to central state agencies for a properly integrated approach to be employed. By contrast, those states with centralized authorities tend to have too little technical capacity or incentive to enforce a universal and integrated approach throughout the territory. However, there are opportunities to do so at lower or smaller geographical scales and these are opportunities that should be explored as far as possible. Even when a full IWRM approach cannot be implemented, the effort to conceptualise how it might be put into place will be a useful one in developing local capacity.

References

Bakker, K. (2003). Archipelagos and networks: Urbanization and water privatization in the South. *The Geographical Journal*, 169(4), 328-41.

Barlow, M. (2009). *Blue covenant: The global water crisis and the coming battle for the right to water*. New York, NY: The New Press.

Biggs, D. (2011). *Quagmire: Nation-building and nature in the Mekong delta*. Chiang Mai: Silkworm Books.

Biswas, A.K. (2004). Integrated water resources management: A reassessment: A Water Forum contribution. *Water International*, 29(2), 248-56.

Boomgaard, P. (2006). *Southeast Asia: An environmental history*. Santa Barbara, CA: ABC-Clio.

Dressel, B. (2010). When notions of legitimacy conflict: The case of Thailand. *Politics and Policy*, 38(3), 445-69.

Falvey, L. (2000). Self-sufficiency or Buddhism? Applied agricultural ethics in Thailand. *Tai Culture*, 5(2), 15-34.

GWP-TAC (Global Water Partnership Technical Advisory Committee) (2000). *Integrated Water Resources Management*, Stockholm: TAC Background Paper No. 4.

Global Water Partnership (2008a). Philippines: Watershed rehabilitation and management strategies in Davao City Water District (#293). Retrieved from: www.gwptoolbox.org/index.php?option=com_case&id=183&itemid=46.

Global Water Partnership (2008b). Vietnam: IWRM principles strengthen sustainability of rural water supply and sanitation, case #122. Retrieved from: www.gwptoolbox.org/images/stories/cases/en/cs%20122%20vietnam.pdf.

Gössling, S. (2001). The consequences of tourism for sustainable water use on a tropical island: Zanzibar, Tanzania. *Journal of Environmental Management*, 61(2), 179-91.

Hanks, L.M. (1972). *Rice and man: Agricultural ecology in Southeast Asia*. Hawthorne, NY: Aldine Publishing Co.

Henderson, J.C. (2007). Corporate social responsibility and tourism: Hotel companies in Phuket, Thailand, after the Indian Ocean tsunami. *International Journal of Hospitality Management*, 26(1), 228-39.

Hensengerth, O. ((2009). Transboundary river cooperation and the regional public good: The case of the Mekong River. *Contemporary Southeast Asia*, 31(2), 326-49.

Jenerette, D.G. & Larsen, L. (2006). A global perspective on changing sustainable urban water supplies. *Global and Planetary Change*, 50(3-4), 202-11.

Johnston, R. & Kummu, M. (2012). Water resource models in the Mekong basin: A review. *Water Resources Management*, 26(2), 429-55.

König, K. (1997). Entrepreneurial management or executive administration: The perspective of classical public administration. In W. Kickert (ed.). *Public Management and Administrative Reform in Western Europe*. Cheltenham: Edward Elgar, 217-236.

Long, J. (2001). Desecuritizing the water issue in Malaysia-Singapore relations. *Contemporary Southeast Asia*, 23(3), 504-32.

MacLean, Ken (2007). Spaces of extraction: Governance along the riverine networks of Nyaunglebin district.' In Monique Skidmore and Trevor Wilson (eds.), *Myanmar: The State, Community and the Environment*, Canberra: Asia Pacific Press, 2007, 246-70, available at: http://epress.anu.edu.au/wp-content/uploads/2011/03/whole_book22.pdf.

Malano, H.M., Bryant, M.J. & Turral, H.N. (1999). Management of water resources: Can Australian experiences be transferred to Vietnam? *Water International*, 24(4), 307-15.

Murdiyaso, D., Lebel, L., Gintings, A.N., Tampubolon, S.M.H., Heil, A. & Wasson, M. (2004). Policy responses to complex environmental problems: Insights from a science-policy activity on transboundary haze from vegetation fires in Southeast Asia. *Agriculture, Ecosystems and Environment*, 104(1), 47-56.

Preecharushh, D. (2009). *Naypyidaw: The new capital of Myanmar*. Bangkok: White Lotus Books.

Ratner, B.D. (2003). The politics of regional governance in the Mekong River basin. *Global Change*, 15(1), 59-76.

Santasombat, Y. (2011). *The river of life: Changing ecosystems of the Mekong region*. Chiang Mai: Mekong Press.

Skinner, G.W. (1957). *Chinese society in Thailand: An analytical history*. Ithaca, NY: Cornell University Press.

Stålnacke, P. & Gooch, G.D. (2010). Integrated water resources management. *Irrigation and Drainage Systems*, 24, 155-9.

Ten Brummelhuis, H. (2006). *King of the waters: Homan Van Der Heide and the origin of modern irrigation in Siam*. Leiden: Koninklijk Instituut Voor Taal Land.

Tortajada, C. (2006). Water management in Singapore. *International Journal of Water Resources Development*, 22(2), 227-40.

Vörösmarty, C.J., Green, P., Salisbury J. & Lammers, R.B. (2000). Global water resources: Vulnerability from climate change and population growth. *Science*, 289, 284-8.

Wittfogel, K.A. (1957). *Oriental despotism: A comparative study of total power.* New York: Vintage.

Chapter 6

Improved leadership in the Lao PDR

Developing a framework for sustainable development

VORADA SAVENGSEUKSA

ABSTRACT

In a time of rapid change and globalization, the Lao PDR (or hereinafter referred to as Laos) stands in a unique position in the world of development. This paper examines INGOs as non-state actors in Laos who aim to contribute to the public service sector through a variety of projects. Country directors and program managers from seven INGO entities shared their insights on their thoughts of organizational success, sustainability, and leadership as it relates to working within the political context of Laos. From the findings, it is recommended that aspiring organizations consider these guidelines: to strengthen engagement with government; build capacity of Lao leaders and staff; incorporate research and technical skills for organization improvement; position foreign administrators and staff to financially sustain the agency; and explore partnerships in the private and non-profit sector. We hope a discussion of these themes will support the development of a strategic framework that supports in-country leadership and capacity building for INGOs.

Introduction

In a place where customs and rituals remain rich and vital, globalisation, transnationalism, and pressing goals for development have made an impact on Laos culturally, socially, and economically. This chapter will begin with a brief history of the country and how it has played a crucial role in defining what is Laos today, including its political structures and investments in human resources.

Laos has had a long, turbulent past, and we will focus on its history starting at the end of French colonial rule and an era of state independence during the 1950s. This period had experienced shifts in ideology and nationalism while the nation searched for a new identity as an independent country (Evans, 2002). When Communist forces seized power in 1975, a substantial number of exiles fled the country in response to political instability and turmoil. This group included highly educated individuals in business, law, health, art, education, and more - individuals who had a wealth of expertise and specialisation. This exodus had a significant impact on the domestic human resource capacity to work in areas of high demand (Holland, 1995), contributing to a significant *brain drain* from Laos to more developed nations in North America, Europe, and Australia. Although it has been over 36 years since the governing Communism began, the land-locked country of approximately 6.6 million continues to experience challenges in economic and human development, especially as it relates to shortages of highly skilled personnel in the public service sector (Holland, 1995).

Laos began to gradually open its doors to the rest of world as part of their economic reform agenda in 1986 by moving from a centrally focused economy to a more market-oriented one (Asian Development Bank; Andriesse, 2011; Evans, 2002). In the following years of reform, more private businesses, non-profit organizations, and social enterprises began to tap into Laos' private market as well as initiate public interest projects. Of the many industries in Laos, agriculture has been vital to livelihoods given that it makes up approximately 75 percent of employment (CIA World FactBook, 2012). The rapid economic growth in Laos has led to better living standards in some parts of the country (Epprecht, 2002). However, despite these improvements, Laos as a whole is still relatively poor (Epprecht, 2002; UNDP Lao, 2012) and heavily reliant on foreign aid to support its infrastructure and human development sector.

In response to new economic agendas, Laos and its neighbouring countries have partnered to make substantial private investments in Laos' big industries such as hydropower, mining, and construction projects. Forging bonds with countries like China, Thailand, and Viet Nam has been one way to finance projects and enhance trade in the mainland Southeast Asian region (CIA World FactBook, 2012). It is also probable that these countries have an influence on Laos' development policies and initiatives provided that they have a critical stake in large-scale projects across different industries.

Although the injection of financial capital from outside sources appears to be helping Laos economically, the externalities of these developments have negatively affected communities living in rural areas and created unsustainable environmental pressures (UNDP Lao, 2012). Rural areas lag significantly behind the rest of the country while larger urban cities have improved robustly in their standard of living (Epprecht, 2002). Moreover, it is evident that the impact of a rapidly developing economy has contributed to greater income inequalities in Laos (Government of Lao PDR). Andersson *et al.* (2006) analysed Lao Expenditure and Consumption Survey (LECS) data in a recent paper observed that 'the differences between rich and poor in each individual region are larger than the differences in the averages between regions'. Disparities in income and consumption vary more within specific areas than when compared between regions, requiring a different approach to reducing and evaluating poverty measures disaggregated by geography.

Another imperative subject relevant to the development policy is Laos' adoption of the Millennium Declaration as set by the United Nations (UN) in 2000. Laos has committed to reaching the eight Millennium Development Goals (MDGs) by 2015, including an additional 9th localised goal in clearing unexploded ordnance (UXO) leftover from the Viet Nam War era (UNDP Lao, 2012). Dependence on foreign assistance is substantial overall; for example, the OECD (2012) reports that in 2009, nearly US$543 million was Laos' net official development aid (ODA), and its ODA that year averaged 86 percent of central government expenditures. With 2015 approaching, Laos is struggling to quickly achieve the majority of the MDGs, let alone stay on track to meet them (Government of Lao PDR & the UN, 2008). Even though the country faces considerable obstacles working towards the Millennium Initiative, it has demonstrated some success such as staying on target to reduce extreme poverty, preventing the spread of communicable diseases, and ensure environmental sustainability by providing improved drinking water and sanitation to urban areas (Government of Lao PDR & the UN, 2010; World Bank, 2013). For Laos, the progress towards the MGDs has been moving, but at a very slow rate, and there are possible challenges in balancing said progress with cultural vitality and preservation. More advancement seems promising given recent development reforms such as the 7th National Socio-Economic Development Plan (NSEDP) (World Bank, 2013) laid out for 2011 through 2015.

On the note of the NSEDP, the government's plan includes a priority for better infrastructure and technological systems (World Bank, 2013). While cities and urbanised areas are moving towards modernisation, road systems in rural areas are far from developed. Technology is similar to road infrastructure in that it is not widespread to all residents. As of 2010, electricity coverage in Laos reached 71 percent of the population, and the Government of the Lao PDR is making a goal to reach 90 percent of the population by 2020 (World Bank, 2011). Lack of access to electricity, technology, and transportation routes are found to be some of the main determinants of poverty in these areas. This may continue to raise concerns about investing and implementing plans for building sustainable technological and physical infrastructures that would increase access in rural environments.

Provided some context in Laos' development affairs, this does have some implications about the sustainability of practices, policy, and systems when implementing social and public initiatives. We will focus primarily on the status quo of the human development sector and capacity building in the INGO sector of Laos. The following background information will provide more substantive context in light of the research carried out, all of which will be explained in the next section.

Laos' current domestic workforce continues to face a shortage of highly skilled professionals working in both the private and public sector, perhaps as a consequence of historic brain drain and now having such a young population, among other systemic factors. Over half of the residents of Laos are under the age of 21 and are largely rural, and this suggests that the majority of the population lacks sufficient formal education and professional experience to contribute to mainstream workforce (CIA World FactBook, 2012). Moreover, provided that about 75 percent of workers are in agricultural activities (CIA World FactBook, 2012), other areas of work such as government/social service and businesses both big and small make up for the remaining quarter of workers, likely stretching these industries thin with fewer employees.

When discussing the historical roots of the limited in-country human development, it is important to bear in mind the limitations of the current school systems. Laos has dealt with barriers in education at the primary and secondary levels (Asian Development Bank; Sisavanh, 2003; Adams *et al.*, 2001), including access, quality, enrolment, and retention particularly among females and ethnic minorities. The shortage of primary and secondary school teachers, high dependency ratio, tuition expenses, and family dynamics may be considerable obstacles in retaining students and preparing a young population for professionalism and leadership. For instance, the social norms of family preservation may lead to decisions ceasing children's enrolment in schools so they can support agricultural activities and income-generation.

With regards to salient aspects of Lao cultural life, Lao culture may be characterised as being community-minded and focused on family preservation. Theravada Buddhism is widely practiced in Laos, and Lao Buddhists have retained customs in their communities over generations. While it is devoutly Buddhist, it is also home to a large number of ethnic minorities coming with their own customs, rituals, and traditions. While the exact number of ethnic minorities is still disputed, there are no fewer than 49 officially recognised ethnic minorities, thus making Laos rich in its diversity (UNESCO, Bangkok Office, 2012). Much of the poverty in Laos is concentrated among ethnic groups and also the most severe forms of poverty. Globalisation and industrialisation have also changed sustainability of livelihoods of ethnic groups residing in remote villages, showing concerns about shifts in cultural preservation and poverty reduction strategies among Laos' poorest members.

Subject background: Human development sector of Laos

The *status quo* of the human resources sector may suggest that Laos is still dependent on foreign assistance to ensure that systems management and administration in the public service sector are up to speed in meeting the needs of its mandates. The conversation on sustainability has shifted to not only bringing in a wealth of fiscal resources to the country, but, more importantly, to provide technical assistance and training to boost domestic workforce skills. Moreover, specialised management, leadership, and strategy to oversee complex operations are areas that have substantial room to improve, although at current, the number of Lao nationals with these skills seems to be severely lacking.

There are policies that have emerged from the Lao government in response to the MDGs and to the pressure from the international community to meet those goals. Therefore the climate of public service and community work has changed substantially for INGOs in carrying out their activities. With regards to the shifts in managing policy, strategic planning, and leadership, administrators must be able to design strategic frameworks that can be applies to non-governmental organizations and community-based initiatives specific to Laos and mainland Southeast Asia. This chapter will focus on sharing research from seven international non-government organization (INGO) entities and developing a preliminary framework that touches on key themes in organizational structure, internal capacity building, and managing processes. This research includes organizations representing many public sector activities such as primary and secondary education, UXO clearance, environmental and wildlife conservation, land rights, health and sanitation, child welfare, human trafficking and sexual abuse, and alternate livelihood creation. For reasons of confidentiality, the names of these agencies will not be disclosed in this chapter.

Research materials and methodology

Seven public sector entities were contacted as part of this process. Six of them are registered INGOs operating in Laos and one was the advocacy network that serves as a liaison between all member INGOs and the Government of the Lao PDR. As mentioned previously, the names of these organizations will not be disclosed in this chapter. The seven groups focus on multi-sector work and have had a presence in Laos for at least fifteen years with the exception of a non-direct service advocacy group established approximately seven years ago. The six organizations run social programs targeting the most vulnerable and needy, covering primary and secondary education, microfinance, capacity building for water and sanitation, UXO education and awareness, land rights, women and child welfare, environmental conservation, and more.

A general interview guide was created and focused on three key areas: (1) organizational impact, (2) managing processes and politics, and (3) internal capacity to manage processes in the long term. It should be noted that the interview guide was used to facilitate the conversation with each respondent and not every question was asked verbatim; nonetheless, the three broad areas were discussed with respondents. Hand-written notes were taken during each interview.

Respondents held managerial or administrative positions for at least one year, either being country directors, coordinators, or program managers. All were expatriates from the US, Australia, or France and have had previous experience working in other developing nations within and outside of Asia Pacific. Each interview was conducted in English, in-person, and lasted between one hour and one and a half hours.

Findings

The findings revealed a number of important themes in development work in Laos. Each of these themes are described in detail based on interviewee responses.

Common models of public service

Respondents shared that there are, in general, two main modes of service delivery in Laos for most INGOs, and a third mode is a combination of the first two. Each of these models have different implications for how effective they are in strengthening diplomacy, in-country capacity building, and foreign human resources; we will also discuss their tradeoffs given the political context for each approach.

Model 1: INGOs as fiscal agents, governments as implementers

The first model insists that INGOs are only a fiscal agent that supports government projects and services and INGOs must have a memorandum of understanding (MOU) with the relevant ministry it intends to support. Often times funding and assistance will go towards government activities and capacity building for public employees. In one interview, a respondent shared that through this model, INGOs may be part of the planning and pre-evaluation phase of the process, but they are not responsible for the direct implementation activities, and this is the duty of the Lao government administration. It supports an approach that ideally would use funds to bolster the capacity of government workers and ensure a more sustainable in-country approach. As one interviewee put it, many INGOs say they would like to be 'out of Laos sometime soon', pointing to an end-in-sight where INGOs have done their work building a functional in-country system for public service carried out by civil society. On the other hand, while this model supports building in-country systems for public service workers, there are drawbacks for INGOs having significantly less involvement in the implementation process. Interviewees expressed that this model is the most preferred approach by the Lao government in that it gives them the resources to do their work, and it enhances the diplomatic relations between government departments and INGOs. However, there are few accountability mechanisms in place for INGOS to know where their monetary sources are going, how public value is defined and created by the government, and how governments as implementers will measure their impact.

Model 2: INGOs as a fiscal agent and as implementer

The second model suggests that INGOs are both the fiscal agent - acquiring funds through grants, private donations, etc. - and the primary implementer that hires its own staff, managers, and administrators to carry out activities. This also means the INGO does not require the support of government workers on the frontline activities. INGOs who aspire to operate with this approach must be approved by local and national governments and have memorandums with relevant ministries also. In the context of the political climate, Model 2 is less preferred by national governments because of the lack of control they may have in how INGOs are involved with the development agenda. Because INGOs are seen as decentralised entities that often serve as an in-between role for business and government, there is not a consistent, direct accountability mechanism between INGO workers and their national counterparts. In reality, there are very few organizations that solely provide services without the direct participation of government workers; if they exist, they operate inconspicuously and at the risk of expulsion. While this model would be preferred by most INGOs, there are far and few in between that actually operate on their own with the approval of political authorities.

Model 3: Building INGO-government partnerships

A third model (Model 3) is a fusion of both, where the INGO acquires funds to operate, manages direct-service projects that use its own staff, yet still supports government staff by building capacity in partnership. The third model is often called a 'partnership' model where both internal (i.e. in-house INGO staff) and external (i.e. government workers) participation in public service delivery and programming.

Model 3 is the most ideal for both sides of INGOs and government as it is a way for both to meet in the middle. However, there are many different ways a partnership can form. Some INGOs experience much frustration as the authority over a partnership agreement is rarely symmetrical in power dynamics - that is, government still has control over the legitimising processes (i.e. signing on memorandums, approving permits, etc.) that often delay the ability for organizations to carry out their work. On the other hand, some INGOs find that the partnership model works extremely well for them, and they have had more positive experiences working with a variety of ministries in education, health, agriculture, welfare, rural development, and planning/investment. More importantly, government workers have a chance to learn competencies through INGO-led training and hopefully return to their jobs as government workers with a more valuable skill set. Successful INGOs who have used this approach have built a strong reputation over time - at least over a 15 year period - where their influence in the public sector is well known and legitimising processes can be less difficult with governments. In some cases, when INGO's influence over policy processes is weak, they still continue to maintain mutually favourable relations with government agencies if they have a strong reputation in public service and uphold a collaborative approach in their mission.

Working with governments: Factors making implementation feasible

There are several factors that contribute to the feasibility of working with governments. One of those factors includes *an understanding and adherence to government policy on monitoring*. INGOs are required to have a government counterpart present during major activities to monitor compliance. Collaboration with local-level government is much more *user-friendly* to INGO workers, although policies across districts and provinces still need to be standardised. For INGOs working in multiple villages and provinces, the lack of standardisation can make communication and compliance challenging even at the local perspective. On the other hand, interviewees expressed that working at the ministerial level is much more challenging given the level of scrutiny and the added layers of bureaucracy in the authorisation process, often running into impracticality.

Overall, from the respondents, it appears that INGOs that emphasise partnership with government – whether local or nation-wide – usually experience more advantages than disadvantages. INGOs are in a unique position to directly engage with those at the local level, and local authorities are also in a unique position to advocate for the services of INGOs to their nation-wide counterparts. Therefore, this is a symbiotic relationship between local government agencies and international non-profit organizations. The partnership at the national level poses bigger challenges mostly because of more bureaucracy, difficulties to find a point of entry, slower processes and more likelihood of corrupt practices (i.e. bribery, laundering, etc.). As one respondent said, 'the higher you go, the harder it becomes' to gain legitimacy as an INGO. Although in some cases climbing higher into nation-wide bureaucracies is avoided, INGOs must understand and comply with national policies (such as registration, activity monitoring, etc.) due to risk of violating Lao PDR laws and expulsion.

For those who have more positive experiences partnering with higher level government ministries, there are a number of factors that make their activities feasible in the context of Laos' way of policy and practice. First, *professional and personal connections to insiders of the relevant ministries can facilitate communication and expediting processes* without resorting to corrupt practice. Another factor of feasibility is having *strong leadership and knowledge base among Lao nationals*, especially if pre-existing connections do not exist. Leaders with a great level of knowledge in their field and a forward-thinking perspective are highly valuable when working with government agencies. Over time, they have built a reputation as one of the experts in their profession and leverage their specialisation as a way to maintain government collaboration. Third, timing is critical factor. Some organizations experience less difficulty because they have *demonstrated impact over a number of years and have effective advocacy methods to show for their milestones*. A combination of these factors – connections to the government, strong leadership capacity, and demonstrated results over time can support better collaboration with government agencies for INGOs.

It is worth mentioning that respondents shared that the Lao government overall tends to focus more on the inputs of the development process (i.e. fiscal resources and government staff). Most INGOs currently in Laos focus on implementing its activities, outputs, and outcomes to produce their intended impact. This disconnect in thinking can be a challenge, and having this conversation with government officials can be, at times, very frustrating for some INGO leaders. However, there are a number of directors that assert their focus on implementation processes and outcomes in government agreements. Given more time, greater reputation, and stronger leadership, INGOs can work to keep governments accountable and transparent. For instance, an interviewee reported that their contracts can become 'very detailed and meticulous' because government agencies may have challenges in 'keeping up their end of the bargain'. Young and aspiring INGOs may not experience these interactions with the Lao government immediately but over time, they may contribute to enforcing accountability as the organization matures and as they develop a communication strategy.

Lao leadership development within INGOs

As mentioned previously, strong leadership capacity is a factor that contributes to effective partnerships with government officials. At each of the six INGOs, there is at least one appointed Lao national leader who facilitates communication with a range of high-level representatives. One would observe that successful INGO-government partnerships normally have a team of Lao coordinators/managers that are required to liaise with the governments rather than having only one appointed Lao leader. Moreover, some expatriate country directors choose to liaise with government at a very minimum, not because they may not have the skills, but instead they prefer a *hands-off* approach. For some expatriate administrators, stepping back means that Lao nationals in leadership roles will adapt to working with their government counterparts and get involved in creative problem-solving when challenges in collaboration arise.

The structure of these Lao leadership teams is very flat at some INGOs; that is, all have equal authority and influence in decision-making among each other. They also routinely convene for the purpose of information-sharing, peer and social support. Expatriate country directors often play an advisory role if they participate in these Lao leadership teams. The hope is that if managers coordinate among themselves to meet routinely and plan collective together, they can innovate freely without relying on the expatriate authority. Moreover, it gives them a greater sense of ownership of their work because they can build more expertise, a more unified voice, and a support system for one another.

On the contrary, for Lao leadership that is not structured in teams, one may observe higher potential for burn-out. That is, the Lao leader acting alone may experience an increased workload mitigating processes with government officials, and therefore they may require greater social and emotional support from their superiors. Those superiors are likely the expatriate directors who often play a role in advising/mentoring their staff and managers, and in turn, expatriate administrators may also feel an increase in their workload to support their Lao nationals. However, Lao nationals made into teams could be associated with better moral and social support, and thus dependence on executive directors to provide managerial and social support may become less so.

INGO leaders shared that other organizations choose to build leadership capacity through mentoring and support systems. Part of the organization is designated as 'senior staff', while the other recent incoming or younger employees are 'junior staff'. By empowering others, senior staff can empower themselves and hold each other accountable to lead by example. Junior staff is able to learn from those who have been with the INGO longer and can later fill roles as senior staff mentors, reinforcing institutional knowledge and social support. The staff are not only mentored in technical trainings (i.e. computer systems, data analysis, communications), but what makes them unique is a 'critical thinking' approach around having a deeper understanding of the field they are working in. For example, organizations focused on women & child welfare often link their projects to *big picture* subjects such as education, family values, single parents, and economic livelihoods at their monthly meetings. Holistic approaches such as this support comprehensive learning, thus the intention is to give Lao staff a chance to make connections in their work in public service. Ultimately these models of continuous training and mentoring are meant to develop and retain staff by building peer support, to produce opportunities for multidisciplinary knowledge, and to share leadership among all employees (as opposed to concentrating it all at the top).

Roles of foreign leadership in INGOs

Provided that many organizations have an expatriate presence usually in an administrative role, the dynamic between foreign managers and local staff should be explored. The following highlights the most salient themes when discussing the role of international managers and directors at INGOs.

Social support for Lao nationals in leadership

Many expatriate administrators see themselves informally providing social support to Lao nationals in leadership roles. This is especially the case for Lao managers or coordinators who are at the forefront of decision-making with government agencies. Working directly with Lao governments is perceived as having a heavy workload as it requires much patience, persistence, and morale. This work burden may potentially lead to burn out among individuals, whether foreign or national; however, Lao national leaders may seek more encouragement and support from their organizational peers to make tasks more feasible and satisfactory. Despite the social needs of Lao nationals, some respondents also shared that they would prefer to establish boundaries between Lao leaders and themselves in order to maintain a professional working relationship. That is, some foreign managers would rather provide technical support and programmatic details so that Lao leaders and nationals are well-informed when speaking with government counterparts; in other words, it is important in professionalism to leave 'the emotions at the door' as one interviewee shared. It is possible that being a source of emotional support is an unintended outcome of working as a foreign director or manager; it is also probable that some directors may be more sensitive to this more than others, and therefore sets the professional (and personal) expectations between international directors and Lao leaders.

Advisory role to guide operations

Some expatriate administrators prefer to take on a more removed advisory role to provide Lao nationals with more autonomy. In practice, advisory roles include giving guidance to program details of current operations and any feedback on the design of future projects. In many ways, an advisory role is much more hands-off – the directors who adopt this practice believe it is deliberate and necessary to the organization's mission of adaptability and sustainability. While expatriate administrators want to stay involved in helping the organization, they often defer to their Lao national leaders to be the real experts in public service work and to take ownership of the decision-making process. Expatriates navigate to strike a balance of being immersed and being *removed* from much of the programmatic decision-making. Having balance is an attempt to dissolve some of the power asymmetries between foreigners and locals in development work, allowing more Lao nationals to weigh in more on organizational operations.

Problem solving and conflicts

Social norms play a considerable part in how people discuss problems and conflicts as they emerge. Respondents in this research shared that they usually intervene when 'big problems' arise related to the use of financial resources or risk of staff reputation and safety. Other times there may be unexpected changes in the implementation of activities where Lao nationals may call to expatriate leadership to address the problem. Some respondents have theorised that the collectivist culture strives to maintain harmony and to dissolve tension; therefore Lao nationals may look to expatriates to step in as 'outsiders' of the culture and relieve the pressure since being a member of the out-group (instead of in-group as a Lao national) helps expatriates discuss sensitive issues when warranted.

However, while the expatriate role is effective in some cases, they may not suit all problematic scenarios and therefore do not require a response from an out-group foreigner. Respondents have also shared that despite these cultural norms, some Lao nationals adapt quickly and practice addressing issues on their own, in spite of risking their reputation, safety, or friendly collegiality. As one interviewee shared, 'Lao nationals know more about the cultural norms of respect' and conflict; they should be trusted to create their own ways of mitigating a serious problem, whereas a foreigner, no matter how long they are living in the country, will not ever 'completely understand' how to navigate the cultural aspects in confronting others. Some expatriate administrators step back in the majority of conflicting situations to empower Lao nationals by letting them learn from the experience.

Bridges between INGOs and funders

The majority of respondents expressed that foreigners have an essential responsibility in the funding process. Presently, much of civil society has little training or experience in grant writing, philanthropy, or reporting financial records back to funders. Because of the lack of training in fundraising, some foreign administrators with better access to information and processes believe that this is one of the primary roles in supporting the organization in the long-term. At a minimum, expatriates can help finance the agency's operations and ensure funds are efficiently spent to carry out services in a sustainable way.

Conclusion and implications

Based on the findings from this research, there are a number of implications on how aspiring INGOs can proceed to structure their organizations with regards to leadership and management. Below are recommendations for newer INGOs working in Southeast Asia, and in particular the Lao PDR. While the recommendations do not serve as a strict guide for development work and has not accounted for a wide range of external factors, they are worth considering as an INGO becomes more established, matures over time, and undergoes different stages of its mission, operational capacity, and political environment.

Strengthen engagement in government affairs

Forging partnerships with governments can support the INGO's sustainability. Collaborative work will strengthen an INGO's understanding of government monitoring and the guidelines to adhere to policies to the best of their capacity. Engagement on the local *and* national level is necessary for successful INGOs. Also stay connected with local governments since they are in a unique position to advocate as beneficiaries in their communities. Moreover, foster communication with government works to make connections inside of the agency; they may serve as a valuable resource in addressing any bureaucratic challenges. If making connections is not feasible, build expertise within the INGO to strengthen its reputation in specific policy fields. Lastly, agencies may develop a strategic communication plan to frame their organizational objectives to align with national objectives – especially if national priorities seem to be centred on private sector development. Pursuing these goals will hopefully establish a strong rapport in INGO-government partnerships to sustain the INGO in its future of public service work.

Emphasise building capacity for Lao leaders and staff

Leadership development among Lao INGO managers and staff is important for sustaining an agency's operations. Opportunities to problem-solve and provide peer support within teams may encourage adaptability and better morale. Such opportunities may require less administrative control from the top of the organization and greater autonomy for Lao nationals as they work with governments and projects. Designing and enforcing support systems among Lao staff and managers can also strengthen the organization's comprehensive learning from each other.

Incorporate research and technical expertise in relevant fields

Research is a strong component that will support an organization with the most current information on policy, practice, and lessons learned with other agencies and programs. Encouraging local leaders to engage in information seeking and sharing will allow them to become experts in their area of work. Moreover, interdisciplinary research may also inform creative project design and implementation that can be carried out alongside other INGOs and/or government agencies.

Utilise the role of expatriates in advisory work and revenue generation

It is inevitable that expatriates will have a presence in INGOs until the systems in place will support a stronger domestic workforce in public service. Taking into account the aforementioned elements, it would be best to support INGOs in its fund raising, financial management, and reporting relevant to operational capacity of the agency. Financial management and revenue can also support enhancing the skill set of both INGO workers (national and foreign) and their government counterparts.

Explore different ways to partner with other entities – both in the public and private sector

As INGOs continue to think about sustainability of their operations, they must consider different modes of collaboration. Hybrid models, where both business and traditional non-profits merge to have an interest in making a commercial *and* social impact, have emerged recently and they should be examined for best practices. Forging networks with other agencies, be it INGOs, civil society organizations, businesses, or government, may bring about more collective benefits than drawbacks in the long-term.

These recommendations are a starting point for aspiring international agencies to consider as we all continue to work towards bolstering the public service systems in Laos and Southeast Asia, especially in leadership, management, and capacity building. The hope is that these framework elements will guide us to critically think about what it means to be a sustainable organization working in development.

References

Adams, D., Kee, G.H., and Lin, L. (2001). Linking Research, Policy, and Strategic Planning to Education Development in Lao People's Democratic Republic. *Comparative Education Review* 45(2): 220-241.

Andersson, M., Engvall, A., and Kokko, A. (2003). Determinants of Poverty in Lao PDR (Working Paper). Stockholm School of Economics, Stockholm, Sweden.

Andriesse, E. (September 2011). State capitalism and vulnerable livelihoods in the Lao PDR. Unpublished conference paper presented at EADI/DSA General Conference 2011: Rethinking Development in an Age of Scarcity and Uncertainty. University of York, United Kingdom.

Asian Development Bank. Year unknown. Chapter 1 Education in Lao economy and society.

CIA – The World FactBook (2012, October). East & Southeast Asia: Laos. Retrieved from the CIA website https://www.cia.gov/library/publications/the-world-factbook/geos/la.html.

Epprecht M., Minot N., Dewina R., Messerli P., Heinimann A.,(2002). The Geography of Poverty and Inequality in the Lao PDR. Swiss National Center of Competence in Research (NCCR) North-South, University of Bern, and International Food Policy Research Institute (IFPRI), Bern: Geographica Bernensia.

Evans, G. (2002). A short history of Laos: The land in between. Singapore: Southwind Production.

Government of Lao PDR & the United Nations (2008). Milleneum Development Goals 2008: Progress report – Lao PDR.

Government of Lao PDR & the United Nations (2010). *Accelerating Progress Towards the MDGs: Innovative options for reaching the unreached*. Retrieved from UN website http://www.undplao.org/.

Government of Lao PDR. Year unknown. National Growth and Poverty Eradication Strategy (NGPES). Retrieved from UN website www.undplao.org.

Holland, S. (1995). Impact of the economic and institutional reforms on the health sector in Laos: Implications for health system management. Brighton, UK: Institute of Development Studies, University of Sussex.

Organisation for Economic Co-Operation and Development (OECD). (2012). Aid Effectiveness 2005-10: Progress in implementing the Paris Declaration, Volume 2. Retrieved from OECD website www.oecd.org.

Sisavanh, K. (2003). Educational Research, Policy and Practice: National Report on Secondary Education in Lao PDR. *Educational Research for Policy and Practice* 2: 3–11.

United Nations Development Programme (UNDP) Lao PDR. (2012, November). United Nations Development Programme Lao PDR. Retrieved from UN website www.undplao.org.

UNESCO Bangkok Office (2012). United Nations, Country Background, Lao PDR. UN Education, Scientific, and Cultural Organization. Retrieved from UNESCO Office website www.unescobkk.org/education/resources/country-profiles/lao-pdr/country-background.

World Bank (2011). Lao PDR: Rural Electrification Program. Retrieved from WB website http://web.worldbank.org/WBSITE/EXTERNAL/COUNTRIES/EASTASIAPACIFICEXT/LAOPRDEXTN/0,,contentMDK:22858227~pagePK:141137~piPK:141127~theSitePK:293684,00.html.

World Bank (2013). Lao PDR Overview. Retrieved from WB Group website www.worldbank.org/en/country/lao/overview.

Chapter 7

Supporting development of local enterprises

Bamboo forests, sustainable livelihoods and civil society organizations in the mountainous region of Thanh Hoa province, Viet Nam

PATRICE LAMBALLE

ABSTRACT

This chapter is set in Thanh Hoa in Northwest Vietnam, bordering Laos. The region is a mountainous region and is home to ethnic minorities (90 percent Thai and Muong minorities). The region remains one of the poorest regions in the country. This chapter describes the region's strategies to develop social and environmentally sustainable enterprises and describes efforts to establish a sustainable bamboo industry.

The importance of individual differences

Thanh Hoa is one of Viet Nam's most populous provinces (4 million inhabitants) (General Statistic Office of Vietnam, n.d.). Located between the northern Delta and the central northern coastal area, 150-200 km south of Hanoi, the Province's total area is 11,000 km^2, stretching from the Pacific Ocean to the Lao border. Northwest Thanh Hoa, bordering Laos, is a mountainous region of ethnic minorities (90 percent *Thai* and *Muong* minorities), and remains one of the poorest in the country (more than 50 percent of people below the poverty line) (Vogel, Lamballe, Castell & Renard, 2010; Ly, Pillot, Lambelle & Neergaard, 2011).

The bamboo industry emerged spontaneously in the early 2000s, and is currently based on seven processing and 18 pre-processing workshops located in the three main valleys of Quan Hoa District (Renard & Lamballe, 2009). 1,500 workers use machines to process about 25,000 bamboo culms a day, mainly producing chopsticks and soaked wastes for the paper pulp industry. Raw products for paper pulping are necessary to make chopsticks production profitable, since chopsticks use only 15 percent of the volume of harvested culms. The same volume of culms is sold direct to the construction sector in the delta, raising concerns on low added-value and sustainability for bamboo forests. Poor farmers cut young culms to get money for short-term needs, but bamboo clumps need enough mature culms to nurture the new shoots, i.e. the culms of following years.

Short-term cash crops, such as maize and cassava, tend to become widespread. They generate erosion and soil degradation, putting strong pressure on the edges of natural forests. Rice-fields in narrow valleys are limited in area, and yield only one or two crops per year. Net incomes from animal husbandry are quite low (due to high mortality, expensive inputs, low selling prices, and high transportation costs). Districts 'import' commodities like vegetables, pigs and chicken for meat from the delta region for day-to-day meals, yet quality and safety of these commodities is not ensured (this may be due to a lack of administrative or social control).

The current agricultural support system is not very efficient and has not yet impacted on bamboo forests or mainstream agricultural production. Agricultural innovation is limited to the introduction or maintenance of certain hybrid rice seeds or exotic high-productivity pig breeds. In this region, there is almost no State regulation, be it for agriculture, animal husbandry (animal health) or bamboo industry (carbon emissions).

The first priority of the Gret LDP (Luong bamboo Development Project)/Green Bamboo Project has been to support bamboo cultivation (plantations) and processing (for flooring), since it is the most sustainable economic activity in the region. Although not the most profitable crop in the short run, bamboo procures environmental advantages such as water regulation and protection of soils, landscapes and carbon sequestration.

Since 2007, the Project developed a comprehensive approach to support local actors and farmers on four main issues: 1) bamboo industry (processing workshops), 2) bamboo forest sustainable management, 3) local and sustainable livelihoods (as an alternative to harvesting immature bamboo culms), and 4) social enterprises and civil society organizations. The main drivers of the support are diversification, innovation, integration and structuring of activities aiming at poverty reduction, together with sustainability both economically and ecologically.

Country background and context

Population dynamics and social context

The population of Viet Nam is close to 90 million, with a growth forecast of 93M by 2015 and 98M by 2020 (Central Intelligence Agency, 2013). The population growth rate is 1.05 percent and total fertility rate is 1.89 (Central Intelligence Agency, 2013). The mortality and malnutrition rate of children under 5 years are respectively 21/1000 and 18 percent, with average life expectancy 73 years (Ministry of Health, 2010). The current density is about 270 inhabitants per km^2 projected to approach 300 by 2020 (General Statistics Office of Vietnam, n.d.a). However, population is essentially concentrated in both large deltas - the Red River Delta in the North and Mekong Delta in the South - and along the narrow coastal strip.

Mountains and hills represent about 80 percent of the 330,000 km^2 of the country (Asian Studies Center, n.d.). The mountain regions, essentially areas close to the Lao, Cambodian and Chinese borders, are populated by more than 50 different ethnic minorities. This population of 13 million persons represents 15 percent of the total. 50 percent of ethnic minorities are poor (earning less than one dollar per day per person) (Ly, Pillot, Lambelle & Neegaard, 2011), whereas the ratio is about ten percent in the delta regions and cities (with an average of about 15 percent at country level) (General Statistics Office of Vietnam, n.d.c).

Policy dynamics and political structure

During the last 60 years Viet Nam has been run by a one-party regime, but there are changes under way, especially on designation of local authorities at commune and district level (United Nations, 2004; Fforde, 2003). The main transformations of the *doi moi* were Directive 100 in 1981 and Resolution 10 in 1988, opening the door for the de-collectivisation of agriculture. New policy thus considers agricultural households as primary actors for developing production.

Aside from State or Central level authority, the main administrative and political management operates at the level of province (63), district (10 per province as average), and commune (20 per district as average); additionally, the village/hamlet level is particularly important in mountainous communes, with the village leader holding an important position. There is a strong structuring of society at all levels (through Party and mass organizations), which leaves little room for independent civil society organizations (CSOs). One of the main consequences is the almost total absence of independent base organizations, farmers' groups or even production cooperatives.

Access to healthcare has significantly increased: 100 percent of communes have health stations, and 75 percent of communes have doctors (Ministry of Health, 2010). But healthcare for the poor and for people in remote and minority ethnic areas is still difficult. The proportion of women taking part in economic activities in 2010 was 83 percent, nearly equal to men (85 percent) (Ministry of Health, 2010). 100 percent of districts have ethnic boarding-schools allowing ethnic minority children to benefit from education (Ministry of Health 2010).

There are specific policies for rural areas (*Nong thon moi*), mountain provinces and regions, and for the poorest districts (30 A), ethnic minorities and poor people (e.g. Bank for Social Policies, budget support to build or improve houses, etc.). While some policies benefit the population in real life, many of the policies officially announced for mountainous zones are not enforced or implemented.

Economic conditions

The last 20-25 years have seen rapid and dramatic economic development in Viet Nam. Economic growth is slower in mountain and ethnic minorities zones; development is more focused on infrastructure than industry and as a consequence few jobs are created in these regions. Fifty percent of the population in these areas lives below the poverty line (Renard & Lamballe, 2009; Ly, Pillot, Lambelle & Neergaard, 2011). However, few households suffer from hunger. In this area, with 50 percent poor, we can estimate average household income at $1,600 per year (1$/day x 365 x 4.5 persons/household) (Renard & Lamballe, 2009; Ly, Pillot, Lambelle & Neergaard, 2011).

In Quan Hoa District, industry is limited to bamboo processing workshops (about 1,500 jobs) (Renard & Lamballe, 2009). In neighboring districts, cassava or sugar processing are the main industrial employers. Another feature of Quan Hoa is the large areas of natural forest (protected by karstic mountains and cliffs), covering about 55,000 ha (55 percent of the total area of the district) and including two nature reserves.

The district has the country's largest area of giant bamboo forest (*luong – Dendrocalamus barbatus*), approx. 23,000 ha (Baulch, Marsh, Nguyen, Nguyen & Vu, 2009). The Northwest region of Thanh Hoa Province has the largest planted bamboo forest in continental Southeast Asia (70,000 ha). This forest is split into small plots of 0.5 to 5 ha, owned by 40,000 farming households (Baulch, Marsh, Nguyen, Nguyen & Vu, 2009). In 2008, Luong bamboo contributed an estimated US$22 million to the household economy of the Luong growing communities in northern Viet Nam (Ly, Pillot, Lamballe & De Neergaard, 2011). Besides bamboo growing and harvesting, short-term crops like cassava or maize are the main sources of income. Animal husbandry is the third source of revenue, together with rice (in larger valleys) and off-farm incomes (Vogel, Lamballe, Castell & Renard, 2010).

Technology and infrastructure

The region is quite isolated, being far from the deltas, cities (150-200 km) and export facilities. Districts and small cities in the valleys benefit from (narrow) asphalted roads. But the other villages, not located in the valley bottoms, are reachable only by tracks, which can be difficult during the rainy season. Bamboo is harvested manually (using machetes) whereas processing is almost exclusively done by machines (cross-cut saws, splitters, planing machines, etc.).

Transportation is quite developed, with plenty of trucks and excavators, as well as buses with daily trips to Hanoi or Thanh Hoa City. More than 90 percent of the population now has electricity (The World Bank 2010). In parallel, there is quite good provision of schools and primary health care (in each commune), though most of these services are not free.

Issues of sustainability faced by the country

Vietnam faces growing pollution concerns: extractive industry, industrial pollution, tremendous increase in traffic, construction, pollution of rivers and water tables, more and more solid waste generated by households, etc. In Northwest Thanh Hoa, the main concern stems from medium level industrial bamboo paper pulp manufacture, with soda discharged into the Ma river, the region's main watercourse.

There are various environmental policies together with nature reserves, parks and large areas of natural forest distributed to farmers so as to ensure conservation. Development of short-term crops (cassava and maize) on slopes is an important ecological concern in terms of soil degradation and decreasing yield, strong erosion and run-off during the rainy season causing dramatic flooding in the Ma river delta region, Vietnam's third major delta.

Investigation issues and outcomes

Support to local bamboo industry and processing workshops

To increase prices paid to farmers for culms, and to improve profitability of enterprises, build resilience to market instability and reduce transportation costs, the project worked on four complementary tracks:

1. increase the price of chopsticks through higher added-value products (Japanese chopsticks earned 220 VND/per pair against 110 for normal chopsticks);
2. diversify markets and products to give higher value to culms (planed slats for flooring, in three enterprises, as a complement to chopstick production, using bottom lengths and increasing the value of raw products from US$1.20 to 1.60 per culm);
3. innovate by developing alternative products (woven slats for panel boards, thermo-treated (carbonized) culms) that use more mature culms from better managed forests, and by increasing the utilization rate (from

20 or 25 percent to 60 percent), and increasing labor and added value per culm (from US$1.20 or US$1.60 to US$2.40 or US$4);

4. test and propose other ways of using waste products (bamboo charcoal, sawdust briquettes, fibers).

The first two activities have delivered quite good results and are being implemented by several enterprises. Activity 3 is less developed (processes and markets are known, but there is low investment capacity). Activity 4 is still at the experimental stage. The problem is not competition or market-related as such (there is strong demand, at least from Japan). Rather, it may be one of costs compared to charcoal obtained from degraded wood forests. Physical measurements/procedures to certify quality and production capacities (investment, equipment, cash-flow, etc.) can pose problems in this regard.

To support the region's processing enterprises, several interventions were developed on local value chains:

1. institutional support (to set up processing cooperatives, Association of Entrepreneurs);
2. links with finishing enterprises (with the long-term goal of finishing products locally), local or foreign buyers, markets or even potential investors;
3. experimentation with new equipment, processes or products, together with entrepreneurs, including local fabrication tests and practical training; and
4. awareness-raising among entrepreneurs on FSC[7] standards to access certification mechanisms, plus support for safe working and equipment.

Priority to support local small and medium enterprises against large external factories

Operating through large industries from outside the region brings few positive impacts locally. Take the example of pre-processing of raw thin slats for one big company in Hanoi, which has acquired a monopoly in producing 'strand woven' products, (now stopped). The assumption was that higher demand would increase culm prices and thus 'naturally' reduce poverty. However, when the demand was quite high, there was no significant increase in culm price, no requirements in regard to quality and maturity of culms (thus threatening sustainability), poorly managed local relations and threats to move production if prices increase, no support to local industry, no capacity building and even problems of late or withheld payment. This kind of model showed a clear absence of social or environmental responsibility and was not a sustainable one.

Strengthening local enterprises and increasing capacity of local entrepreneurs are much more efficient for local industrial development (local jobs, salaries, incomes)

[7] Forest Stewardship Council (FSC) is an independent, non-governmental, not for profit organization established to promote the responsible management of the world's forests.

in the valleys. To some extent, these actions lead to higher social and environmental responsibility. This process can be brought about with support or contracts for products delivered to local or external developed companies. Increasing capacity of entrepreneurs enhances their status, creating more choice, higher resilience, and adaptability to different market situations.

Although FSC or carbon finance on bamboo are not yet possible in this region, we can observe some improvement in terms of social and environmental responsibility among enterprises:

1. more local concern and responsibility about resource sustainability (bamboo culms); and
2. local management with minimum level of welfare, so as to maintain skilled workers in the enterprise.

Lessons learned – What works or doesn't work in such a situation

1. Markets, most of the time, can be found, but they require high volumes and guaranteed quality: the main challenge is to forge a link between the players and provide support for the increase in volume.
2. Most of entrepreneurs are not very keen to carry out trials if there is no immediate market, especially with large volumes involved. Work is needed to select actors and prepare specific budgets.
3. Opportunities to build concrete advocacy and practical support are more useful than traditional courses.
4. A comprehensive approach across the value chain is required, giving most support to the weakest points - not just to one link in the value chain, one product, enterprise or market.

Support for bamboo forest sustainable management

In this isolated region, close to the border, environment and forest sustainability have to be ensured, as well as strengthening local industrial development. Both require sustainable bamboo forest management. Bamboo growers need clear signals from industry (price, quality). We need to work on all links in the bamboo commodity chain at local level.

Sustainability across all 70,000 ha of luong bamboo forest is in question for different reasons:

1. There are few if any new forest management or sustainable management inputs (the same is true of investments in bamboo forestry).
2. There is heavy pressure on young culms, close to the roads, and particularly, for poor families; this leads to decreasing yields and will increase poverty in the future.
3. For exportation of raw culms or processing for chopsticks, mature culms (three years and older) are not needed, whereas sustainable bamboo forest management demands that these culms alone be harvested.

4. In some locations, there are dangers of non-sustainable short-term crops like maize or cassava displacing bamboo.

The Project carried out a number of activities to ensure sustainability and maintain the potential of bamboo forests:

1. advocacy at provincial and district authorities level (discussion, steering committee meetings), though there have been very few active results in the field four to five years later, since the budget is still not released;
2. support for setting up of farmers' organizations for better protection and management (see 3.4);
3. organization of trainings and practical visits for farmers on demonstrations or external models;
4. introduction of other livelihoods (see 3.3), to offer alternative short-term incomes; and
5. clusters, operating within confined areas: discussion/negotiation at local level, with markets, through enterprise; 'clusters' rarely works as foreseen, but can often create conditions that encourage the emergence of local initiatives and prominent actors (such as small entrepreneurs or farmers' leaders).

The last three activities have yielded quite good results, particularly in terms of gradual change in bamboo forest management. However, it is not easy to upscale such clusters and livelihoods to benefit thousands of households.

Integration of bamboo forests in the local cropping system has also been an issue. The Project tried to advocate planting of bamboo directly in degraded forest (to avoid the impact of short-term crops) or growing mixed forest with short-term (Acacia), and long-term (Chukrasia) trees for timber. Groundnut was chosen as an intercrop during the first two years to avoid planting cassava, for its income potential, adaptation to weather and resistance to pests. Where bamboo plantations are close to farmhouses the most interesting association to emerge has been the bamboo-chicken rearing pattern (see 3.3).

Lessons learned

- Pioneer farmers are not too difficult to find but they need clear, ongoing support year on year.
- Working with farmers on fertilizer solutions (chemical or organic) is neither achievable nor sustainable since they never invest in inputs for forest or plantations (old habits of subsidies).
- Efforts have been made to integrate all these activities into an institutional agenda but it is difficult to coordinate with State programs (lack of transparent support, programs rarely carried out or not on time).
- Credit schemes begun by cooperatives and local or foreign NGOs seem ill-suited and/or unsustainable: farmers often borrow to reimburse loans they took out with State-owned banks.

- Clusters can work if there is at least one dynamic enterprise involved. Direct involvement of an entrepreneur (social enterprise) is a plus (e.g. paying premium prices for higher quality culms).

Support for local and sustainable livelihoods

Thai or Muong communities were supported to introduce or develop local livelihoods (vegetables, 3-crop systems, chicken rearing, etc.), as alternative income to bamboo, so as to ensure more sustainable bamboo forest management. Section 2 briefly illustrated the main limitations of local livelihoods: bamboo, rice, cash crops on slopes, animal husbandry and off-farm activities. Moreover, the region 'imports' vegetables, rice and chicken from the delta 100-150 km away; raw cassava and maize are sold at low prices to the town, whereas buying industrial animal feed is very expensive.

Vegetables

Vegetable production does not need a large cultivation area or high technical skills, but water must be available all year round, as well as quality organic fertilizers like manure. To be efficient, it has to be conducted in groups (10-25 households). This is why the action was implemented generally at village level with women's unions. Vegetables of different species (from 5 to 15) can be grown and used to provide nutrients and vitamins for the household and neighborhood, or for wedding parties, or to sell to markets. These safely grown vegetables can replace products brought in from the delta, which come from intensive agriculture grown with pesticides. In mountain areas chemicals are rarely used on vegetables.

In such remote areas, it is possible to give value to endemic species, which are very tasty and suited to local conditions. Communities at higher altitude can also grow several species of 'European' vegetables out of the winter season, thus benefitting from higher prices. Vegetables are short term (3-4 months) or very short term (1.5-2 months): they can adapt to very different situations, crop systems and calendars. It is possible to grow three seasons per year with different species suited to each season (spring-summer, summer-autumn and winter). 200 m^2 of vegetables, three seasons per year, will yield an income to farmers equivalent to that of 1-1.5 ha of bamboo. Such short-term cycles are favorable also in motivating farmers and allowing developers to support and readjust on time.

Three-crop systems (three crops per year, in lowland rice-fields)

Besides proposing other livelihoods for better management of bamboo forests, the objectives are to decrease pressure on slopes, protect natural forest and then ensure available water for irrigation in the dry season. Where forest still surrounds the village it is thus important to raise awareness among local communities and intervene at an early enough stage. The 'three crops' system has been tested with different communities and women's unions. It is a feasible approach but requires dynamic and charismatic village or group leaders. In mountainous zones with less sunlight and a colder winter climate it is difficult to cultivate maize as a third (winter) crop. But in its place very short-term vegetable species can be grown. Numerous possible combinations of crops may be adapted, according to calendar or water needs.

The three-crop system presents many advantages:

1. significant income increase , thus decreasing pressure on slopes, bamboo, forests, etc.;
2. improved value and efficiency in lowland narrow rice fields;
3. strengthened fertility and reduced pest influence for subsequent rice crops; and
4. suitability to weather conditions (drought, rain, floods, etc.) and even to climate change.

Tests done in the zone in 2011, with groundnut or maize grown in spring, rice in summer, and cabbage in winter, on 500 m^2 rice-field plots, yielded net incomes equivalent to 2 or 2.5 ha of *luong* bamboo.

Chicken rearing

Chicken rearing is particularly suitable for poor farmers and/or women. A farmer can start with very low investment (20-30 chicks); there is no shortage of small-sized areas around the house or maize/cassava as animal feed. Both local (higher prices) and local-hybrid fowl are suitable and sold at a much higher profit than industrial chickens in the delta. Three cycles per year, of 40 chickens per cycle, brings in a net income equivalent to the harvest of 1 ha bamboo culms in the same period. As with vegetable growing, farmers don't need external support for such a simple activity. However, there are serious problems of availability of chicks, high mortality rates, and lack of support services. For the communities, it is a classic 'chicken and egg' situation: there are not enough layers (females) to produce eggs or chicks, and not enough chicks to develop into layers afterwards.

To break this vicious cycle, lots of eggs and layers have to be introduced from outside, along with equipment such as incubators; good animal health protection, feed and relevant technical advice must be available. Different interest groups have been supported with some success, but the activity only really became sustainable when a new (social) enterprise specializing in the incubation/hatching of chicks and ducklings arrived on the scene.

Lessons learned

- Short-term support is not enough; distributing some seeds or chicks periodically in some communities, as governmental bodies have typically done, does not work. As people say in Vietnam: 'don't provide the fish unless you can help make the rod to catch them'.
- Such activities, particularly on animal husbandry, need comprehensive support, not only regarding breeds but also for veterinary protection, feed, technical guidance, and information on markets.

- Prioritizing only hybrid or high performance seeds/breeds is not suited to mountain zones, with ethnic minorities. It is important to have specific, technically relevant programs and activities for such beneficiaries.
- Development of indigenous animal breeds or vegetables is very well suited to local conditions, improving nutrition and minimizing chemical food imports from the delta.
- In mountain zones, value addition should focus on specific conditions: 1) cropping systems only possible at altitude, with early cycles in summer/autumn, 2) low needs/use of pesticides allow selling local, organic or 'green' products, 3) food processing should use with locally available products.

Local institutions, civil society organizations and social enterprises

The success and sustainability of interventions in industry, forest management and livelihoods depend essentially on the presence and quality of civil society and social enterprises. We can draw, in few lines, a picture of what existed in the region before intervention:

1. Local political and administrative institutions (Party and People's committee) at provincial, district and commune levels,
2. Mass organizations (Women, Farmers, Veterans, Youth) at equivalent levels (it can be useful to identify dynamic leaders at district/commune level before choosing partners)
3. Local small enterprises (workshops) and a very small number of pre-existing civil society organizations, etc.

Farmers' organizations

In Vietnam, and particularly in this region, very few organizations existed beforehand: the project had to start from zero and took time to become established. If only bamboo groups were created, there would be a risk of not having enough dynamic groups (out of selling quality bamboo at higher prices). So it is important to integrate livelihood support activities, with short-term incomes and greater dynamism, concurrently with exchanges between groups in the region. Work can be accomplished through existing or new groups if there are dynamic, credible leaders to engage with.

Association of (bamboo processing) entrepreneurs

It is in fact very difficult to change behavior in just one or two enterprise; hence the project's support for the setting up of an Association of Local Entrepreneurs in bamboo processing (25 enterprises so far). The main activities are:

1. lobbying/advocacy activities (on taxes, prices) with local (district) authorities;

2. trying to define common policy on purchasing of raw materials or attracting potential customers; and
3. facilitating more cooperation between members.

The preconditions for this type of integration are: common objectives or constraints, low level of competition inside the group, charismatic group leadership and the real concern of local authorities.

The Association is also the institution most suitable for integrating social and environmental concerns. At association level, the members decided not to buy young culms any more so as to ensure long-term forest productivity. They also exerted some pressure on those enterprises that continued to pollute water systems, by highlighting the negative image this creates to the bamboo industry.

Social enterprise(s)

Such an enterprise depends on the director's capabilities (open-mindedness, prior experience in NGO context, readiness to embrace new initiatives). Tre xứ Thanh[8] (TXT) implement pioneering actions, complementary to what already exists in the zone, with greater reach in environmental, agro-ecological and sustainability terms. Priority is given to practical training and capacity building of workers/managers, to improve efficiency and long-term vision with provision of services to farmers that the State does not offer – such as technical advice, quality control or monitoring.

Lessons learned

- Local institutions/mass organizations (particularly farmers' organizations) are not enough by themselves to support development efficiently.
- Attention must be paid to composition (gender, age, social function), particularly of group leaders.
- Practical training, capacity building and creation of specific conditions to make them be autonomous (for instance, building independent capacity for seed production and breeding).
- Strong, close support and monitoring of these nascent organizations is essential.
- A long-term vision is required if building CSOs is to be a priority, but more profitable short-term activities are also needed as part of the mix.

Implications for the field/lessons of experience

Despite constraints on the bamboo value chain, this holistic approach has produced a practical change in the zone towards more sustainable development.

[8] A company, social enterprise, that was established in Northwest Thanh Hoa province in 2010. It is an organic farm, bamboo processor and provides other services to farmers. *Tre xứ Thanh* literally means 'Bamboo originating from Thanh Hoa'.

Jobs, higher added-value products requiring mature culms (i.e. more sustainable management) and higher prices for quality culms have ensued. Experience from the past year however shows that external industrial development has not lived up to expectations.

Such results require flexibility and adaptability (of project and staff) to local institutional conditions, objectives of entrepreneurs, market and economic situation, priority processes and products, etc. Work with enterprises needs to build strong links with issues of quality in agriculture/forestry production and develop institutional aspects. Recent projects focus on markets, but the cases illustrated here show that local markets and consumption already exist; poor communities need support primarily in terms of production capabilities. Social enterprise is an emerging actor in the local institutional landscape, and the most relevant player for developing efficiency and sustainability.

Change has also been possible through alternative livelihoods that offer more choice to farmers in terms of earning a living, resulting in more a sustainable local economy and more appropriate bamboo forest management. For instance:

1. real improved capacity among poor local communities to adapt to change and to diversify production systems;
2. significant local markets and real needs for fresh vegetables, chicken, etc., being satisfied;
3. short value-chain circuits shown to be feasible, cheaper, with lower impact in terms of transport to and from the delta, and often more profitable outcomes;
4. awareness of the need to increase capacity and autonomy of farmers and expanding their productivity options.

In terms of support and institutions, our main findings are:

1. local presence (including easy day-to-day contact and credibility) and long-term commitment of organizations in charge of support actions have to be ensured;
2. testing and support have to be maintained over several seasons – it is a mistake to think that early withdrawal means greater sustainability of actions;
3. work must be undertaken across a spectrum of different groups (from a minimum of communes/districts) so as not to depend on specific conditions, or the goodwill of particular stakeholders;
4. work is more efficient if groups are identified, with dynamic farmers groups supported for a 'critical mass' effect and to avoid pressure on individual households (social pressure, thefts, cattle, pests, etc.).

Such an approach could be applied at least to mountain and hill regions of Vietnam and even Laos. In these areas there are few investors, processors and companies. Populations are over-dependent for local economic development on these actors coming from deltas and cities.

In theory, the State can make this happen, but grass-roots level experience shows how limited State input can be and how an external stimulus can bring benefits. Current experience suggests that a committed NGO (foreign or local) or social enterprise (or branch of one set up elsewhere), working towards dynamic development through re-skilling farmers as micro-entrepreneurs, can bridge the gap.

Conclusions

In conclusion, we advocate a new rural development agenda in poor regions integrating local commodity chains and processing, working on the weak points of value chains and labor intensive small-scale diversification, together with strengthening actors and developing sustainable local livelihoods.

Necessary steps include identification of concerned actors, organisation of visits in relevant zones, participatory discussions with people, design of programs, (flexible) plans and activities, defining participation of social enterprises as well as State and/or CSOs, scoping needs for funding and support, organization and synergies between components, support system and monitoring/evaluation scheme.

Other long-term benefits for individuals and communities include limiting rural exodus and social evils, maintaining skills, generating capacity for innovation at countryside level, creating dynamic elements for autonomous, self-centred development, with a more long-term vision than that of 'outside' companies/actors with short-term commitments.

References

Asian Studies Center. (n.d.b). *Vietnam – Geography*. Retrieved from http://asia.isp.msu.edu/wbwoa/southeast_asia/vietnam/geography.htm.

Baulch, B., Marsh, J., Nguyen, B. L., Nguyen, H. T. & Vu, H. L. (2009). *Key findings from the second Thanh Hoa Bamboo Survey: Second Prosperity Initiative Impact Assessment Report* (Unpublished draft report). Commissioned by Prosperity Initiative.

Central Intelligence Agency. (2013, February 11). *The world factbook: Vietnam*. Retrieved 27 MARCH 2013 from https://www.cia.gov/library/publications/the-world-factbook/geos/vm.html.

Danon, S. (2011, January 17). Possibilities for payments for environmental services and carbon market projects in bamboo forests of Quan Hoa District, Thanh Hoa Province, Vietnam (Master's thesis). AgroParisTech, Paris. Retrieved 27 March 2013.

Fforde, A. (2003, November). *Decentralization in Vietnam – Working effectively at provincial and local government level – a comparative analysis of Long An and Quang Ngai Provinces*. Retrieved from AusAid: www.ausaid.gov.au/Publications/Documents/decentralisation_vietnam.pdf.

General Statistics Office of Vietnam. (n.d.). Average population by province. Retrieved 27 MARCH 2013 from GSO website: www.gso.gov.vn/default_en.aspx?tabid=467&idmid=3&ItemID=12939.

General Statistics Office of Vietnam. (n.d.a). *Area, population and population density in 2011 by province*. Retrieved 27 MARCH 2013 from GSO website: www.gso.gov.vn/default_en.aspx?tabid=467&idmid=3&ItemID=12941.

General Statistics Office of Vietnam. (n.d.c). *General poverty rate by residence and by region*. Retrieved 27 MARCH 2013 from GSO website: www.gso.gov.vn/default_en.aspx?tabid=474&idmid=3&ItemID=12651.

Lamballe, P. & Francois, M. (2011, January). *Territorialised value chain (supply chain) – Example of bamboo value chain in North-West THanh Hoa – Gret – Vietnam*. Unpublished paper presented to MARD Seminar on Rural Development, Hanoi.

Ly, P., Pillot, D., Lambelle, P. & Neergaard, A. (2011). Evaluation of bamboo as an alternative cropping strategy in the northern central upland of Vietnam: above-ground carbon fixing capacity, accumulation of soil organic carbon, and socio-economic aspects. *Elsevier Agriculture Systems and Environment*, 149, 80-90.

Ministry of Health. (2010, December). *Five-year Health Sector Development Plan 2011-2015*. Retrieved 27 MARCH 2013 from http://www.wpro.who.int/health_services/viet_nam_nationalhealthplan.pdf.

Renard, O. & Lamballe, P. (2009). Creating sustainable jobs and incomes to reduce poverty: lessons from bamboo supply chain development project in North-West Vietnam, *World bamboo congress (WBC)*. Bangkok, Thailand.

Renard, O., Lamballe, P. Nguyen, T.H. & Vogel, A. (2010). Developing bamboo supply chain in North West Vietnam: benchmarking the Chinese model?. *INBAR Congress on Bamboo and Rattan*. Shanghai, 20-22 May 2010.

Samarasinghe, B., Tran, VA., Nguyen, V.A. & Lamballe, P. (2011, December), *Policy Action Research on bamboo contracts in mountainous districts in the North-West of Thanh Hoa*. Revised interim report for ADP/M4P II.

Steer, L. & Sen, K. (2010, November). Formal and Informal Institutions in a Transition Economy: The Case of Vietnam. *World Development*, 38 (11), 1603-1615.

The World Bank. (2010). Access to electricity (percent of population). The World Bank. Retrieved 27 March 2013 from http://data.worldbank.org/indicator/EG.ELC.ACCS.ZS.

United Nations. (2004, February). *The Socialist Republic of Vietnam: Public Administration Country Profile*. Retrieved from http://unpan1.un.org/intradoc/groups/public/documents/un/unpan023247.pdf.

Vogel, A., Lamballe, P., Castell, F. & Renard, O. (2010). Understanding the role of bamboo in farmers' livelihood and strategies: towards a comprehensive approach to reduce poverty in North-West Vietnam. *Shanghai semina of INBAR Congress on Bamboo and Rattan*. Shanghai, 20-22 May 2010.

Annexure 7.1 Map of the region and project zone

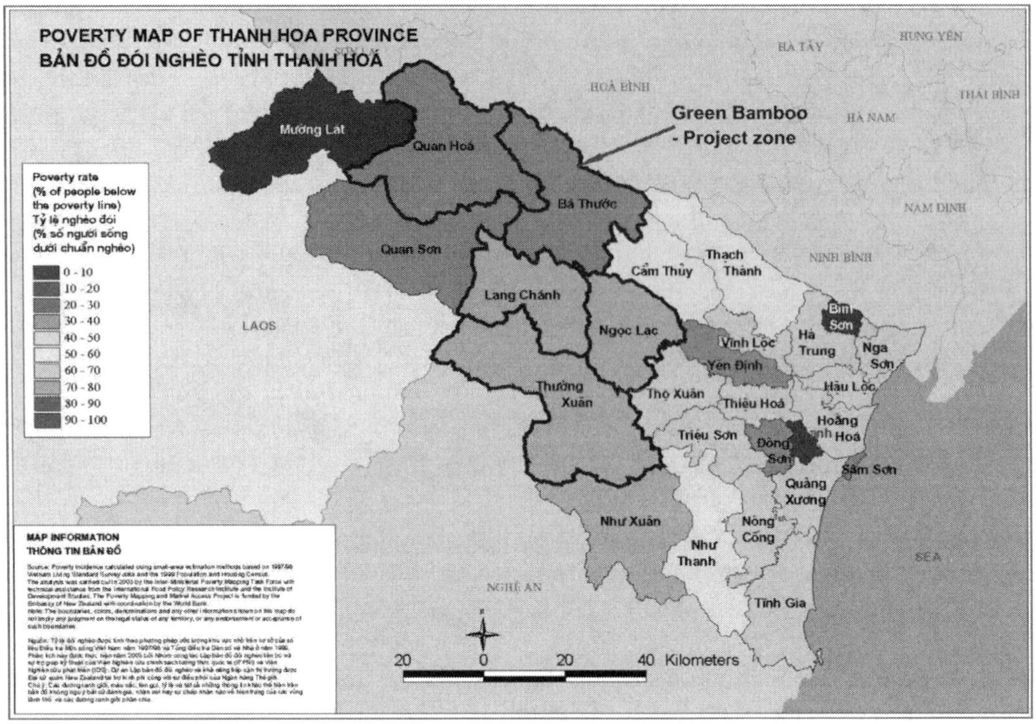

Chapter 8

Sowing sustainability

Rice commodity pathways, NGOs and farmers' engagement with alternative agriculture in northeastern Thailand

LIZA WOOD

ABSTRACT

Rice is the cornerstone for much of Thailand's agricultural development. However, moving from subsistence farming to commercial agriculture has greatly altered its role in the country's northeast region. Particularly, the Green Revolution impacted farmers' livelihoods, environment, health, and culture. Farmers in non-governmental organizations base their rice variety choices primarily on factors of price and marketability. This market-based motivation is critical for NGOs to consider, particularly on balance with their larger goals of environmental and cultural sustainability.

Introduction

Thailand is divided between two development paradigms. One calls for rapid neoliberal development, and the other for a more sufficient economy with a focus on equitable progress. Grassroots non-governmental networks have played a critical role in representing the focus on equality over industrialization, as they emphasize environmental sustainability, maintenance of culture, and human rights. To contextualize the efforts of these NGOs, I outline Thailand's social, political, and economic dynamics, and then present my case study concerning agricultural NGOs in the Northeast area so to make recommendations for organizations looking to work in this area.

Contextualizing Thailand

Population dynamics and social context

Thailand's history is based in a rich cultural tradition, representative of the various ethnicities and geographic regions. Today, Thailand's population is estimated to be about 67 million with about 7 million (11%) being 'other' ethnicities (Central Intelligence Agency, 2012). These 'other' ethnicities include Thai-Khmer and Thai-Laos of the Northeast, Thai-Muslim along the southern Malay border, and the 'hill people' of the northern and western borders, comprised mostly of the Karen in the east and Lahu and Lisu in the North (Baker and Phongpaichit, 2005). In this paper I focus on the population in the Northeast, referred to as Isaan, which is strongly influenced by the culture of its neighboring countries, Laos and Cambodia. Relative to the country's five regions, Isaan has the largest population of 18.8 million (28.7%), followed by the central region with 18.1 million (27.7%), and Bangkok 8.2 million (12.6%) (National Statistical Office (NSO) 2010).

Isaan is considered the rice basket of the country, as it constitutes half of the country's rice fields (Feeny, 2003). Much of the population lives in rural areas and in 2002 more than 90 percent of rural households produced rice, illuminating the fact that agriculture plays a major role in daily Isaan life. Of these households, 60 percent are subsistence, producing rice primarily for their household, while the other 40 percent are commercial (Ekasingh *et al.*, 2007). However, the dynamics of these traditional agricultural communities are changing, as financial and social pressures to modernize and urbanize are beginning to stratify the rural age demographic and reduce the practice of traditional agricultural methods.

Policy dynamics and political structure

Thailand is a constitutional monarchy, in which King Rama IX, Bhumibol Adulyadej, serves as a stable and nearly worshipped figurehead of the country. As such, he has a tremendous amount of indirect influence over its political dynamics. Much of this indirect power stems from Thailand's *lèse-majesté* law, which imprisons anyone who defames or insults the King or his royal family. Furthermore, the King and his appointed Privy Council are closely linked to the military, allowing them to act as a triad of non-elected elites with unparalleled political influence (Chambers, 2010). Though Thailand as been declared a democratic nation since 1932, the indirect power of the elite triad in combination with the country's history of unstable, money-driven politics, has been an impediment to establishing a true democracy (Chambers, 2010).

The divide between Thai political parties can be crudely described as a rift between the elite conservatives (yellow-shirts) and a newly politically empowered rural sector (red-shirts). While political parties are frequently being dissolved and reinstated under proxy names, the most recent party titles have been the red United Front for Democracy Against Dictatorship (UDD) and Pheu Thai Party (PTP), and the yellow People's Alliance for Democracy (PAD) and Democrat Party (DP). The red-shirts aim to eliminate corruption and money politics from Thailand's democratic system, and promote populist policies in favor of the rural poor. This group is influenced by their party's previous Prime Minister, Thaksin Shinawatra (2001-2006), who changed the game of Thai politics by combining populist policies for the rural poor with an opening of the global market for the business middle-class (Hewison, 2010). The yellow-shirts, however, are anti-Thaksin, as they aim to maintain the country's tradition of elite rule and object to dramatic neoliberal development schemes (Hewison, 2010). The divide between these two groups has been particularly hostile since 2006, at which time the ousting of Thaksin by the military began a sequence of violent and tumultuous coups until 2010 (International Crisis Group, 2010). Elections were held in 2011, putting Yingluck Shinawatra of the Pheu Thai Party in place.

Economic development

The social and political divide between the elite of central Thailand, and the rural poor of outlying regions is representative of the country's developmental history and current economic dynamic. There is considerable degree of economic inequality between the country's regions, as the three richest regions – Central, Southern, and Bangkok as its own region – share 70 percent of the country's income among only 30 percent of the population, while the Northeast shares only ten percent of the country's income among over a third of the population (International Monetary Fund (IMF), 2012). This economic divide between regions has been the trend since Thailand began exporting rice in the mid-eighteenth century (Baker and Phongpaichit, 2005). The economic success the country's early trade was confined to the Central region, as the Northeast was notably disconnected and disadvantaged in comparison. Its limited infrastructure for transport, in combination with poor environmental conditions, barred it from exposure to the global economic growth experienced by the Central region (Feeny, 2003).

It wasn't until after the Second World War that infrastructure began to expand beyond central Thailand to the Northeast, and with it came education, urbanization, and industrialization of agricultural practices, ultimately facilitating the region's move from subsistence living to conventional agriculture (Feeny, 2003). This nation-wide expansion led to an increase in the national and regional

GDP, but the benefits were not equally distributed. Rather, the rural regions remained comparatively poor, as the mean household income in the Northeast was still only 66 percent of that in the central region in 1975 (Ikemoto, 1991 in Feeny, 2003). Later in the 20th century, Thailand's industries began changing, and while it is still a front runner for the world's largest exporter of rice (United States Department of Agriculture, 2013), its role in the export economy has declined. In its place, machinery and transport materials, petroleum oils, electronic circuits, and rubber products all place above rice in terms of Thai exports (United Nations, 2010). The trend of growth between regions has shifted accordingly, with central and southern Thailand now representing much of the country's industrial sector, while the North and the Northeast remain the country's agricultural regions.

Sustainability issues

With such a rapid move towards modernization and global development during the mid-20th century, non-governmental organizations (NGOs) began to form, protesting the government's lack of consideration for environmental sustainability. Most notable is the Assembly of the Poor (AOP), a nationwide grassroots network formed in 1995 to oppose the government's neoliberal development schemes (Missingham, 2003). The AOP rallies around issues of environmental human rights, and acts as a network to connect groups that represent various sectors, such as fisheries and water management, land use, and agriculture. These groups represent the issues of environmental sustainability in Thailand, as well as their link to human rights. For example, the construction of dams on wetland environments impacts the traditional culture of wetland foraging, chemical agriculture and mono-cropping threatens environmental and human health, and logging or mine construction denies land tenure to indigenous people. These examples broadly represent the country's environmental human rights concerns with regard to sustainable development, and it is in these areas that NGOs are most active.

In addition to issues of environmental sustainability and human rights, two issues have arisen that pose a challenge to sustainable farming is Isaan – climate change and youth migration. During the fall of 2011, Thailand experienced unprecedented amounts of rain and flooding, greatly impacting the lives of all Thais – urban and rural – and particularly damaging the rice crop (Javier and Suwannakij, 2011). Extreme weather events such as these are becoming more and more common, and both farmers and urban-dwellers alike may struggle to confront future climate change obstacles. Beyond a changing climate, the changing demographics from rural to urban may also impact Thai agriculture. The country's municipal areas hold 44 percent of the population (2010), which is a significant increase from 31 percent in 2000 and 29.4 percent in 1990. (NSO, 2010). As such, the population of youth in farming is dwindling and the average age of farmers is increasing, causing the farming population to confront issues of sustained livelihoods.

Background

This case study takes interest in the Isaan NGOs for environmental human rights, particularly the alternative agriculture movement's focus on native rice varieties. Like potatoes in the Andes and maize in Mexico, Thailand has historically been home to a wide array of rice varieties, many of them playing a particular cultural and environmental role. During Thailand's agricultural modernization, the government began promoting the growth of 'mainstream rice', defined as the rice types selected for quality by the government's Rice Breeding Department – most notably Jasmine rice 105 and Sticky rice 6.[9] These mainstream rice varieties, paired with chemical fertilizers and pesticides, brought about higher agricultural efficiency – rice yields went from an average of 1.55 tons/ha (1961/62) to 2.26 tons/ha (1997/98) – as well as an increase in Isaan's economy (Panyakul, 2003).

Despite the benefits, however, the standardization of rice varieties has also had negative effects, as it has impacted farmers in terms of labor shortage, crop vulnerability, debt, farmer health, and cultural change. Mono-cropping limits the window for harvesting, requiring hired labor or machinery, and the narrowed crop diversity increases vulnerability to pests and disease (Panyakul, 2003; Oukpaew, 2011). Mainstream seeds must be bought every few years and are complemented by chemical inputs, adding costs that contribute to financial insecurity for farmers (U. Yoowah, personal communication, June 16, 2012). These chemical inputs (many of which have been banned from other countries) impact farmer health through muscle aches and rashes (AAN *et al.*, 2011). Furthermore, the limitation of varieties effects cultural practices, as certain varieties play different roles in spiritual and community ceremonies, such as alms giving and wedding ceremonies (W. Tongnoi, personal communication, June 16, 2012). With such dramatic shifts in agriculture and the livelihood of farmers over the last half-century, my research turns to the local agricultural NGOs to assess their impact on farmers' agricultural practices and values.

Case study: Alternative agriculture in Isaan

In light of the Northeast's agricultural development and its impacts over the past half-century, this study focuses on the non-governmental groups that emerged to oppose such changes. Through in-depth interviews with stakeholders in the agricultural NGO arena, and surveys with farmers in varying capacities of NGO involvement, I aim to understand the organizational dynamic of the rice commodity system, as well as well as draw conclusions with regard to the role of NGOs, markets, and government in the alternative agriculture movement.

[9] Other mainstream varieties include Kor Khor 10 and Kor Khor 15, which are white rice varieties, non-glutinous and glutinous, respectively. I term all varieties other than mainstream as 'native varieties', as this is the term used by Thai farmers to represent the rice types that had traditionally been grown before government's breeding initiatives.

Rice commodity pathways

The 'rice commodity pathway' (Figure 8.1), provides a generalized look at the relationship between the organizations that commercial farmers are involved in and the available types of rice mills and markets. Though this visual representation does not reflect the percentage of farmers involved in each of these groups – as the vast majority of farmers belong to government organizations and are involved in the middle, conventional pathway[10] – the rice commodity pathways figure captures the relationship between organizational involvement and mill and market access.

Figure 8.1 Rice commodity pathways

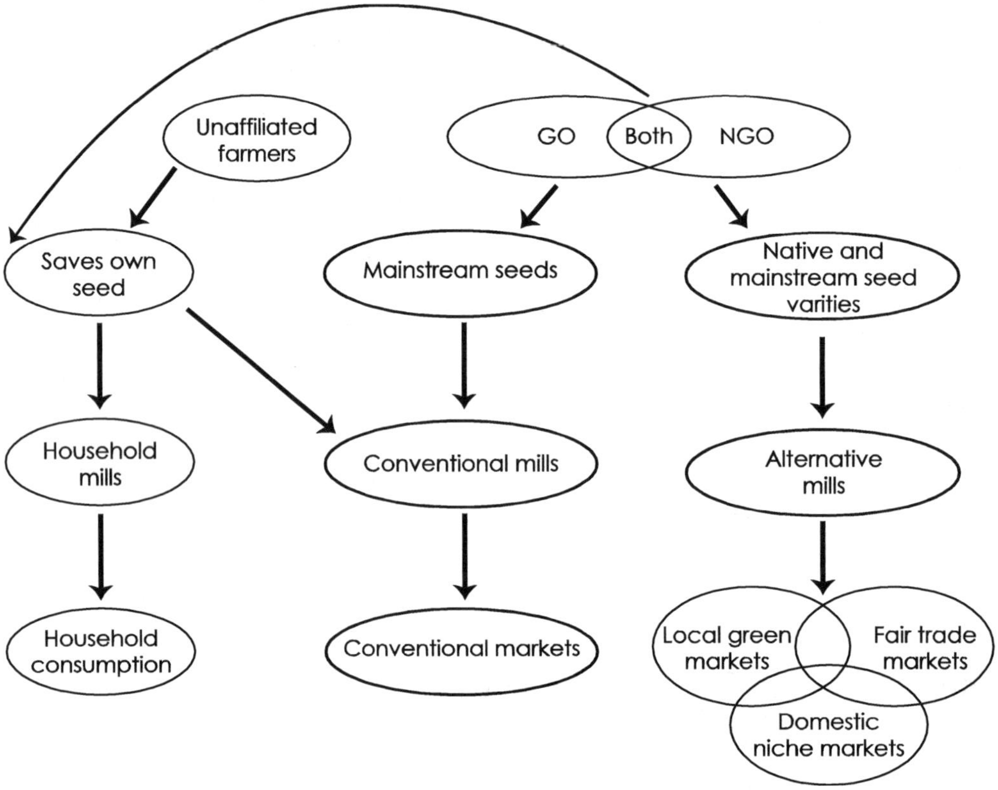

Based on my survey sample, most farmers are growing the government's mainstream rice varieties, which means that they are likely interacting with, buying from, or selling to a government organization (GO). Government farmers' organizations can include agricultural extension offices, cooperatives for loans, or milling groups (Ekasingh *et al.*, 2007). Involvement in these groups is common, as their presence is accessible in nearly every district and made convenient to the farmers. However, such involvement impacts farmers' options along the commodity pathway, from seed selection to market outlets.

---

[10] While no exact data could be found on the percentage of farmers involved in NGOs in Isaan, I estimate that less than 3% of the country's farmers are members of these alternative groups based on discussions with NGO leaders about their membership relative to their province.

Mainstream rice varieties are promoted along the governmental pathway (the middle group in the figure), first by providing only these seed types at extension offices and cooperatives. Farmers in these organizations then sell their rice to government or privately owned mills, which I term 'conventional mills', because they accept primarily the government-approved mainstream rice and have no regard to chemical use.[11] The government and private conventional mills sell rice to various wholesalers, after which point the rice goes to 'conventional markets', which distribute one third of the rice to domestic regions outside of Bangkok, one third to Bangkok, and the final third exported internationally (Ekasingh *et al.*, 2007).

The alternative to these conventional practices and pathways promoted by government organizations, however, is often through involvement in a non-governmental organization (right-most path in the figure). Membership in a non-governmental organization provides services similar to that of GOs, however these services are usually more diverse in their seed access, mill, and market options. Moreover, NGOs also provide farmers with educational resources for alternative farming methods (e.g. organic), and an extended network of alternative farming support. It should be noted, however, that not all farmers who are NGO members utilize all of the options available to them in the alternative pathway, as many still grow mainstream seeds and sell their crop to the government's conventional pathway.[12]

Among non-governmental organizations, a greater variety of seed types are available and often promoted for the sake of diversity maintenance. If growing these native seeds, or even mainstream seeds organically, NGO members then have the option of selling their rice crop to an 'alternative mill'. These mills are either NGO, community, or privately owned, and are considered alternative because they accept rice types other than mainstream varieties, and may also distinguish between organic and inorganic. Many NGOs and alternative mills then give access to alternative market options, such as local and domestic niche markets, or international fair trade, which specialize in native and organic rice.[13]

Outside of governmental and non-governmental organizations, farmers can also choose to be unaffiliated with any formal network. Typically, unaffiliated farmers save their own seeds from their community or family, then sell to private

[11] A recent example of government promotion of mainstream rice is Prime Minister Yingluck Shinawatra's rice price guarantee, which was put in place for the past year (2011-2012), and again renewed for the following year (2012-2013). Through this guarantee, the government mills buy Jasmine 105 rice at 20% above the global market price. While this policy was put in place to create financial benefits for farmers, the cost to the government is extreme, estimated at 1% of the country's GDP (IMF, 2012).

[12] Based on my sample, 47% of NGO members are still utilizing resource or mills of government organizations.

[13] Local and domestic niche markets include local NGO-established Green Markets, hospitals, and specialty health food stores in metropolitan areas, especially Bangkok. The two international fair trade organizations in my study include Green Net (Yasothon) and Alter Eco (Surin), which sell in various outlets in the EU and US.

conventional mills or process their rice at a household mill for their own consumption. It should also be noted that the option of household milling for personal consumption is a route available and utilized by most farmers,[14] and it is common for at least one community member to have a small household mill who will share with community.

Having a general sense about the paths that farmers can choose in terms of organization involvement, seed selection, and subsequent mill and market-related steps, we can now move forward to analyze how engagement with these pathways impacts farmers in terms of their agricultural practices and values, as they relate to the alternative agriculture movement. This allows us to assess the role of NGOs in facilitating education and change within the Thai agricultural sector, as well as the potential roles of markets and government-NGO cooperation.

Methods

Six locations across northeastern Thailand were intentionally selected to represent varying degrees of NGO involvement: Yasothon, Surin, Khon Kaen, Kalasin, and Chaiyaphum provinces (Figure 8.2). Surin and Yasothon represent the two major strongholds of the alternative agriculture movement – the Alternative Agriculture Network (AAN) and Natural Agriculture Group (NAG) – and Roi Et and Khon Kaen are developing small 'daughter' organizations in relation to the AAN. In Kalasin, a progressive government official recently worked with farmers to establish a group, now independent from the government, that practises alternative agriculture within the AAN network. And lastly Chaiyaphum has a number of farmers who neither affiliate with governmental nor non-governmental organizations (not shown in figure).

Figure 8.2 Network relationship between the sampled alternative farming NGOs

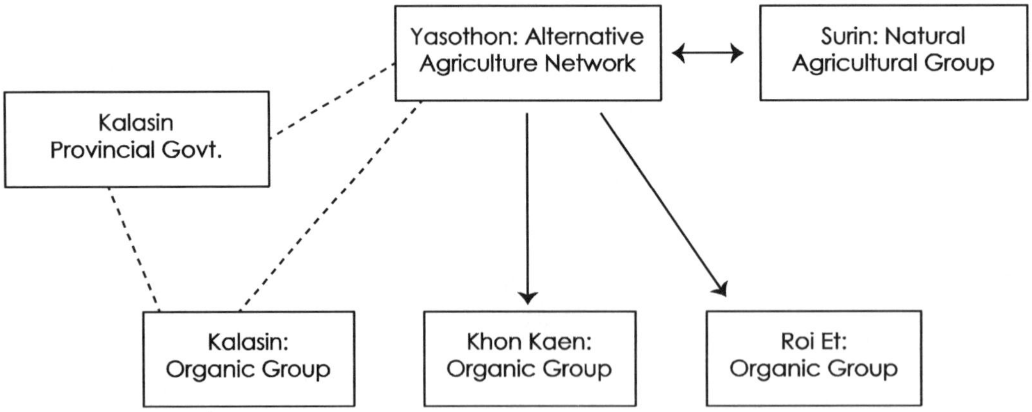

In each location I conducted in-depth interviews and surveys, in addition to ethnographic immersion, working on farms and living with families involved in

[14] In 2005, one fifth of the rice production in Isaan was kept for household consumption (Ekasingh *et al.*, 2007).

NGOs. The interviews were conducted with over 20 key players such as NGO representatives and mill managers in order to understand the structure and goals of different organizations. The surveys were conducted throughout the villages, and the sample farmers (n=84) were randomly and non-randomly selected so to represent those involved and not involved in the non-governmental networks.

The survey addressed questions of organization membership, rice-growing practices with regard to the types of rice being grown, the motivations for growing certain rice, the perceived importance of growing native rice, and the type of market pathways in which the farmer was involved. Furthermore, the survey asked about the value of rice varieties in Thai tradition, and the degree in which the farmer practises these traditions.[15] Using these variables, my research analyzes how organization, market, and government involvement affects farmers' crop choice, perceived importance of native rice varieties, practice of traditional rituals related to agriculture, and motivation for the growing of certain rice-types.

Results

The effects of non-governmental organization involvement are quite significant when it comes to alternative farming practices and values (Table 8.1).[16] First and foremost, farmers in alternative agriculture NGOs are significantly more likely to be organic, or in transition to organic (meaning no chemical fertilizers or pesticides) than farmers in GOs. And while mainstream varieties account for the majority of all farmers' land, my surveys indicate that non-governmental farmers grow a greater number of native varieties, and use a significantly greater portion of their land for them (21 percent of land) compared to farmers in governmental organizations (four percent of land). NGO farmers also place a significantly greater importance on the growing of native varieties (3.58 of 5 on Likert scale) when compared to GO farmers (1.87 of 5), demonstrating a stronger commitment to native varieties in terms perceived value. A greater engagement with native varieties in term of number, percentage of land, and perceived value may indicate greater access to alternative types of seeds, a greater degree of freedom in growing choices based on expanded market options, or simply a greater interest and understanding of growing multiple seed varieties.

[15] In order to measure the practice of traditions relative to agriculture I combined responses to three highly correlated questions ($p<0.001$) on the subject, including whether or not the farmer practices any agricultural rituals (0-1: yes/no), how seriously and passionately these rituals are practiced (1-5: Likert scale), and what particular rituals are practices (0-2: 0=no practices, 1=only a fraction of the practices such as only planting or only checking the 'good day' on the Buddhist calendar, and 2=doing all of the practices). Agricultural rituals-passion level: $p<0.001$, $r=0.893$, agricultural rituals-practices: $p<0.001$, $r=0.874$, passion level-practices: $p<0.001$, $r=0.915$. The number of respondents who fully answered the survey with enough data to complete this measure of culture was smaller in proportion to the full sample (n=33).

[16] I ran independent t-tests using governmental and non-governmental membership as independent variables, which excludes unaffiliated farmers and farmers involved in both GOs and NGOs, so to get a clear look at the effects of each group independently.

Table 8.1 Independent t-test for NGO and GO farmers on alternative growing practices and values

Survey questions	Organization	n	Mean	Significance
Grows rice organically (Rank 0-2)	GO	24	.33	
	NGO	29	1.55	.000*
Land area with native varieties (%)	GO	24	3.71	
	NGO	29	21.07	.003*
Number of native varieties grown	GO	24	.13	
	NGO	29	.86	.012*
Native varieties are important to grow (Rank 1-5)	GO	23	1.87	
	NGO	26	3.58	.001*

Note: Significance column is two tailed, equal variances not assumed.
An asterisk (*) indicates a statistical significance ($p < 0.05$).

Beyond the effectiveness of NGO involvement and alternative agriculture practices, a major focus of my research was to determine the factors contributing most significantly to the farmers' rice variety choices so to understand their priorities and opinions in terms of agricultural development. In the survey farmers were asked an open response question about why they chose to grow certain types of rice, and I categorized their responses into five groups: price and marketability, personal taste or health related preferences, environmental suitability, seed and resource accessibility, and convenience or habit-related reasons. The results showed no significant differences in any of these motivations between NGO and GO farmers, indicating that motivations are generally equal between groups. As a whole group, 43 percent of farmers were motivated by reasons related to price and marketability, and 25 percent were motivated by personal preference for taste or health. These categories exceed the three other response categories,[17] indicating that both groups are equally motivated by price and marketability as the primary factor, and personal preferences secondarily, in their rice-growing decisions.

The motivation rankings reveal that farmers are practical in their decision-making, such that they respond best to non-governmental organizations when they find their involvement provides personal advantage. In many cases, farming is the household's main source of income, and so most farmers feel that they cannot commit to a farming practice or seed variety if it doesn't bring direct benefits. In terms of personal health, many of the farmers in NGOs have explained that they initially joined their group because chemical farming had noticeably harmed their health, and they wanted support and education in their transition to organic practices, as well as grow healthier rice for consumption (B. Mahtkao, personal communication, June 15, 2012).

[17] Environmental: 16%; convenience: 11.1%; rice quality: 3.7%; and seed accessibility: 1.2%.

While market-based factors are governing farmers' growing decisions, values of crop biodiversity, environmental resilience, and community food sovereignty are often espoused by local NGO representatives (U. Yoowah, personal communication, 16 June 2012). NGO leaders also emphasize the importance of keeping native rice varieties for their use in celebrations and spirituality, as traditions are becoming fewer and fewer as the proper rice is no longer available (S. Jangsri, personal communication, June 23, 2012). Overall, NGO leaders often communicate values beyond basic market needs and farmer practicality, as they discuss the importance of alternative agriculture in terms of food security and sovereignty, environmental sustainability, and maintenance of communal and cultural traditions.

This emphasis on more abstract values by NGO leaders turns my research to question whether or not the NGO member farmers share similar cultural values and practices. To do so, I measured the perceived importance of native rice in culture, and practise of traditional methods and ceremonies (Table 8.2). My data indicates that farmers involved in NGOs did not believe native varieties to be important to traditional culture significantly more than those in GOs. Instead, the opinions of NGO farmers are across the board. Some excitedly describe, 'Having the local varieties helps us keep up with the cultural activities. We need *Khao Jow Deng* [soft red rice] to make noodles. We need *Khao Gum* [black sticky rice] to make *Khao Thom* [rice treat] and black sticky rice can also be used as medicinal food for healing.' In other cases, farmers don't think much of different varieties, explaining, 'Whether it is a local variety or a new variety, it is just about rice.'

My survey data also indicates that NGO membership has a marginally significant positive relationship with the practice of traditional ceremonies and rituals related to agriculture, indicating that NGO involvement is related to more frequent practice of, and greater dedication to, the traditional ceremonies of farming. This relationship may reflect a more fundamental trait of alternative farmers in Isaan; that those more engaged with the spiritual and ritual aspects of farming more readily connect with the values of alternative farming.

Table 8.2 Independent t-test for NGO and GO farmers on perceived cultural values and traditional practices

Survey questions	Organization	n	Mean	Significance
Native varieties are important to my culture (Rank 1-5)	GO	24	2.96	
	NGO	29	3.48	.295
Practice of traditional ceremonies (Rank 1-10)	GO	12	4.83	
	NGO	21	7.29	.051

Note: Significance column is two tailed, equal variances not assumed.
An asterisk (*) indicates a statistical significance ($p < 0.05$).

Taken together these results indicate that while NGO members are perhaps slightly more focused on the cultural values of native and traditional agricultural practices, average members do not share the NGO leaders' larger visions and values of fostering food sovereignty, rice diversity, and traditional cultural practices, particularly when balanced with market pressures. However, this disconnect of priorities between leaders and members seems to have resulted in an NGO development model that finds a middle ground between the two parties. I find that the NGOs aim to provide the direct benefits needed to incentivize farmers, while also fostering education with regard to environmental and cultural values in the hope that these ideas will eventually be taken on by members.

In addition to understanding the leader-member dynamics, I was interested to know whether or not government involvement plays a significant role in NGO farmer practices or values. In my research, the Sai Na Wang organic group in Kalasin province is an exceptional and unique organization, such that its establishment was largely facilitated by the governmental initiatives of a social activist turned local governmental official. When compared to other non-governmental organizations, there are few differences between the two groups in terms alternative practices and values, as both grew similar numbers of native varieties on similar amounts of land, as well as placed the same relative importance on native varieties (Table 8.3).

Table 8.3 Independent t-test for Sai Na Wang community

Survey questions	Organization	n	Mean	Significance
Land area with native varieties (%)	NGO	22	16.73	
	Sai Na Wang	9	27.11	.277
Number of native varieties grown	NGO	22	.64	
	Sai Na Wang	9	1.67	.124
Native varieties are important to grow (Rank 1-5)	NGO	21	3.48	
	Sai Na Wang	6	3.33	.902
Market growing motive (Rank 0-1)	NGO	22	.55	
	Sai Na Wang	9	.11	.010*
Native varieties are important to my culture (Rank 1-5)	NGO	22	3.68	
	Sai Na Wang	9	2.22	.149
Practice of traditional ceremonies (Rank 1-10)	NGO	14	6.21	
	Sai Na Wang	8	9.50	.006*

Note: Significance measures are two-tailed, equal variances not assumed.
An asterisk (*) indicates a statistical significance ($p < 0.05$).

The major differences are that Sai Na Wang farmers are significantly less motivated by the market and tend to engage more with the practice of traditional agricultural ceremonies. Based on these findings I contend that strong government support, particularly local government policy, gives NGOs an advantage in terms of resources and educational networks, improving their ability to foster a range of alternative values and traditional practices. In this case, the local government was able to provide the farmers with funding for resources such as mills and seeds, and also facilitated a variety of workshops to educate farmers about native seeds - all while having the government seal of approval. The success of this organization in facilitating alternative farming and cultural practices, particularly a shift away from market-based motivations, indicates that government support can aid NGOs in dispersing and reinforcing education about native seeds. However, it is important to note that the small sample from Sai Na Wang (n=9) may also be responsible for the marked significance in the research findings. In small communities there is limited opportunity to attract larger sample sizes.

Ultimately, my research indicates that non-governmental organizations in Thailand play a unique and prominent role in the country's move towards sustainability. Particularly in the field of agriculture, NGOs are making a concentrated effort towards organic growing and agro-biodiversity, specifically native rice diversity, as a strategy for environmental resilience and cultural preservation. In doing so, the organization promotes the health benefits of organic farming, supports the creation of local organic markets, and educates farmers on low-income ways to improve and diversify farmland. This tactic of combining goals of environmental sustainability with practical support for farmers is a balance critical to the success of an NGO, and moreover, the NGOs in this field that are progressing furthest may be those that are paired with local governments, as they can benefit from their resources, networks, and policy influence.

Implications for the field

My research findings lead to three major recommendations for current and future regional and international non-governmental organizations looking to work in the Isaan area and beyond. First, the general success of the organizations in my case study can be largely attributed to their grassroots networking and educational outreach, and the value of these practices cannot be understated. Though the directionality of the NGO-alternative practices relationship is unknown, its clear that a critical part of the alternative movement is the network relationships, and how those relationships facilitate a more diverse and engaged education, set of values, and practices. As such, NGOs should establish and continually improve these networks, as it fosters participation and a sense of communal support among members. Furthermore, NGOs should aim to foster participation in educational workshops and community based projects, such as seed banks and experimental plots in the case of agricultural NGOs. Continuing education for sustainable farming methods, and particularly sharing information about native seed value, culturally and environmentally, is critical to continue strengthening the network and its goals.

Secondly, my research demonstrates that NGO-government relationships can facilitate network development, provide funding and resources, and ultimately lead to a more engaged membership. Government relationships may also lead to increased support of NGO initiatives through policy, which make the movement more sustainable through longer-term, systematic change (A. Saengubon, personal communication, July 20, 2012). While NGOs should be careful not to lose autonomy through dependence on funding or resources, finding a balance with the local government could help relieve some of the institutional roadblocks, such as government promotion of pesticides in the case of agriculture. Ultimately, NGOs should aim to carefully utilize the help of government offices in an effort to advance their goals.

Lastly, it is critical for NGOs, local and international, to understand its participants' primary motivations – as they are not always congruent with those in leadership – and work to find a middle ground between the needs of its members and the values of the organization. Based on my research findings, to gain and maintain membership, the use of incentives that relate directly to the participants' needs should be proposed as primary goals. For example, the health benefits from organic farming and opportunities to sell at alternative markets with higher prices are the strongest motivators for membership in an alternative agricultural NGO. Pairing members' well-being, financial and otherwise, with educational outreach and support related to goals of sustainability is a balance critical to the success of an NGO.[18]

This realization of members' practical realities is not to say that goals of environmental or cultural sustainability should be forfeited. Rather, the hope of this balance is that in time, NGO members will become more educated about values beyond just their direct personal gain, to include environmental and cultural significance. In this way, the non-governmental organization can serve as an access point for farmers to transition to organic farming and connect to alternative markets, both of which serve as a means of achieving longer-term goals of sustainability education and policy change.

References

(AAN) Alternative Agriculture Network Isaan, Khok Pak Good-Pong Daeng Farmers Network, Thai Baan Association, Mahasarakam Hospital Chemical-Free Market Network, Mahasarakam Green People Network, Isaan Contracted Farmers Network, Isaan Thai Farmers Networks Association, Isaan 'Noat' Sustainable Agriculture Local Research Network, Mahsarakam Health Promotion Network, Mahasarakam Green Market Network, Man Yuen Network, Organic Group of Nong Paen Sub-District, Yang Ta Lad District, Kalasin Province, Isaan Farmers Generation Network, and Isaan Young People Group. (2011). 'Open Letter to

[18] An example to be aware particularly of in Thailand is the role of the recent rice price guarantee on organic farming. Because the guarantee incentivized the growing and selling of mainstream Jasmine rice 105 to government mills by purchasing it at 20% above the global market price (IMF, 2012), this policy cancelled out the premium associated with organic or native rice. As such, a large number of the NGOs' organic farmers defaulted back to chemical agriculture, as it is less work for the same amount of money (V. Panyakul, personal communication, July 4, 2012). It is important for non-governmental organizations to be conscious of maintaining a benefit to its member farmers in general, and must be even more vigilant in the face of such policies.

Prime Minister Yingluck Chinawatra' presented at Organic Farmer Protest, September 20, 2011.

Baker, C. & Phongpaichit, P. (2005). *A History of Thailand*. Cambridge and New York: Cambridge University Press.

Central Intelligence Agency. (2012). World Factbook: Thailand. Retrieved from https://www.cia.gov/library/publications/the-world-factbook/geos/th.html

Chambers, P. (2010). Thailand on the Brink: Resurgent Military, Eroded Democracy. Asian Survey, 50, 835-858.

Ekasingh, B. Sungkapitux, C. Kitchaicharoen, J., Suebpongsang, P. (2007). Competitive Commercial Agriculture in the Northeast of Thailand. Department of Agricultural Economics and the Multiple Cropping Center. Faculty of Agriculture, Chiang Mai University, Thailand.

Feeny, D. (2003). The Political Economy of Regional Inequality: The Northeast of Thailand 1800-2000. *Crossroads: An Interdisciplinary Journal of Southeast Asian Studies*, 17, 29-59.

Hewison, K. (2010). Thaksin Shinawatra and the reshaping of Thai politics. *Contemporary Politics*, 16, 119-133.

Ikemoto, Y. (1991). *Income Distribution in Thailand: Its Changes, Causes, and Structure*. Tokyo: Institute of Developing Economies.

International Crisis Group. (2010). Bridging Thailand's Deep Divide. Asia Report N 192. Retrieved from http://www.crisisgroup.org/~/media/Files/asia/south-east-asia/thailand/192_Bridging%20Thailands%20Deep%20Divide.pdf.

International Monetary Fund. (2012). Thailand: Article IV Consultation. Retrieved from www.imf.org/external/pubs/ft/scr/2012/cr12124.pdf.

Javier, L.A. & Suwannakij, S. (October 26, 2011). Floods Ruining 14% of Thai Rice May Erase Global Export Glut: Commodities. Bloomberg. Retrieved from www.bloomberg.com/news/2011-10-25/floods-ruining-14-of-thai-rice-may-erase-global-export-glut-commodities.html.

Missingham, B. (2003). Forging Solidarity and identity in the Assembly of the Poor: from local struggles to a national social movement in Thailand. *Asian Studies Review*, 27, 317-340.

National Statistical Office. (2010). Population and Housing Census, Executive Summary. Retrieved from http://popcensus.nso.go.th/file/popcensus-08-08-55-T.pdf.

Oupkaew, P. (2011). Complexity and adaptability of a traditional agricultural system: case study of a gall midge resistant rice landrace from northern Thailand. *Genetic Resources and Crop Evolution*, 58, 361-372.

Panyakul, V. (2003). Thai rice: the rice of freedom. Green Peace Southeast Asia. Green Net, Thailand.

United Nations. (2010). *Country Profile: Thailand Trade Profile*. Retrieved from http://data.un.org/CountryProfile.aspx?crName=THAILAND#Environment.

United States Department of Agriculture Foreign Agricultural Service. (2013). *Grain: World Markets and Trade*. Retrieved from www.fas.usda.gov/psdonline/circulars/grain.pdf.

Chapter 9

Asset-based community development in Myanmar

Theory, fit and practice

ANTHONY WARE

ABSTRACT

Highly participatory and community-led approaches to development have previously been shown to be effective forms of poverty mitigation and community empowerment. This chapter explores the applicability and effectiveness of the most highly participatory and community-led approach to development, Asset Based Community Development (ABCD) in Myanmar both theoretically and in practice.

Introduction

Effective community development empowers the marginalised, powerless and poor to achieve better life outcomes and a higher level of well-being for themselves. This requires imagining their world differently and taking action to change their circumstances, implying a high level of participation and empowerment (Eyben, Kabeer & Cornwall, 2008, p. 3).

Myanmar has been a highly complex and very restrictive socio-political context for poverty alleviation and development activity over the past two decades. Attempts to address the high levels of poverty in the country were frustrated by a government highly suspicious of the motivations of international agencies, by a domestic priority on security over poverty alleviation, and by strained international relations over human rights concerns[19], which resulted in economic sanctions and restrictive international assistance policies. Recent political reform is bringing very welcome change, however research conducted prior to this reform (Ware, 2012) found highly participatory, community-led approaches to development to be effective forms of poverty mitigation and community empowerment even within this restrictive context. One of the more highly participatory approaches first researched then is now the focus of the discussion in this chapter.

This chapter explores the applicability and effectiveness of Asset Based Community Development (ABCD) within this context, both theoretically and in practice. After this introduction, the chapter is divided into four sections. The first section provides an overview of the socio-political context of Myanmar within which the case studies of ABCD take place. The second section offers a brief overview of ABCD theory, from Nietzsche to Freire and Chambers, and then the literature on Asset Based Community Development itself. The third section examines the effectiveness of ABCD within this context by offering two case studies, the Action Aid Myanmar Change Maker Fellowships Program, and the GraceWorks Myanmar Community Development Education program (with which I am personally involved). The final section concludes with implications and lessons learned from the case studies.

Background: Myanmar context

Poverty is significant issue in Myanmar, and the poor in Myanmar suffer deep multidimensional poverty. According to the UNDP (2011), almost a third of the estimated 55-60 million population are multidimensionally poor, with 45 percent poor in at least one dimension and facing significant risk of multidimensional

---

[19] The Human Rights Council and the UN General Assembly passed resolutions condemning human rights abuses in the country at every sitting from 1991/2 until recently. I would say that this issue of human rights violations and how it was being addressed was a central driver for the strained international relations and sanctions, whether we think they originated from an overly western perspective or otherwise. This is taken up in the background section.

poverty. The UNDP report also finds that those who are multi-dimensionally poor in Myanmar typically suffer a particularly high intensity of multidimensional deprivation, with almost ten percent of the population living in 'severe poverty'.

The most recent and thorough poverty data on the country, the *Integrated Household Living Conditions Survey in Myanmar (2009-2010)* (IHLCA, 2011) concludes that 26 percent of the population live in absolute poverty, unable to purchase the minimum food and non-food items required to maintain a basic calorie intake while continuing to subsist. As a result, 39 percent suffer moderate-severe malnutrition, while almost one in five have no access to healthcare, 30 percent lack safe drinking water, and almost a quarter have no toilet or sanitation. More than half the population does not have more than a grade four education, with two-thirds having no access to secondary education. Economically, Myanmar is so far behind its neighbours that U Myint, chief economic advisor to the new president, has suggested that even if double-digit GDP growth could be sustained (which is unlikely based on the performance of other Asian economies), 'it would take 39 years to catch up with the level of per capita GDP that Malaysia hopes to attain by 2020' (U Myint, 2010, p. 22).

The poverty and vulnerability of the people was highlighted in 2008 by Cyclone Nargis, which resulted in 140,000 deaths and caused 'unprecedented destruction', affecting 2.4 million people across the Delta region of Myanmar (TCG, 2008). Nargis was only a category-3 storm, the same strength as Hurricane Katrina in New Orleans or Cyclone Yasi in northern Australia: Hurricane Katrina hit a more densely populated urban center with higher wind strength and a storm surge of similar magnitude and only killed 75 people, and Cyclone Yasi resulted in only one fatality.

International attempts to provide relief to this poverty have been frustrated over most of the last two decades by a combination of domestic and international restrictions. Poverty in Myanmar is the result of decades of isolation, poor governance, failed policies and inept bureaucracy, characterised by the personal power politics of authoritarian military-led regimes (Ware, 2012). The military took control of the state five decades ago on the mantra of preventing the breakup of the union due to civil conflict, and preventing neo-colonial subjugation to a foreign power. Civil conflict continued in many parts of the country, largely unabated since Independence until the ceasefires of the last decade, and claiming an estimated million casualties—almost a third of all civil conflict casualties in Southeast Asia during that time (Steinberg, 2010). Foreign backing for these insurgencies, particularly during the Cold War, reinforced the idea of being surrounded by enemies and the danger of foreign domination, driving the polity of isolation and fuelling the fears of the political elite (Selth, 2008a). Thus when the new regime came to power in 1988, they again claimed they were saving the country from disintegration or foreign subjugation (Taylor, 2009).

International ire against this new regime was kindled by their perceived close association with the massacre of thousands of civilian demonstrators in 1988, even though the massacre itself occurred immediately prior to their coup. The regime's ongoing authoritarian crackdown on dissent, culminating in the arrest of opposition leader Aung San Suu Kyi in 1989, and failure to transfer power after legitimate democratic elections in 1990, turned international opinion strongly against them. Tough economic sanctions were then applied by many Western governments after an attempt on Suu Kyi's life and her re-arrest in 1995, and were only strengthened during the intervening years prior to the current political reform. The seriousness of international opprobrium is illustrated in that the United Nations General Assembly and Human Rights Council passed resolutions condemning human rights violations in Myanmar at every sitting between 1991 and 2011.

The impact of the resultant international tension can also be highlighted by the standoff which occurred immediately after Cyclone Nargis. Apparently paralysed by the need to allow an international presence to assist with the emergency response, the regime delayed in responding to international offers until ASEAN intervened. In the meantime, the alarm the international community felt at the difficulty of obtaining permission to deliver aid and bring in expertise led to calls by numerous Western politicians and activists for an armed incursion into Burmese sovereign territory, to deliver aid under the *Responsibility to Protect* mandate (Selth, 2008a, 2008b). Neither domestic fear and restrictions, nor Western confrontation and conditionality, were helpful in alleviating the immediate needs of the poor victims.

International attempts to help alleviate poverty have thus been frustrated on the one hand by a government highly suspicious of the motivations of international agencies, and by domestic priority on security over poverty alleviation, and on the other hand by strained international relations which resulted in economic sanctions and restrictive international assistance policies.

Anthropological research during this period suggested that the psychological impact of five decades of military rule on the wider population was an aversion to risk trying new things, and they people felt highly disempowered in decision-making (Fink, 2000, 2001; Skidmore, 2003, 2005). Aung San Suu Kyi (1995) spoke of the people living under constant fear, leading, she suggested, to the poor having pronounced, learned helplessness and dependence. She argues that a chain of command culture trivialised people who did not enjoy formal positions, de-motivating initiative and independent self-help action.

This is exemplified by the response to protests such as the Saffron Revolution in 2007, so-called because it was led by large numbers of monks in robes. The campaign began as a series of peaceful protests through the streets, initially over price rises caused by the removal of a fuel subsidy, and it was led by the monks as they were thought to be relatively immune from military oppression. The 'revolution', however, failed, and large numbers of monks were disrobed, with an estimate of hundreds of protesters killed and thousands more arrested in the subsequent crackdown, accentuating a reversion to non-confrontation with authority.

It was particularly surprising, therefore, when my previous research found that INGOs widely reported highly participatory, community-led approaches to development were particularly effective in Myanmar, even prior to the current political reform (Ware, 2012). With minimal government assistance, few formal civil society organisations beyond religious institutions, and little by way of international assistance, people apparently learned to depend on themselves and one another. Agencies reported that with deliberate planning and time dedicated to getting the process right, and through elite cooption to create a safe space and assist, the fear of risk and self-initiation could be overcome and self-reliance could turn into effective community leadership. This readiness for self-reliance was illustrated in the spontaneous emergence of civil-society assistance after Cyclone Nargis (CPCS, 2008). Buddhism, the dominant religion, has also taught people to be self-reliant.

This chapter examines in more detail one of the more highly participatory development approaches observed in Myanmar during this earlier research, Asset Based Community Development (ABCD). It explores the practice and reasons for effectiveness of the Action Aid Myanmar's highly effective *Change Maker Fellowships* program, as well as GraceWorks Myanmar's *Community Development Education* program, with which I am involved.

Asset-based community development (ABCD) theory

Highly participatory development based on empowerment has a long history within philosophy, sociology and development studies. Nietzsche's critique of modernist thought, for example, called for individuals and communities to be empowered such that people are able to reclaim ownership of their own futures; utilising their own strengths, resources and culture to move beyond oppression and deficiency (see Hipwell, 2009). Nietzsche's ideas of *active ethics* and the cultivation of the *will to power* are reflected, at least implicitly, in the rationale of ABCD.

Freire, in his *Pedagogy of the Oppressed* (1972), similarly argued that traditional processes of teaching in which a teacher transfers knowledge to students is both ineffective and a form of oppression. This, he suggests, is especially true in development, which assumes professionals from a more 'advanced' position provide solutions. Rather, Freire argues, learning should be a process of people rethinking their assumptions and acting upon their own ideas, more than of consuming the ideas of others. This paradigm has become a foundation underlying all participatory approaches to development, including ABCD. Freire's (1972, 1974) primary contribution is the concept of *conscientização* (Portuguese), translated as critical consciousness, conscientisation, or awareness-raising, which refers to a process of facilitating people becoming aware of oppression, its sources, and the means available to them to do something about it. Education or development, then, should not revolve around the transmission of preselected knowledge but the facilitation of self-discovery of circumstances, and how to act upon the material situation and social structures.

Participatory Action Research (PAR) (Fals-Borda, 1987, 1991), and its subsequent incarnations as Participatory Rural Appraisal (PRA), Participatory Learning and Action (PLA), et cetera, have argued development professionals need to shift from being on 'on-top' to 'on-tap', emphasising they should approach their role with the values and disposition of facilitator rather than expert (Fals-Borda, 1987, 1991). Building on this foundation, Chambers (1983) conceptualised poverty as powerlessness due to marginalisation, rather than as a lack of income, assets, services or even knowledge. Highlighting the often inappropriate knowledge outsiders bring to development contexts, Chambers argued for a reversal in the management of development, transferring decision-making primarily into the hands of recipients.

ABCD is a coherent development approach which includes a set of participatory tools, built on the premise that recognition of strengths and assets is more likely to inspire positive action for change than is a primary focus on needs and problems. The significant innovation of ABCD beyond most participatory development practice is thus its focus on the appreciation and utilisation of otherwise unrecognised community assets, both tangible and social, as the primary resources for self-managing their own development, and reliance on community leadership, social networks and advocacy to bring about substantial change (Kretzmann & McKnight, 1993, 1997; Mathie & Cunningham, 2003). It encourages active citizenship in both the sense of citizen-to-citizen ties and citizen-state relations, and thus involves working at the community level in two dimensions, one to create and seize contextual opportunities for sustainable development, and the other being to help people leverage outside assistance and claim the rights and entitlements of state and global citizenship.

In practice, ABCD therefore replaces professional development workers in the communities with individuals trained and willing to facilitate community processes. Such facilitators do not necessarily need the same level of education, status or access to finance as community development professionals. However, rather than replace them, facilitators network with development experts to the community relationally. Thus, the community is empowered to access their resources or the resources of others on an as-needed basis.

ABCD seeks to reignite hope and release an entrepreneurial imagination that empowers people to look for ways they can take control of their own futures, with outside workers acting as facilitators in a process of deliberate capacity building focussed on community processes and empowerment rather than largely being a conduit for financial assistance. 'The appeal of ABCD lies in its premise that people in communities can organise to drive the development process themselves, by identifying and mobilising existing (but often unrecognised) assets, thereby responding to and creating local economic opportunity' (Mathie & Cunningham, 2003, p. 474).

> *This community development strategy starts with what is present in the community: the capacities of its residents and workers, the associational and institutional base of the area – not with what is absent, or with what is*

> *problematic, or with what the community needs. . . . The development strategy concentrates first upon the agenda building and problem-solving capacities of local residents, local associations, and local institutions (Kretzmann & McKnight, 1993, p. 9).*

The application of ABCD therefore commences with either the training of local community members to function as facilitators – or a period of relationship building by a trained outside facilitator – followed by the development of community processes and planning in which assets are identified, a new story of the community is formulated, and new community skills and relationships are developed (Ennis & West, 2010). This involves both internal-focussed community work (such as asset mapping and developing community processes), as well as external-focussed activities (such as understanding and entering into dialogue with political, economic, cultural, and legal structures).

The greatest criticisms of ABCD are made when the focus on internal assets obstructs impact upon the external structures affecting communities (Mathie & Cunningham, 2003). This is an easy imbalance to slip into in practice, given the distinctive focus of ABCD is on reliance upon previously unrecognised tangible and social community assets. However, the focus on assets is to combat a deficit and dependency mindset, and is only the first step of effective *conscientização*. Successful ABCD thus involves both efficient application of local assets to address local needs, as well as active citizenship, advocacy and engagement with authorities and others, to bring additional resources to the community and create change in oppressive structures.

Case studies

Case study 9.1

Action Aid's 'Change Maker' Fellowships program

Program description

The Action Aid 'Change Maker' Fellowships program is the largest ABCD program in Myanmar. It commenced in 2006, in partnership with local NGOs Metta and Shalom (Nyein) Foundation. Based on early successes, the program was quickly expanded to now have numerous local partner organisations, and more than six hundred young 'agents of change' supported to work full-time in communities.

As with many highly participatory development programs in Myanmar, the 'Change Maker' Fellowships program has both local grass-roots development and broader democratisation goals. It seeks to both stimulate positive change at the local level through ABCD, based on the communities' priorities and resources, as well as contribute to broader macro change through community empowerment in their contact with government agencies and by developing the potential of idealistic and passionate, educated young people (ActionAid, 2010).

Fellows are recruited by local partner organisations through their direct contact with communities. Most commonly, an advocate from a local partner facilitates an open community meeting, explains the program and invites the community to nominate suitable young people to receive intensive training with Action Aid. Nominated fellows must be under twenty-five years of age and have commonly completed a tertiary degree. Many graduates in Myanmar don't have good employment opportunities in the narrow and poorly-developed economy, and a good number return home after completing tertiary studies. However, given almost two-thirds of the rural population do not have more than a grade four education (IHLCA, 2011), these tertiary-educated young people are a potentially powerful force for community empowerment despite their youth.

Fellows are recruited for a two-year placement and are commonly placed in their own village area or are at least sent back to their own region and ethnicity. Thus, despite their youth, they start with a measure of credibility and program understanding by their communities. Action Aid provides a month of intensive training to the fellows, which includes training in participatory development tools as well as personal development before they are sent back to facilitate participatory processes in the community for two years (Ferretti, 2010; Löfving, 2011). Fellows are provided a minimal support salary and little additional financial resource, but are given personal support through networking with other fellows and intermittent ongoing training opportunities.

The program then '[throws] the fellows in at the deep end … [providing] fellows with tools and capacities to mobilize people, but with no blueprint on how mobilization should proceed' (Ferretti, 2010 p.2). Described as a learning program, focus is on building the capacity of the fellows and not on prescribing change. Given freedom in the tools and types of activities they initiate, they most commonly commence by facilitating some of a range of self-help groups with interested community members, ranging from savings and loans groups, to literacy groups, to rice banks. Only after they have built credibility do they seek to form and train village-level community development organisations to take responsibility for the planning and implementation of projects and processes. Over time, fellows then seek to establish community based organisations (CBOs) out of these committees. This is an express goal of the program.

Action Aid emphasise rights and advocacy in their training, together with personal development for the fellows. Fellows report that one of the biggest challenges is to change attitudes about the authorities, to convince themselves and communities that engagement through non-confrontational strategies is possible (Ferretti, 2010). Such engagement involves adopting methods often referred to as 'elite co-option', noting that even when their vested interests may lie elsewhere, constructing 'persuasive narrative around notions of joint gains' rather than by attempting to blame or shame, can result in officials becoming involved in 'constructive dialogue about the nature, causes of and solutions to poverty in ways that will maximise their empathy and engagement with the issue, and minimise the danger that they will feel railroaded into responding' (Hossain & Moore, 2002 pp.5, 10). One of the most oft-reported outcomes at fellows' conferences, and the most surprising outcome for most new fellows, is their increased confidence to engage with authorities in this manner (Ferretti, 2010; Löfving, 2011). While initial suspicion of the fellows has at times resulted in threats, even arrests, and while describing engagement with state actors as a long and complex process, a real strength of the program is this extent to which it has successfully engaged the structures affecting communities.

Fellows usually start by promoting community action around tangible areas such as health, education, livelihoods, and developing an environment of cooperation and social cohesion, through the self-help groups as above and by use of participatory development activities with those open to work with them. Later, as they develop a track record, they shift the focus more to development of community-wide inclusive participatory decision-making structures, and community engagement with state and non-state actors to obtain the space and resources required for larger-scale development activities:

> *The programme views communities as inherently resourceful and capable of identifying their own needs, formulating ideas and initiating and leading processes of change. … [It] seeks to inspire communities to realize their development aspirations through advocating to and forging linkages with state and non-state actors. … Underpinning [the program] are the complementary concepts of self-reliance and empowerment (Löfving, 2011, p. 2).*

Where support is achieved from government officials, this most often comes from seeking assistance after the community has demonstrated how much they have already achieved on their own (Ferretti, 2010). Communities that could demonstrate a self-reliant approach, that were well organised, and which had a long-term plan for their village were more likely to have their requests taken more seriously by officials and other external actors (Löfving, 2011).

Fellows are seen as catalysts for change, as opposed to field staff, and work alongside local village volunteers. It promotes a model of low cost interventions that emphasise self-reliance. It makes a 'conscious investment in the long-term empowerment of communities … the processes of community led development are anticipated to extend far beyond the duration of the program itself' (Löfving, 2011, p. 2).

Effectiveness

Yeneabat & Butterfield (2012) propose evaluating the effectiveness of ABCD programs against five key building blocks of the ABCD approach, namely: effectively mapping the capacities and assets of individuals, citizen associations, and local institutions; convening a broadly representative community group who plan and build community vision; building relationships for mutually beneficial problem solving within the community; mobilising the community's assets for information sharing and economic development; and, leveraging activities, resources, and investments from outside the community to support locally defined development. On this set of criteria, these ABCD programs have proven highly effective in Myanmar.

External evaluations of the program find that that almost all communities develop a representative committee within the life of the 2-year fellow's presence, and the mobilisation of local assets plus those from outside the community has results in very impressive outcomes (Löfving, 2011). They had 160 fellows in communities by their first national fellows' conference in January 2011, when they compiled reported outcomes to that point. In the education sector, results included the opening of 40 early childhood centres, the construction of schools in 30 villages (with a mix of government and non-government funding), local community members providing voluntary teaching in 30 underfunded primary schools, 22 villages negotiating for government-paid teachers, and over 1,600 people in adult literacy groups. Health and sanitation outcomes included 77 wells in 33 villages, well cleaning in another 50 villages, 45 ponds constructed in 26 villages, 1,500 new toilets across 75 villages, health clinics built and staffed in 11 villages, vaccination programs in 44 villages, and 19 villages obtaining health workers, with another 27 villages negotiating new mobile health services from other NGOs. Similar outcomes were seen in the livelihood sector, with, 152 savings and loans groups established, plus 60 rice banks and many other self-help groups supporting livestock, farming, and so on. These outcomes are based on facilitators self-reporting of their achievements to external evaluators, and have not been verified in the communities, but they are nonetheless significant.

These results are significant across a broad range of sectors, particularly given the minimal level of funding supplied by the international agency and the youthfulness and relative lack of training of the fellows. Also significant is the impact of this ABCD on the external structures affecting communities, through the use of community social assets to co-opt officials, government agencies, or sometimes other NGOs. Based on the significance of these outcomes, Action Aid have subsequently almost quadrupled the number of fellows in this program since the January 2011 conference.

Case study 9.2

GraceWorks Myanmar's Community Development Education program

Program description

Developed independently, GraceWorks Myanmar's Community Development Education (CDE) program is remarkably similar to the Action Aid program in aims and approach. The CDE program seeks to empower local communities to pro-actively organise, make decisions and implement their own development according to priorities they determine, starting with effective utilisation of their own assets and resources, then moving quickly to leverage this through engagement with officials and other outside assistance.

A primary difference between the GraceWorks and Action Aid programs is that GraceWorks sets no age or educational criteria in the recruitment of facilitators. GraceWorks likewise recruits facilitators via local partner organisations, but the criteria are focussed on motivation and personal attributes. As a result GraceWorks' facilitators are, on average, considerably older and less well-educated than those of Action Aid. Based on the dynamics of their partner organisations, CDE facilitators are also noted to more often have been recruited from outside the communities they work within. Who the facilitators are in relation to the community, and how they relate to local community members, is therefore significantly different. Bringing a good deal more life experience and social status with them, GraceWorks facilitators can sometimes quickly gain acceptance and influence with community leaders and local authorities. However, the older they are and more status they bring, the more easily they default back to an outside expert role, and they may also be less innovative as a result.

Countering this, many GraceWorks facilitators don't have a secondary education, and some are functionally illiterate, helping them connect with the poorer members of the community more as peers than experts. To address the functionally illiteracy of some of the rural adult facilitators, and also to train those facilitators in using the same style with which they will need to train functionally illiterate committee and community members, GraceWorks' training emphasises oral learning techniques. GraceWorks also adapt the training to a just-in-time training format. Rather than providing a month-long intensive to train facilitators, GraceWorks provide one week training per quarter, every quarter, with the training matched to the implementation stage the facilitators face. GraceWorks believe this caters better for rural adult oral learning styles.

Like Action Aid, GraceWorks implements their program through local partner organisations that are very grassroots, very close to the local people and communities. Facilitators also commit to four years in a community, rather than two, allowing a longer project cycle, and as in the ActionAid program facilitators are only supported with a minimal, subsistence level of financial support. GraceWorks' CDE program facilitators are chosen by the local partner organisations through their membership networks, rather than directly from the community. Facilitators are, however, usually from the same geographic region and ethnicity as the communities they work with. Nonetheless, because of this recruitment method many of the facilitators are single (or single again), with minimal family commitments.

With most facilitators being outsiders, avoiding potential community resistance is important. This has been achieved in the experience to date by spending time slowly building trust over the first half-year to full year, building a track record through a series of simple 'seed projects' planned and implemented together with community members whom they have most quickly established rapport. These seed projects include self-help groups similar to those of Action Aid, or simple community repairs to local infrastructure, or things like organising classes for children in the absence of a government-appointed teacher. After six to twelve months of informal work in the community in this manner, in an act of deliberate empowerment, facilitators arrange a series of open community meetings to communicate in detail what a full CDE program could look like. These awareness meetings run for several hours, often over several evenings, and clearly communicate ABCD principles and the details of the operation of the proposed program. At the conclusion of the meetings, communities are given an opportunity to invite a full CDE program to commence in their community, or politely decline. Communities who decline may choose to participate in a CDE program at a later date if they desire, without prejudice, subject to availability of a facilitator, and facilitators who face such an outcome move to commence with a new community. Where communities do request a full program, facilitators are encouraged to relocate, at least part-time, into the community.

Effectiveness

No external evaluations of GraceWorks' CDE program have yet been compiled. As of early 2013 the program has eighteen full-time facilitators, and the early results are encouraging in terms of community ownership, and the breadth and effectiveness of the program. According to self-reporting by facilitators during quarterly training and internal reports accumulated by staff from the local partner organisations, communities have accepted the outside facilitators quickly, mobilised representative committees, and chosen to work on projects such as road repair, sanitation, water purification and preventative health awareness programs, for example, as well as repair of preschools and schools, placement of community teachers, construction of a jetty and footbridge, and planning for a community blood-type register for emergency transfusions. The program has also seen functionally illiterate facilitators function effectively, and facilitators work successfully in regions like rural Rakhine State, where the formal illiteracy rate is 25 percent and functional illiteracy is closer to 90 percent (IHLCA 2011).

These results are encouraging in the extent to which implementation has remained highly participatory and community-owned even in the very poorest communities. Based on the informal evaluations of the program to date, the two major changes are being recommended: a) to further increase the use of oral tradition, narrative-based means of communication of program principles, and b) to move to having more facilitators chosen directly by communities themselves, from the community, rather than chosen and sent by the local partner organisation.

Conclusions and implications for the field

This chapter demonstrates that ABCD can be implemented very effectively and at a very minimal cost in poor Asian contexts, and is very adaptable in its implementation. These two case studies are most illustrative of the principles and possible implementation modes of ABCD generally, despite being very grounded in and developed specifically for the restrictive context of Myanmar as it was prior to the political reform that began in 2011.

ABCD is a coherent development approach built on the premise that appreciation and utilisation of otherwise unrecognised assets inspires positive action for change. It draws heavily on Friere's *conscientização* as the model for facilitating communities' self-discovery of their true situation, and self-reliant action to change both their material situation and the social structures affecting them. It therefore involves empowering the community to sustainably improve their material circumstance by drawing on their tangible and social assets, leveraging outside assistance from the state and global community, and working confidently to change oppressive social structures.

The Action Aid and GraceWorks Myanmar case studies illustrate a number of keys to successful implementation of an ABCD program. Of greatest importance is the placement of facilitators rather than development experts into communities, whose focus is on process and relationship more than program, and these facilitators working through extended involvement in communities. Both programs suggest that it is not the amount of training the facilitators receive which is important, as much as the character, approach and personal development of these people, and their ability as facilitators. Also key is the focus on community mobilisation around previously unrecognised assets, drawing in the resources of other actors after commencing with their own. Both programs alike illustrate that it is helpful to limit the resources easily available to facilitators from the international organisation, as too much outside resource could undermine this community asset focus. These examples show, however, that

ABCD can be implemented to avoid the trap of dependency, and can preserve, even capitalise on, a strongly self-reliant culture. Both programs also highlight that concurrent with a focus on self-reliance as a basis to address material concerns, an equal focus must be maintained on engaging with the state and other actors to seek changes to oppressive social structures.

As well as illustrating key principles, these two case studies also illustrate the degree of flexibility and diversity possible in implementation of ABCD programs. For example, Action Aid and GraceWorks Myanmar select and train facilitators quite differently. The key for both is the care taken to negate personal power and status issues that could see facilitators elevated to the role of experts by communities, rather than facilitators. Action Aid use youth, education and unemployment as strengths in selection of their fellows, and turn a lack of life experience and low status due to age into assets to help negate power and assist fellows be related to as facilitators. GraceWorks reverse this, turning the lower level of education and sometimes even functional illiteracy of adult facilitators into assets to negate the greater status and positive skills that greater age and life experience can provide. Their age and states are an advantage in communicating with community leaders and local authorities, but careful selection of facilitators and careful focus in training is required to ensure they facilitate, not lead. Either model appears to work well. What stands out is the different but significant contextualisation of both models, and the important catalytic rather than expert role the trained fellows/facilitators play in community development.

Returning to the Myanmar context in particular, a number of conclusions and observations can be made about the effectiveness of these programs in that context. Firstly, the emphasis given by these two programs on building trust and respect, both internally within the community and with officials and other stakeholders, is a significant contributor to their success. In a context in which significant tension between the state and the international community resulted in suspicion of international agencies, officials appear to have been a little less suspicious about community-led approaches. Seeking to work with, rather than shame officials was also important, as was the building of social capital within communities in a context with deep political and ethnic tensions. Secondly, in a context where authoritarian rule created an aversion to risk trying new things and people highly disempowered in decision-making, using the international agency and the facilitator to assist create a space for action, and facilitators talking about engaging with officials reduced fear and empowered decision-making.

The third factor in the effectiveness of these ABCD programs, and the one most emphasised by NGO managers interviewed for this research, was the power of *conscientização*, awareness-raising. This factor relates strongly to the above point. For a population long fearful of authority and scared to risk change, awareness-raising of the way the local political and civil service processes work, and the opportunities available under the current political context, demonstrated great effectiveness in empowering communities even prior to the recent political reform process in the country. Now, in the midst of the rapid and wide-ranging socio-political reforms in the country, such awareness-raising of ways to affect change has become even more effective. Action Aid in particular, an organisation which has adopted a rights-based approach to development globally, has demonstrated that this awareness-raising training about active citizenship, ways to approach officials, and forms of advocacy can be very effective in helping communities mobilise necessary resources and take control of their own developmental future. In many ways, ABCD practice is summed up in Friere's concept of *conscientização.*

References

ActionAid. (2010). The Fellowships Programme in Myanmar: Critical Stories of Change. Yangon: ActionAid.

Aung San Suu Kyi. (1995). *Freedom from Fear and Other Writings*. London: Penguin Books.

Chambers, Robert. (1983). *Rural Development: Putting the Last First*. London: Longman.

CPCS. (2008). Listening to Voices from Inside: Myanmar Civil Society's Response to Cyclone Nargis. Phnom Penh, Cambodia: Centre for Peace and Conflict Studies [CPCS].

Duffield, Mark. (2008). On the Edge of 'No Man's Land': Chronic Emergency in Myanmar. Bristol: Department of Politics, University of Bristol.

Ennis, Gretchen & West, Deborah (2010). Exploring the Potential of Social Network Analysis in Asset-Based CD in Research and Practice. *Australian Social Work, 63*(4), 404-417.

Eyben, Rosalind, Kabeer, Naila & Cornwall, Andrea. (2008). Conceptualising Empowerment and the Implications for Pro Poor Growth: A paper for the DAC Poverty Network. Brighton, UK: Institute of Development Studies, University of Sussex.

Fals-Borda, Orlando. (1987). The Application of Participatory Action-Research in Latin America. *International Sociology, 2*(4), 329-349.

Fals-Borda, Orlando. (1991). *Action and Knowledge: Breaking the Monopoly with Participatory Action Research*. New York: Apex.

Ferretti, Silva. (2010). Fellows and Civil Society. Yangon: ActionAid Myanmar.

Fink, Christina. (2000). Burma: Human Rights, Forgotten Wars, and Survival. *Cultural Survival, 24*(3).

Fink, Christina. (2001). *Living Silence: Burma under Military Rule*. London: ZED Books.

Freire, Paulo. (1972). *Pedagogy of the Oppressed*. Harmondsworth: Penguin.

Freire, Paulo. (1974). *Education for Critical Consciousness*. New York: Continuum.

Hossain, N. and M. Moore (2002). Arguing for the Poor: elites and poverty in developing countries. University of Sussex, UK, Institute of Development Studies.

Hipwell, William T. (2009). An Asset-Based Approach to Indigenous Development in Taiwan. *Asia Pacific Viewpoint, 50*(3), 289-306.

IHLCA. (2011). Integrated Household Living Conditions Survey in Myanmar (2009-2010) Poverty Profile. Yangon: Integrated Household Living Conditions Assessment [IHLCA] Project Technical Unit. Joint Project of Myanmar Ministry of National Planning and Economic Development [MNPED], United Nations

Development Programme [UNDP], United Nations Children's Fund [UNICEF], and Swedish International Development Agency [SIDA].

Kretzmann, John & McKnight, John P. (1993). *Building Communities from the Inside Out*. Chicago: ACTA Publications.

Kretzmann, John & McKnight, John P. (1997). Asset-Based Community Development. *National Civil Review, 85*(4), 158-172.

Löfving, Annami. (2011). The Force for Change: Achievements of the Fellowship Programme in Myanmar Yangon: ActionAid Myanmar.

Mathie, Alison & Cunningham, Gord. (2003). From Clients to Citizens: Asset-Based Community Development as a Strategy for Community-Driven Development. *Development in Practice, 13*(5), 474-486.

Selth, Andrew. (2008a). Burma and the Threat of Invasion: regime fantasy or strategic reality? Brisbane: Griffith Asia Institute, Griffith University.

Selth, Andrew. (2008b). Even Paranoids Have Enemies: Cyclone Nargis and Myanmar's fears of invasion. *Contemporary Southeast Asia, 30*(3), 379-402.

Skidmore, Monique. (2003). Darker than Midnight: Fear, Vulnerability, and Terror Making in Urban Burma (Myanmar). *American Ethnologist, 30*(1), 5-40.

Skidmore, Monique (Ed.). (2005). *Burma at the turn of the twenty-first century*. Honolulu, University of Hawaii Press.

Steinberg, David I. (2010). *Burma/Myanmar: What Everyone Needs to Know*. Oxford and New York: Oxford University Press.

Taylor, Robert H. (2009). *The State in Myanmar*. London: Hurst & Company.

TCG. (2008). Post-Nargis Recovery and Preparedness Plan: Tripartite Core Group [TCG]: Government of the Union of Myanmar, the United Nations and ASEAN.

U Myint. (2010). Myanmar Economy: a comparative view. Stockholm-Nacka: Institute for Security and Development Policy.

UNDP. (2011). Human Development Report 2011—Sustainability and Equity: A Better Future for All. New York: United Nations Development Programme [UNDP].

Ware, Anthony. (2012). *Context-Sensitive Development: How International NGOs Operate in Myanmar*. Sterling, VA: Kumarian Press.

Yeneabat, Mulu & Butterfield, Alice K. (2012). We Can't Eat a Road: Asset-Based Community Development and The Gedam Sefer Community Partnership in Ethiopia. *Journal of Community Practice, 20*(1-2), 134-153.

Chapter 10

Perspectives on multi-sector social partnerships for social change

JOSEPHINE PREVITE

ABSTRACT

The process for developing effective partnerships across sectoral boundaries is an important component of many social change programs. This chapter overviews the rationale and processes for establishing social partnerships and how they contribute to sustainable communities. The chapter provides a framework for partnership formation and guidelines on managing partnership relationships that consider the balance of power between collaborators and how power imbalances impact social change outcomes in Southeast Asia.

Introduction

In the 21st century the growth and prosperity of communities is increasingly influenced by interdependency and cross-sector collaborations between nonprofit organizations, corporations and governments. This accelerated shift to collaborative approaches is occurring as governments realize the limitations in their systems to deliver social services that can address the magnitude and complexity of social and environmental problems confronting communities today (Austin, 2000). Decision-makers across these sectors are therefore seeking new resources and more effective organizational approaches which involve new partnership styles between the three main societal sectors—public, voluntary and private business—that address social issues and causes. Thus partnerships are becoming a key collaborative approach for organizations to address challenges such as economic development, education, health care, poverty alleviation, community capacity building, and environmental sustainability.

The explicit, collaborative intent of cross-sector social partnerships offers decision-makers in regions such as Southeast Asia, who are confronted with complex and interwoven environmental issues and social concerns, with opportunities to open a dialogue about co-operating across sectors in search of sustainable solutions for the region. Thus, the following discussion in this chapter outlines the role and influence of multi-sector social partnerships and how they are capable of being deployed over the long term for the purpose of supporting sustainable community practices in Southeast Asia.

The role and purpose of collaborative partnerships

The social challenges and issues confronting Southeast Asia and other communities today cannot be addressed by one agency, government, or organization alone. In response to today's social complexities, decision-makers are increasingly turning to partnership approaches to provide creative, flexible and resourced solutions based on the involvement of multiple international, national and local actors offering various resources, skills, expertise and interests. Additionally, partnership actors also have the authority to direct change and empower local communities to be informed and involved in discrete social change projects, and other long-term agendas for change. Drawing from this purview then, a partnership is defined as:

> *a dynamic relationship among diverse actors, based on mutually agreed objectives, pursued through a shared understanding of the most rational division of labour based on the respective comparative advantages of each partner. Partnership encompasses mutual influence, with a careful balance between synergy and respective autonomy, which incorporates mutual respect, equal participation in decision making, mutual accountability and transparency (Brikerhoff 2002, 21).*

A partnership is therefore more than a simple relationship, as it is an institutionalized process that incorporates primary stakeholders in the inception of social change project, through to community implementation and development, and beyond to future policy making and directions for community change. Thus, the breadth of the partnership process indicates a continuum of possible interactions from minimal to maximal co-operation and collaboration between organizations and institutions. Himmelman (2001) describes these partnership interactions on a continuum involving:

- **Networking** to simply exchange information for mutual benefit. Organizations may communicate formally or informally to update each other on community program initiatives and future developments. There is little cooperation involved in this partnership approach; rather, the information shared assists internal organizational planning and ensures programs offered to the community do not compete or undermine planned activities by individual organizations aimed at enhancing social change and community well-being. Networking partnerships can enhance community sustainability as they ensure a balance between the supply and demand for community resources, and benefit the community by considering local needs during the design and implementation phases of organizational and institutional social change projects.
- **Co-ordinating** planning to meet shared goals, including co-ordinating projects and activities that have synergistic effects. Fundamental to this process is clearly defined objectives and outcomes that balance partners' needs and local needs with desired project outcomes. At this level partners establish trust based on linkages and personal relationships between people involved in projects.
- **Co-operating** involves organizations and institutions in pooling their resources to conduct projects and events based on common goals. Partnerships involving this level of interaction require transparency and sound ethical practices, which foster openness and good faith in terms of outcomes and shared accountability.
- **Collaborating** involves interactions between partners which provide mutual gain. Enhanced community sustainability evolves from positive collaborations between organizational and institutional partnership processes as they need to focus on internal and external project beneficiaries, which builds local capacities and stocks of social capital in the community.

Partnerships differ greatly in size, scope and purpose. However they all commonly share the following: they are voluntary and collaborative relationships in which the partners work together to achieve an agreed goal, sharing 'risks, responsibilities, resources, competencies and benefits' (Richter, 2004, p. 6). In explaining the scope and purpose of partnerships, Selsky and Parker (2005, 850) explain that collaborative activities involving partnership formation across different sectors can be 'transactional' – short-term, constrained and self-interest oriented - or 'integrative' and 'developmental' – longer term, open-ended, and largely common-interest oriented. Importantly, in differentiating cross-sector *social* oriented partnerships, from conventional arms-length commercial partnerships, Selsky and Parker define CSSPs as 'cross-sector projects formed explicitly to address social issues and causes that actively engage the partners on an ongoing basis'. Seitanidi, Koufopoulos and Palmer (2010) suggest that these socially oriented partnerships have the potential to transform organizations and societies.

Types of cross-sector social partnerships

Different types of partnership may be effective in different conditions and will involve various levels of interactions across partnership stages. The critical point is that through partnership formation, community outcomes should be enhanced due to the joint efforts of organizations across sectors. French (2010) however has pointed out that there is need to move away from passive forms of partnerships that merely seek to secure funding for government-focused initiatives, and towards more active and jointly developed initiatives focused on building community resources and changing community standards. Cross-sector social partnerships that can be implemented to meet this call are:

- Public private partnerships (PPPs) which require coordination between private (commercial) and public (non-commercial organization). PPPs are being promoted as an innovative policy by institutions such as the World Health Organization (WHO), the United Nations Population Fund (UNDP) and the World Bank (French, 2010; Richter, 2004). These institutions increasingly identify the commercial sector as a channel for connecting with different societies, or niche community interests. This is because commercial entities are viewed as having established and alternative relationships with community members and groups. For some decision-makers, however, the establishment of a formal partnership involving commercial interests and non-commercial societal interests create possible tensions and conflicts because of concerns about ethical practices and economic and power imbalances—particularly around potentially vulnerable markets such as children and youth and their consumption behaviours, which are linked to nutrition and alcohol (Hoek & Jones, 2011). The credibility of the commercial sectors contribution to societal problems and issues however is evident in the established Corporate Social Responsibility (CSR) business strategies which have made a valuable contribution to communities through collaborations involving governments, NGOs and commercial institutions over the last decade.
- Nonprofit-Government partnerships make a significant contribution to communities through funding community projects, social and health services, the provision of professional skills (e.g. doctors, nurses, etc.) and education programs offered through voluntary organization, foundations and charities. NGOs typically have developed structures and delivery channels and continue to be significant providers of local, national and international programs, which also drive strong ethical and

humanitarian efforts that sustain communities in both developed and developing countries.

- Nonprofit partnerships with community have been established via individual-focused volunteer programs, and have built strong reputations and NGO brand recognition in many communities. Many of these partnerships embrace a community-based approach focusing on empowerment principles and building local capacity via education and skills programs. The range of activities that has been successful in creating positive partnerships between nonprofit entities and community members includes: volunteer activities, peer programs and the creation of local committees and councils, which invite community members in as key decision-makers when designing community initiatives (French, 2010).

Partners are more than stakeholders

Stakeholders consist of 'any group or individual who can affect or is affected by the achievements of an organization's objectives' (Freeman, 1984, 46). Thus a stakeholder can have a passive or active relationship with community institutions and projects. Whereas, a partnership based on varying levels of shared interactions illustrates that a partner brings different resources, skills and expertise to a relationship, which also engages them in an active and maybe long-term community initiatives focused on sustainable outcomes. Eagle, Dahl, Hill, Bird *et al.* (2013) state that there are many advantages for organizations involved in partnerships: public partners will acquire access to skills, expertise and resources that might be lacking in the public sector. Concurrently, private partners can obtain credibility, access to market intelligence and a way of associating the organization with ethical business practices. Additionally, they also note that community partners could gain insight into the institutional decision-making process and play a unique role in designing and developing local interventions. Overall, however, the key benefit for all partners is synergy –the partnership can accomplish more than individual partners could on their own (Eagle *et al.*, 2013). French (2010, 309) however points out that whilst there is a pervasive rhetoric about 'creating conditions where partners can 'be equals', the reality is rarely that straightforward'. Thus a critical first step in forming social partnerships for positive social change is for decision-makers to engage in 'partnership formation planning' (Steitanidi *et al.*, 2010) which encompasses consideration of organizational characteristics, partners' motives, the history of interactions and assessment of environmental structures that either facilitate organizational and institutional partnerships, or create barriers. Critically, this conceptualization stage in the partnership plan should be completed prior to the enactment of a partnership and its community implementation.

Partnership formations

Developing social partnerships requires a pragmatic approach, which considers outcomes that deliver value for both organizations and society. Figure 10.1 *Partnership formation as an indicator of meso and macro transformative potential*, adapted from Seitanidi *et al.* (2010), outlines indicators that can be used to inform a decision to partner with an organization. The framework explicates (ibid, 152) the meso-level of organizational influence in society based on organizational characteristics, which indicates an organization's capacity to contribute social value to enhance community outcomes; organizational partnering motives indicates the level of transformative intentions; and the history of an organization's social interactions which demonstrates the organization's experience. Also important to the assessment of partnership formation are macro-level environmental influences which shape supportive environments that influence organizations decisions to enter partnerships that address social issues. Environmental structures have transformative potential as they provide structures and policy programs that can either support potential partnerships or put in place barriers to cross-sector social partnerships.

From the social marketing literature 'upstream' pressures involving policy and regulatory elements support and promote organization involvement in social change initiatives, or put in place barriers and conditions that reduce the desirability for partnerships across sectors (Hoek & Jones, 2011). This is pertinent for the private sector, and sometimes the voluntary sector, where official government and public sector agency guidance places restrictive and defensively framed partnership policies in place to minimize the risks associated with partnering. Whilst on the one hand it is important to have in place transparent partnership processes and guidelines that minimize risks, on the other hand, restrictive or onerous partnership policies can reduce organizational intentions to form partnerships. In particular, safeguards for public interests restrict PPPs as decision-makers are driven by conflict of interest considerations which create obstacles towards new innovative way of working with industry. As a result, communities are missing out as regulatory needs and concerns are privileged over the alternative which is to promote social change by harnessing the power, influence and skills of potential industry partnerships.

Figure 10.1 outlines a framework of indicators and factors for considering partnership formation, and provides a process to assess the extent to which a long-term partnership is possible. Such thinking is important during the formative stage, considering research suggests that many partnerships do not last beyond one year (Lasker & Weiss, 2003). Additionally, it is a suitable aide to detect early in partnership assessment if potential relationships with partners' have transformative potential and capacity to be involved in sustainable social change programs. Importantly, the framework can also be used to indicate the partnership potential to deliver both organizational and social change.

Figure 10.1 Partnership formation as an indicator of meso and macro transformative potential

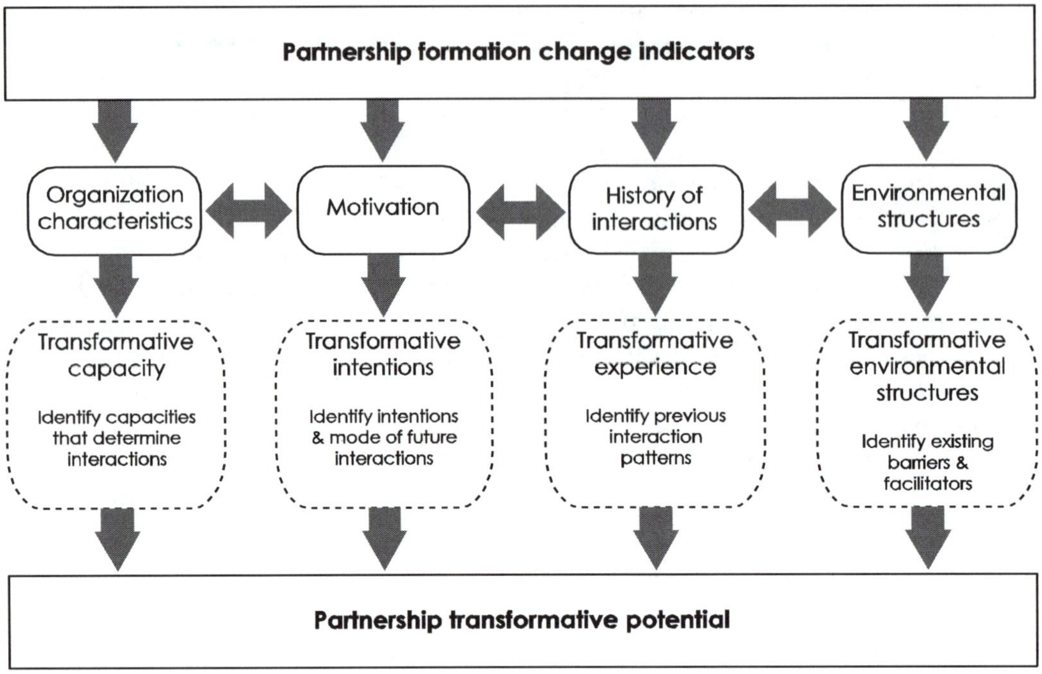

Managing partnerships

Managing social partnerships requires consideration as they involve cooperation and collaboration between diverse interests (e.g. in Southeast Asia partnerships will need to address the sometimes conflicting interests of agricultural providers and local employment interests, versus the future growth opportunities of mining, forestry and urbanization). Additionally, these conflicting interests can also result in misunderstandings and power imbalances when instituted across multiple sectors in society. The risks associated with power imbalances will be a significant challenge for Southeast Asian partnerships as they seek to find solutions to the acute environmental and social problems confronting the region.

When implementing and managing social partnerships there are a number of issues and factors that need to be reinforced to support the social change potential imbued in the partnership relationship. Waddock (1988, 22-23) outlines four key issues for consideration, including:

- Attending to the potential 'fragility' of the partnership. Individuals involved in partnership agreements have their own agendas and interests and whilst partnerships are entered into based on common interests, these can evaporate and change overtime. Also, institutional and environmental barriers can create lengthy timelines that need to be addressed and managed throughout the partnership; they may also reduce interest and capacity for individual decision-makers to maintain a partnership process.

- Social partnerships take time to develop. Trust is a fundamental element of strong partnerships and it takes time for this to build across partners and within the community.
- Cooperation and power balance influence the long-term future of partnerships. Cross-sector social partnerships involve interdependence to achieve social and community goals, therefore mechanisms are needed to facilitate cooperation and consensus building to ensure power is realistically shared.
- The fragility of a partnership is influenced by the collaborative efforts required to balance decision-making power. Therefore acknowledgment of power dynamics resulting from organizational characteristics, which particularly favours industry partnerships (Seitanidi *et al.*, 2010), is needed to ensure transparency via continuous communication and the maintenance of realistic expectations about the partnership.
- Expectations bound partnership communication and processes, therefore realistic expectations, based on the assessment of institutional resources and individual skills, need to be assessed and monitored. 'Understanding the limits of partnership is as important as understanding the potential' (Waddock, 1998, 23).

Conclusion

Partnerships between business, government, and civil society will play a major role in addressing key global and developmental challenges confronting the Southeast Asian region. The dynamic arrangements of interactions across these multi-sector social partnerships have potential to impact micro (individual), meso (organizational), and macro (societal) levels of social reality. The interdependence associated with cross-sector social partnerships can bring benefits to both institutions and organizations involved in a partnership, as well as the communities and issues that are being addressed by partnership efforts. Increasingly, partnerships are being used to implement social change interventions. Whilst there are numerous societal benefits for involving public and private institutions in partnerships that address social change and health issues, a partnership must be seen to be legitimate by the communities they serve, particularly in relation to the closer interaction between social issues and industry interests. The success of partnerships cannot be guaranteed. However, investing in formative planning and considerations about partnership management strategies are important phases that can lead to positive partnership outcomes.

Cross-sector social partnership approaches offer Southeast Asian communities pathways to redress the erosion of local priorities and systems of social ecology which have been undermined by economic progress in the region. Opening dialogues across sectors to establish and sustain partnerships thus require a comprehensive set of approaches focusing on creating comprehensive programs that include practices such as:

- Information sharing and awareness rising, with a particular focus on supporting local communities and people to be active participants in planning and decision-making. Involving local people and communities will encourage dialogue and knowledge sharing about the local culture and land, and ensure that cultural values and skills are embedded in the social change programs implemented in the region.
- Instituting transparent, legal and institutional governance frameworks which document sectorial interests and address the potential impact industry and economic interests may have on local culture and land in Southeast Asian communities. In particular, partnership formation communication should aim to harmonize across sector interests and develop policy frameworks that explicitly address legal boundaries and responsibilities between all actors in a partnership.
- Develop planning and decision-making mechanisms which create multi-sector partnerships that also encourage and support contributions from economists, engineers, urban planners, health and social workers, and social marketers so that the solutions designed to address the complex environmental and social concerns in Southeast Asia provide both social and economic benefits to local communities.

References

Austin, J. E. (2000). Strategic collaboration between nonprofits and business. *Nonprofit and Voluntary Sector Quarterly, 29*(1), 69-97.

Brinkerhoff, J. M. (2002). Government-nonprofit partnership: A defining framework. *Public Administration and Development, 22*(1), 19-30. doi:10.1002/pad.203.

Eagle, L., Dahl, S., Hill, S., Bird, S., Spotswood, F. & Tapp, A. (2013). *Social Marketing*. Harlow, England: Pearson.

French, J. (2010). Partnerships in social marketing. In French, J., Blair-Stevens, C., McVey, D. & Merrit, R. (Eds). *Social Marketing and Public Health: Theory and Practice* (pp. 302-317). New York: Oxford University Press.

Freeman, E. R. (1984), *Strategic management: A Stakeholder Approach*. Boston: Pitman.

Hoek, J. & Jones, S.C. (2011). Regulation, public health and social marketing: a behaviour change trinity. *Journal of Social Marketing, 1*(1), 32-44. Retrieved from http://dx.doi.org/10.1108/20426761111104419.

Lasker, R.D. & Weiss, E. S. (2003). Creating Partnership Synergy: The critical role of community stakeholders. *Journal of Health & Human Services Administration, 26*(1), 119-39.

Richter, J. (2004). *Public-Private Partnerships and Health for All.* Helsinki: Ministry for Foreign Affairs of Finland, Development Policy Information Unit. Retrieved from http://www.ibfan.org/art/538-5.pdf.

Seitandid, M.M., Koufopoulos, D.N. & Palmer, P. (2010). Partnership Formation for Change: Indicators for Transformative Potential in Cross Sector Social Partnerships. *Journal of Business Ethics, 94*, 139-161. Doi:10.1007/s10551-011-0784-2.

Selsky, J.W. & Parker, B. (2005). Cross-Sector Partnerships to Address Social Issues: Challenges to Theory and Practice. *Journal of Management*, 31(6), 849-873.

Waddock, S. A.: 1988, 'Building Successful Partnerships', Sloan Management Review Summer, 17–23.

Part III

Praxis (Case Studies)

Chapter 11

Sustainable change marketing

An approach to development and communications in Indonesia and beyond

Nicholas Goodwin

Abstract

The case study is Indonesia's *Fantastic Mom* health project. The issue is communications and sustainability. The approach uses the sustainable change marketing (SCHEMA) model. Findings include success in changing behaviors but failure to engage authorities, implying participation is vital. The originality is using SCHEMA, providing a management guide as value.

Why can't you sell soap... like you sell brotherhood?

Wiebe (1952)

Can communications and marketing approaches help us address the major sustainability issues facing Southeast Asia? To answer this question, we will examine aspects of social and behaviour change communications (SBCC), with a focus on social marketing. This chapter will draw on the latest evidence and ideas – including on participation and capacity – to introduce the sustainable change marketing (SCHEMA) framework. We will then apply the SCHEMA approach to Indonesia's *Fantastic Mom* program, developed to reduce infant mortality, and discuss the results and the implications for our work. Whether you are a government policy maker, NGO program manager, university researcher or commercial marketing manager, we all need to communicate to effect change.

Context

In 2003, Indonesia was at a crossroads. The nation had begun to emerge from the Asian Financial Crisis and the ensuing social and political turmoil. It faced persistent problems that demanded government and donor investment in order for the country to continue to lift many of its 240 million people out of poverty. This included reducing infant mortality rates. At that time Indonesia ranked 76 in the world, with 41 children for every 1,000 born dying before their fifth birthday (UNICEF, 2002).

During the era of Indonesia's President Soeharto, public funding for health in Indonesia was low and the health services were tightly controlled by the central government. Following the downfall of President Soeharto in 1998 there was sweeping political, economic and administrative reforms. Fiscal decentralization saw delivery of services become the responsibility of district governments. In addition, public funding for health services more than doubled between 2001 and 2006. It was widely hoped that health would improve as district governments now had both more funds and the responsibility for services (Heywood & Harahap, 2009). A group of public health policymakers and practitioners in Jakarta, including USAID, had been analysing the most efficient and cost-effective approaches to development. One of the major issues was political and social sustainability, especially how to ensure community ownership of development programs and the continuation of their impact beyond the life of the intervention.

This approach to sustainability originated in the context of the debate around renewable resources (Lele, 1991). Sustainable development emerged on the global stage in 1980, when the International Union for the Conservation of Nature and Natural Resources (IUCN, 1980) presented its World Conservation Strategy (WCS) with 'the overall aim of achieving sustainable development through the conservation of living resources'. International agencies, such as the World Bank, soon adopted the new thinking, which has evolved to bring us new approaches to progress and prosperity (Jacobs, Munro & Matte-Baker, 1987). One component of sustainable development was the recognition that resources are limited, including public funding. While policy and sectoral support may continue for decades, individual interventions usually have a fixed funding period and budget which cannot be continued forever. Significantly, most projects have an ultimate goal to produce positive and significant change that can be sustained after the external assistance is completed (Khang & Moe, 2008).

An influencing factor on a program's sustainability is the role of a donor country's foreign policy objectives as part of its official international development assistance. Recipient countries and communities, long dictated to through top-down delivery of foreign aid, have resisted a perceived lack of control and demanded a greater role in projects affecting their countries. Focusing on individuals, many disadvantaged and marginalized people at the local level became suspicious of the motivations of international donors and national elites, and have increasingly called for their needs and opinions to be incorporated into the development process. Indonesia, in particular,r had experienced a tumultuous national crisis around the role of the IMF and World Bank, with many calling for Indonesia to refuse the harsh conditions imposed as part of emergency lending facilities (Hutchison, 2003).

With these issues on their minds, USAID and its partners decided to design a project that included technical assistance for a national campaign, grants for community partners and capacity building to support local organizations. And so the Fantastic Mom project was created.[20] It was designed to reduce infant mortality by changing hand washing with soap behaviours among mothers and caregivers in poor communities in priority provinces. But USAID and partners faced significant challenges - people saw hand washing as an 'old' behaviour that had already been taught, mothers were tired of negative health campaigns, communities faced numerous problems and funds were limited - all of which threatened the sustainability of the work.

Social marketing, participation and capacity

Sustainable development has evolved to become the basis for new approaches to poverty and social change. These methods grew from their environmental and development origins and incorporated the latest thinking and practice from political science, psychology, economics, anthropology, sociology and many more fields. In the context of sustainable development, communications and marketing cover a broad collection of models and theories that revolve around the role of information - its production, dissemination and use. It includes media law, technological innovation, social and behaviour change, market segmentation, humanitarian responses, fundraising, product development, organizational communications and many other areas and issues. This chapter will focus on one approach to social and behaviour change communications - social marketing.

[20] The author managed the Fantastic Mom project on behalf of Ogilvy, the communications and marketing firm engaged to provide design and implementation services.

Social marketing and sustainability

Social marketing was conceived as the application of commercial marketing principles to social and behaviour change. Kotler and Zaltman (1971) advised, 'Careful thought be given to the manner in which manageable, desirable, gratifying and convenient solutions to a perceived need or problem are presented to its potential buyers.' It includes methods taken from psychology, communications, economics and sociology. Social marketing focuses on the real-life circumstances of individuals and their communities, and works to overcome the barriers to, and promote the benefits of, the desired change. Leading models include the six points for effective social marketing by Andreasen (2002) and the UK's National Social Marketing Centre's eight benchmark criteria, led by French and Blair-Stevens (2006). The effectiveness of these approaches has been tested on a variety of public issues, from alcohol and smoking to HIV/AIDS and recycling (Bleeker *et al.*, 2009; Evans & Hastings, 2008; Evans, Uhrig, Davis & McCormack, 2009; Flynn *et al.*, 1994).

Community centred social marketing approaches incorporate ideas of partnerships and participation. Of these, the most recognized are by Bryant, Forthofer, Brown, and McDermott (1999) with their 'community based prevention marketing', which borrows from community organizing and capacity building approaches. Another is McKenzie-Mohr (2000) and his 'community based social marketing' which 'merges knowledge from psychology with expertise from social marketing' and provides recommendations for program design and evaluation at the community level. For development and other public programs, these approaches take us from implementing social marketing programs *in* a community to *with* a community.

The most successful projects are those that combine social marketing with community participation and transform these into social movements for change. Examples include Thailand's *100% Condoms* program (Ainsworth, Beyrer & Soucat, 2003), Australia's *Hello Sunday Morning* movement on safe alcohol use and the *Heart Truth* campaign of the USA's National Heart, Lung and Blood Institute. To sustain these types of movements for change, we must ensure the participation of individuals and their communities as well as build their capacity to ensure impact beyond the life of the project.

Empower participation and avoid manipulation

Proponents of participatory approaches to public policy consider participation to be vital to the social sustainability of a program or policy. There are many ways to distinguish participatory development from the approaches it sought to supersede, however there is no universal agreement on its definition. One method examines the type of participation and positions development initiatives on a continuum, such as Arnstein's *Ladder of Citizen Participation*, with manipulation at one end and empowerment at the other (Campbell & Vainio-Mattila, 2003). Manipulating participation is carried out to secure the actor's involvement for the achievement of externally identified project goals. Empowerment of the actors means that they define such goals themselves, as well as make decisions on the strategies and actions required to achieve them. This means a shift from a passive voice to an active one for the targeted individuals and their communities. The difference between the old and new ways is that manipulation considers participation as a means to an end for project success, while empowerment views participation as an end that, when achieved, will result in long-term engagement by those involved in implementing solutions.

Capacity as culture

We can think of capacity building as a process of strengthening the abilities of individuals, organizations and systems to sustainably and effectively respond to their needs. Successful approaches to sustainable development are centred in helping ensure that governments, donors and other change leaders invest in building capacities that both have direct and immediate applications to address the problem at hand. These investments must also contribute to capabilities that have broader and long-term importance. The most successful are those that approach capacity strengthening as culture building.

Capacity building is often described as an external (often foreign) organization or group providing tools and training to individuals and groups with a lack of resources. However, capacity is not something that is provided or produced and then passed on. Rather, it is best and most effective when it is *homegrown*, that is, when it builds on and strengthens something that already exists in some form. Capacity building efforts grow from and seek to strengthen existing resources, skills and knowledge. In effect, then, through capacity building we nurture and grow *seeds* that already are planted among the individuals, organizations and systems we seek to support. The approach to capacity as culture building reflects a commitment to continuous improvement both in people and the work undertaken. The following section incorporates these sustainability issues of participation, social marketing and capacity building and packages them into a model for use in development programs and public service.

The sustainable change marketing (SCHEMA) model

Sustainable change marketing (SCHEMA) is a new concept that seeks to capture the latest in theory and practice, including social marketing and other social and behaviour change communications programs in Southeast Asia and beyond. The ten key elements of the SCHEMA model are as follows:

1. **Individual orientation**: put the individual's needs and behaviours at the centre of the intervention, rather than using top down approaches.
2. **Participation**: interventions must shift from a passive voice to an active one for affected individuals and their communities which means that actors make decisions on the goals, strategies and actions.
3. **Insight** based on formative and behavioural research, using proven theoretical approaches.

4. **Behavioural goals**: these should be clear and quantified - not broad policy or political statements - using the insights derived from research and tracked and adjusted through the life of the project.
5. An understanding of the consumer's **barriers and benefits** to the change, leading to creation of intrinsic and extrinsic value - often through the creation of brands - for which the intended recipient is willing to **exchange** their resources (money, time, etc.).
6. **Capacity**: an evidence-driven process of culture building that strengthens the abilities of individuals, organizations, and systems.
7. **Competition** from opposed interests and behaviours, as well as from other public issues, must be taken into account.
8. A **mix of methods** for communications activities, e.g. media and traditional forms of communication, as well as adjustments to price, place and promotion.
9. **Partnerships** with government, and with community and private sector organizations - they all have their role to play and resources to bring.
10. **Monitoring and evaluation**: knowing how your project is going and reporting back to your community of beneficiaries, funders and partners will improve its impact and reduce the chance of things going wrong.

The next section will examine these sustainability issues in reference to a social marketing project implemented in Indonesia. It will show how the SCHEMA model can be used to analyse completed work as well as plan future programs.

Indonesia's Fantastic Mom project

The Fantastic Mom project was designed in 2004 and aimed to reduce the incidence of diarrhoea in children under the age of five. USAID provided funds to the US-based Johns Hopkins Centre for Communication Programs (CCP) and the Jakarta-based Coalition for a Healthy Indonesia (KuIS) - an alliance of NGOs, community groups and the private sector - to design and execute the project. USAID also funded several international NGOs, such as Save the Children, to integrate the project into their existing development programs. CCP and KuIS also worked with local partners, including NGOs, universities and religious groups, especially those in the project's priority provinces. Other international agencies, such as the World Bank and UNICEF, collaborated and shared results.

Project design

At the individual level, CCP research found that diarrhoea affected three in every 10 people in Indonesia. And it was the number two killer of Indonesian children under five, causing 13.2 percent of total deaths (Rimbatmaja *et al.*, 2007). The research found low awareness among mothers and caregivers of the benefits of washing hands with soap to prevent diarrhoea. Whilst soap was relatively affordable and available, hand washing was considered an old or learned behaviour, something that people had already heard about at school or in the community. However, the connection in people's minds to diarrhoea was not well understood. Getting people to use soap and clean, running water was a challenge.

At the community level, mobilizing action by stakeholders proved difficult. The Indonesian government, whilst committed to this project, was challenged by restricted funds and limited capacity to coordinate several departments at national and local levels, plus coordinate international agencies and local organizations. Other health and social issues, such as natural and human-made disasters, a growing HIV/AIDS epidemic, poor education, corruption and deforestation, also challenged Indonesia. The NGO community was mobilized but lacked capacity and access to the funds to make the impact they desired. The private sector was engaged where they saw business opportunities, especially well known companies and their brands such as Unilever's Lifebuoy soap.

The traditional development approach might have been to distribute information through health workers and government agencies. The existing market would take care of the provision of soap and associated products for those who had access. However, a different approach was required to overcome the significant inertia acting as a barrier to adoption of the new behaviours. The project required the creation of sustained collective action through a hand washing movement that galvanized the parents as well as the key influencers and partners. This included creating the central and aspirational brand of the Fantastic Mom, who was an inspiration for all mothers. Loved by her healthy children, supported by her capable husband and admired by her neighbours - who wouldn't want to be a Fantastic Mom?

Strengthening and supporting this brand platform was a community mobilization program and a media campaign to provide the surround sound effect for the program. Messages on hand washing with soap were delivered through a jingle, music and dance competitions, radio spots and other media. Mothers and other members of the community were able to experiment with soap and the new behaviours at carnival-style roadshows. These featured local and national celebrities and hand washing competitions. Many of these activities were made possible with the participation of members and volunteers from local community and religious groups, engaged as partners in the movement by KuIS.

The international agencies and local organizations were funded to incorporate the messages and materials in their existing programs. CCP convened a working group of international agencies to coordinate this work, often attended by USAID. Limited effort was made to engage the national and local governments. KuIS mobilized its network of NGO and private sector members, including through roundtable discussions and funding partnerships. These local organizations were given the opportunity to attend learning sessions on the campaign, which were generic classes on how to use the materials and tools developed by the project. While effective on this level, the learning sessions were not tailored to the specific needs of the individuals and organizations, nor did these activities take into account other needs of these organizations - and nor the dynamics of building system-wide capacity.

Results

The roadshows and media activities helped the messages reach more than 10 million people in the two priority provinces. The evaluation at the end of the first year recorded an increase of those who reported practicing hand washing with soap from 35 percent to 56 percent. There was also an increase in audience awareness of the benefits of hand washing with soap from 45 percent to 85 percent (Rimbatmaja *et al.*, 2007). Two large companies, Unilever and Wings, launched soap product campaigns utilizing the project's messages in areas not already reached, working with KuIS and partners.

There were several issues identified that affected the effectiveness of the project. One of the key challenges impeding the project included the availability of clean, running water. This shows that while social marketing programs cannot themselves overcome structural issues, such as a lack of adequate infrastructure, they play a vital role in highlighting these issues for governments, donors and partners to address. Thus, sustainability often relies on an interdisciplinary approach. The attempt to solve one development problem must be linked to others. In the best-case scenarios, the larger communities of practice are drawn upon to solve an entire issue - in this case, reducing infant mortality.

Whilst the Fantastic Mom project was limited by the availability of clean water, additional water and sanitation programs undertaken by the World Bank and UNICEF, working with key government agencies, complemented it. Creating demand for services can inform those on the supply side. Another major challenge was the availability of funds from the donor, USAID, and the Indonesian government. These were not available beyond the second year, making it impossible to achieve sustained social and behaviour change, and to expand the coverage of the project.

Government support in this regard was proven to be weak, partly reflecting limited human and financial capacity. The preference of the international development partners to work with NGOs might be the reason that national and local government involvement, and therefore support, was limited. A lack of government support can create an unvirtuous cycle that leads back to a lack of donor support. Programs need to account for and where appropriate be responsive to government strategies and development priorities. It is true that there will be cases where either international negotiations are required to secure government agreement as part of international negotiations on foreign policy and development agendas (the Millennium Development Goals for example) or that there will be resources supplied and assistance given that is without government endorsement - in environments where there are restrictive or authoritarian governments, receptivity to much needed assistance may be deprioritized, or publicly rejected.

The SCHEMA model view of the Fantastic Mom project

Viewed through the lens of the SCHEMA model, the Fantastic Mom project fulfilled most of its criteria for a successful initiative. The focus on the barriers to, and benefits of, hand washing with soap for mothers and caregivers gave it a strong marketing core. The mix of communications activities, including media and community mobilization, ensured the messages reached their intended targets. This core was sustained by capacity building efforts and supported by its partnerships with international NGOs and community partners. One shortcoming was the limited involvement of local and national government agencies, which in turn saw USAID support also weaken. This resulted in the project's funding being reduced and then discontinued after only two years. The following table provides a summary comparison of the elements of the Fantastic Mom program against the SCHEMA model.

Table 11.1 Elements of the Fantastic Mom program vs the SCHEMA model

SCHEMA	Fantastic Mom program
1. Individual orientation	Mothers and caregivers of children under five years.
2. Participation	National coalition of NGO and private sector jointly managed the project. Community organizations helped design local activities.
3. Insight	Formative and behavioural research covered behaviours and stakeholders.
4. Behavioural goals	Increasing hand washing with soap behaviours
5. Barriers & benefits (exchange)	The brand offered the emotional and aspirational value of being a Fantastic Mom in addition to functional health and economic utility.
6. Capacity	General learning sessions for national and local NGOs and community based organizations. Tools developed for use in local activities.
7. Competition	Perception that hand washing was already learned. Emotional appeal cut through other issues.
8. Mix of methods	Advertising, PR, community mobilization, workshops, product, word of mouth.
9. Partnerships	Government, international agencies, NGOs, faith-based organizations, media.
10. Monitoring & evaluation	Baseline, mid-term and post project M&E.

Implications for the field

Projects like Indonesia's Fantastic Mom highlight the importance of addressing real limits on social, environmental and economic resources. Adapting to these limitations – a dramatically difficult challenge given entrenched behaviours and systems along with a growing population – is a priority for the international public policy community. Fortunately, this evolution in theory and practice of sustainability has produced more effective and efficient methods and tools for us to use in our work.

Participation is one of the most advanced and vital elements to emerge from the evolution of sustainable development. Similarly, social and behaviour change communications, including social marketing approaches, reflect a move away from top-down approaches to in order to determine the needs of individuals and their communities. Social marketing is an effective way to make use of scarce resources because it seeks to create value in the form of products, services and behaviours. Combining social marketing and sustainable development into a single model for practitioners to test, refine and integrate into their work, represents an opportunity to address persistent blocks to human prosperity. Capacity building ensures that the capability and resources are available beyond the life of one intervention.

We know from experience and the evidence that social and behaviour change requires time and resources to work, especially for individuals to learn and adopt new beliefs and practices. Attention to strong partnerships is vital to the success of any program. Change leaders, including from government, NGOs, international agencies, universities and the private sector must work together to ensure that programs have adequate resources. With increasing access to a greater variety of communications technology, the nature of participation has significantly changed. New forms of influence need to be researched, tracked and incorporated into program design and execution.

The SCHEMA model has its limits, for example it focuses on the creation of demand and not supply, including the provision of adequate infrastructure for the delivery of products and services. It also does not directly address underlying issues such as economic disadvantage, gender discrimination and threats to security. Further work is needed to understand these issues better and may result in the modification of the SCHEMA model. However it is likely that the supply side of development will be better informed when there is strong demand from individuals, organizations and systems.

Conclusion

Where to from here? Some of you are working in – or considering – social marketing or other development and communications programs, or perhaps just researching or thinking about these issues. One possible first step would be to examine your project, concept or issue through the lens of the SCHEMA model, in the same way that this chapter does with Indonesia's Fantastic Mom project. Look at each element and ask whether it has been addressed. Keep in mind the three key pillars – a core of effective marketing and communications; empowering participation; and building capacity. From there, several options for further work, research or thought will follow. We wish you every success with your endeavours and look forward to hearing of your progress.

References

Ainsworth, M., Beyrer, C. & Soucat, A. (2003). AIDS and public policy: the lessons and challenges of 'success' in Thailand. *Health Policy, 64*(1), 13-37.

Andreasen, A. R. (2002). Marketing Social Marketing in the Social Change Marketplace. [Book Review]. *Journal of Public Policy & Marketing, 21*(1), 3-13.

Bleeker, A., Silins, E., Dillon, P., Simpson, M., Copeland, J. & Hickey, K. (2009). The feasibility of peer-led interventions to deliver health information to ecstacy and related drug (ERDS) users. In N. D. a. A. R. Centre (Ed.), *Technical Report*: UNSW.

Bryant, C., Forthofer, M., Brown, K. M. & McDermott, R. (1999). Community-based prevention marketing. *Social Marketing Quarterly, 5*(3), 54-59. doi: 10.1080/15245004.1999.9961061.

Campbell, L. M. & Vainio-Mattila, A. (2003). Participatory development and community-based conservation: Opportunities missed for lessons learned? *Human Ecology, 31*(3), 417-437.

Evans, W. D. & Hastings, G. (2008). *Public health branding: Applying marketing for social change*: Oxford University Press, USA.

Evans, W. D., Uhrig, J., Davis, K. & McCormack, L. (2009). Efficacy methods to evaluate health communication and marketing campaigns. *Journal of health communication, 14*(4), 315-330.

Flynn, B. S., Worden, J. K., Secker-Walker, R. H., Pirie, P. L., Badger, G. J., Carpenter, J. H. & Geller, B. M. (1994). Mass media and school interventions for cigarette smoking prevention: effects 2 years after completion. *American Journal of Public Health, 84*(7), 1148-1150.

French, J. & Blair-Stevens, C. (2006). Social marketing: National Benchmark Criteria. *National Social Marketing Centre.*

Heywood, P. & Harahap, N. P. (2009). Public funding of health at the district level in Indonesia after decentralization–sources, flows and contradictions. *Health Research Policy and Systems, 7*(1), 5.

Hutchison, M. (2003). A cure worse than the disease? Currency crises and the output costs of IMF-supported stabilization programs *Managing Currency Crises in Emerging Markets* (pp. 321-360): University of Chicago Press.

IUCN. (1980). World Conservation Strategy: Living Resource Conservation for Sustainable Development: Gland, Switzerland: International Union for Conservation of Nature and Natural Resources, United Nations Environment Program and World Wildlife Fund.

Jacobs, P., Munro, D. A. & Matte-Baker, A. (1987). *Conservation with equity: strategies for sustainable development*: St. Martin's Press.

Khang, D. B. & Moe, T. L. (2008). Success criteria and factors for international development projects: A life-cycle-based framework. *Project Management Journal, 39*(1), 72-84.

Kotler, P. & Zaltman, G. (1971). Social marketing: an approach to planned social change. *The Journal of Marketing*, 3-12.

Lele, S. M. (1991). Sustainable development: a critical review. *World development, 19*(6), 607-621.

McKenzie-Mohr, D. (2000). New Ways to Promote Proenvironmental Behavior: Promoting Sustainable Behavior: An Introduction to Community-Based Social Marketing. *Journal of Social Issues, 56*(3), 543-554. doi: 10.1111/0022-4537.00183

Rimbatmaja, R., Pooroe-Utomo, N., Semiarto, A., Adri, A., Lestari, A., Amini, F. & Figueroa, M. E. (2007). Health and Hygiene Behaviors in Indonesia: results of the formative research. Jakarta, Indonesia: Environmental Services Project (ESP).

UNICEF. (2002). The state of the world's children 2003. New York.

Wiebe, G. D. (1952). Merchandising Commodities and Citizenship on Television. *The Public Opinion Quarterly, 15*(4), 679-691.

Chapter 12

Sustainable lifestyles in Vietnamese cities

GIANG WELLS-DANG AND ANDREW WELLS-DANG

ABSTRACT

Rapid urbanization in Vietnam poses multiple risks to environmentally sustainable development. The innovative Green Living program of Action for the City, a Hanoi-based NGO, seeks to change environmental behaviors at the neighborhood and ward levels. Their experiences demonstrate the possibility of citizen action to find cooperative solutions to urban problems.

Introduction

Only a generation ago, most Southeast Asians lived in rural societies based on sustainable, organic agriculture and traditional socio-political structures, with relatively low levels of income. This context has changed dramatically, to the point that the majority (in Southeast Asia and the world) now live, for the first time in history, in cities (UNFPA, 2007). Rapid urbanization poses massive challenges for sustainability: in dealing with pollution, waste and traffic congestion, but also in public services and lifestyle change.

Vietnam is a telling exemplar of the urban trends in the region. Due to the effects of war and collectivized economic policies, Vietnam's urban transformation began later than in other large Southeast Asian countries, but the country now has the highest urbanization rate in Southeast Asia. From a population that was over 75 percent rural a decade ago, Vietnam is now 34 percent urban and expected to reach nearly 50 percent by the year 2020 (Indrakesuma & Loh, 2012). Fueled by migration to industrial zones and other urban jobs, the population of major cities has skyrocketed: Ho Chi Minh City (Saigon) from 3.9 million in 1989 to 7.1 million in 2009, Hanoi from 2.4 to 6.4 million over the same period, including a doubling in size in the last decade alone (GSO 2011, p. 66). Particularly since the 10th Party Congress in 2006, the Communist government has prioritized policies of 'industrialization and modernization' (*cong nghiep hoa, hien dai hoa*), effectively providing official backing for an urban-centered boom.

Both cities and their residents have been unprepared to adapt to rapid economic and population growth. The infrastructure of Hanoi, including transportation, water treatment, and housing as well as social services such as education and health care, was originally designed by the French colonial administration to sustain a population of about 500,000 (AFP, 2007). The city expanded somewhat on this base after independence, but until the mid- and late 1990s, the urban core of four districts remained within tight boundaries. Life in the surrounding villages beyond the city limits remained predominantly agricultural. These areas have now become sprawling industrial zones and construction sites, albeit with roads, utilities and public services still designed for the rural conditions of the recent past. Environmental consequences have also been immense: Vietnam now ranks 79 of 132 studied countries around the world in Environmental Performance Index (EPI), and ranks in the bottom ten countries on air pollution effects on human health, below any other country in Southeast Asia, though ahead of China, India and Bangladesh (Yale Center, 2012).

Migrants arriving in such burgeoning cities are also often not prepared for changes in their lifestyles. City life requires compliance with impersonal regulations, not just negotiations among neighbors. The effects of bringing essentially rural behaviors into the city can be seen in disregard for traffic rules, haphazard construction of apartment buildings and other housing, and uncoordinated waste management, all of which affect urban quality of life. Dumping trash in an unused lot in a village with several thousand residents often causes no serious problem, but the same action in a city of millions multiplies its effects to become a public nuisance that no one takes responsibility for cleaning up. In a documentary film entitled 'Who Does Hanoi Belong To?', for instance, most migrants interviewed see themselves as temporary residents or second-class citizens; although they live in the city, it is not really theirs (Action for the City, 2007). Most migrants' residence permits (*ho khau*) remain in their rural communities of origin, limiting their access to many city services, although city governments have taken some steps to relax these restrictions in recent years.

In the process of urban expansion, hundreds of thousands of farmers have lost their land and become city-dwellers, in what researchers elsewhere describe as 'de-peasantization' (McMichael, 2012). This also has consequences for the cities' food supply, which used to be sourced from the nearby villages but now must be shipped from further away. No longer able to be self-sufficient and grow their own food, they must compete in wage markets with other recent arrivals, leading to a loss of resilience and a sense of insecurity: families may have higher incomes in the non-agricultural sector, but they have nothing to turn back to should their money run out (Oxfam & ActionAid, 2012). With a limited public safety net, those who fall on hard times typically rely on extended family or people from the same village or region for mutual help and short-term loans. Yet this unregulated informal credit system is also fertile ground for exploitation and even criminal behavior.

The Vietnamese government has adopted a mixture of policies towards urban growth that have not always been applied consistently. On one hand, policies have promoted economic development and job creation. Most foreign and domestic investment has centered in or around main cities due to the availability of infrastructure, transport links and the large labor pool. On the other hand, authorities have historically tried to restrain migration through the *ho khau* registration system and have not encouraged private charity or citizen initiatives to strengthen or replace government social programs. Among the hundreds of Vietnamese NGOs that have formed in the past decades, few focus on urban issues. The methods and approaches that have proven successful in reducing rural poverty, through both government and NGO programs, may not apply easily to new forms of urban vulnerability that are characterized less by monetary poverty than by relative deprivation in quality of life and access to services (World Bank, 2012; UNDP, 2010). The complexity and dynamic nature of urban social issues cannot be addressed through charity or government alone: these challenges require cooperation among multiple stakeholders, most importantly including the participation of urban residents themselves in actions that affect their lives.

Concepts of sustainable urban living

Urban sustainability is both an environmental and a social idea, consisting of people's relation to their physical and natural surroundings (Evans, 2002). It may be conceived as the sum of three elements: governance, environmental balance, and lifestyles. *Governance* in this context means how people make decisions about public issues. Voices of all groups in society must be heard in the governance process, especially the most marginalized, so that outcomes can be negotiated to serve everyone's interests, not only the powerful and influential. For instance, where should roads, sanitation facilities, parks and public buildings be sited? How are such decisions made? If a new park is located near poor people's housing, this can have a direct positive benefit on the neighborhood's quality of life. On the contrary, a garbage dump in the same location might bring harmful health and environmental consequences.

Such small-scale decisions take on greater importance in the context of an entire city plan: designing a transportation system, making zoning decisions, locating industrial estates and other far-reaching changes to the urban structure. Responsibility for such planning may rest with a higher administrative level, but in a sustainable city, community members may nevertheless provide input into decision-making and hold city authorities accountable. Planning decisions should be determined by a set of fair rules agreed by all stakeholders, including neighborhood representatives. Such public participation provides the best grounds for freedom and happiness of all citizens (Sen, 1999).

In environmental terms, cities are engines of consumption with large resource use concentrated in a small area. The water, electricity, and waste generated by a city affect the soil, rivers, and air not only inside the city limits but in surrounding areas. A city that produces a portion of its own resources, grows food, recycles water and garbage, and saves on energy use brings benefits not only to its environment, but also the economy through the creation of 'green jobs' and fairer opportunities for the poor. The exchange of services within the city and nearby rural areas where this is feasible and efficient leads to increased social equity, as urban residents trade in relationship with each other and rely on services and goods each other produce. It is possible that a sustainable city will grow at a slower rate than one based solely on export production and resource extraction, but the benefits of growth will be better distributed among all citizens who are involved.

The third element of urban sustainability is individual or household lifestyles, which is the main focus of this chapter. Choices of lifestyles are conditioned by social norms, government policies, and economic opportunities. Yet even given structural pressures and limitations, people in any city maintain the ability to select a lifestyle that either supports or hinders sustainability. By starting with individual lifestyles, a sustainable model of urban living builds input for more participation in governance, without necessarily challenging or replacing existing political systems.

'Green and healthy living' in Hanoi

Based on the core values of urban sustainability, one Hanoi-based NGO, Action for the City (*Trung tam Hanh dong vi su Phat trien Do thi*) has developed a household- and community-driven program of behavior change). Action for the City's innovative model of bottom-up environmental action starts with formation of neighborhood-level 'Green and Healthy Living Teams' (*Nhom Song xanh Song khoe*, hereafter 'Green Living Teams'). The eight to ten members of each team cooperate to reduce electricity, gas and water consumption, recycle waste, and improve health in each household. Teams then come together to form ward-level Green Living Clubs that design community projects to improve quality of life, such as a youth-led green transport campaign and efforts to transform abandoned land into community gardens. The results of community projects are then documented and presented as advocacy messages to local government, the private sector and other organizations in order to promote replication and build support for improved urban environments.

Action for the City was founded in 2006 by one of the co-authors of this chapter (Giang) together with colleagues and associates in Hanoi. Like many Vietnamese NGOs, the organization is registered with the Vietnam Union of Science and Technology Associations (VUSTA). Its initial projects focused on promotion of green transportation, organic vegetables, and other quality of life related topics. In January 2009, Action for the City began a three-year Neighborhood Empowerment project in four low-income Hanoi wards, aiming to improve the living environment of urban communities and urban governance through promoting bottom-up residents' actions. Since then, 80 Green Living Teams have formed with nearly 1,000 members in Hanoi, plus an additional 300 participants in Hue, Danang and Ho Chi Minh City. The vast majority of members (90 percent) are women; most members join through word of mouth, since team members often talk about their involvement to their families and neighbors. If other residents are interested in joining, they contact the community coach and sign up to take part in a new team in their ward. Participation is a choice that emerges from the starting point of individuals' own concerns for their families, communities and countries.

Action for the City has benefited from international experience on individual and community behavior change on energy use, environmental protection and sustainable living, adapted from the Global Action Plan (GAP) international network. Partners from GAP Ireland supported training and adaptation of the GAP model in Hanoi during the first two years of the Neighborhood Empowerment project, after which Action for the City continued on its own. Costs for the program are low: about $100 per team for start-up in the first year and $50 per team thereafter (Action for the City & Irish Aid, 2012). This is a modest budget that can be raised locally and does not depend on external donor resources. Each team has a coach (shared among several teams in one ward) who is trained by Action for the City as a resource person. These coaches, who are paid a nominal stipend to cover expenses, can become part of the resources for replication. Most coaches actually contribute much more time than is required, and some even put their stipends back into team activities as seed funding. Most meetings are held at people's houses, so there is no cost for a venue. Materials are contributed by participants themselves.

Green living: Results and impacts

The immediate impacts of green living teams come in energy savings and garbage reduction. The participating households from 2009-11 saved an average of nine kilowatts of electricity per month, two cubic meters of water, 38.5 kg of garbage, and 90 plastic bags. These may not sound like large changes, but over three years, green living team members saved a cumulative 333,720 kw of electricity, 74,160 m^3 of water, 1,427,580 kg of garbage and 3,337,200 plastic bags. In terms of CO_2 equivalent, this resulted in savings of over 8,000 tons of carbon emissions (Action for the City & Irish Aid, 2012). An example of these savings is presented in the following table:

Table 12.1 Monthly energy saving results for 19 new Green Living Teams, 2011 (185 households)

	Ward A	Ward B	Ward C	Ward D
Number of Green Living Teams (8-10 hh/team)	6	4	5	4
Electricity savings (Kw) per household	13.5	24	20.83	30.65
Water savings (m3) per household	1.8	3.1	1.9	2.73
Waste reduction (kg) per household	38	49.3	27.6	49.3
Plastic bags reduced per household	27	42.7	50.4	71

When more people joined the program, the residents decided to form larger green living clubs. At this meso-level of change, citizens come together for collective actions to improve the environment in their communities. Unlike the top-down propaganda organizing model, these clubs are self-organized, funded partly by Action for the City and partly through contributions from members. To date, clubs have completed 20 small projects to preserve and upgrade public spaces in their neighborhoods. These projects have left physical impacts in the form of new or cleaned up community centers, gardens, playgrounds and lakes that are used by thousands of Hanoi residents. Green living activities also resulted in increased neighborhood pride, participation and governance. In some wards, authorities responded positively to club initiatives, leading to cooperative structures between citizens, local government, and mass organizations such as the Vietnam Women's Union. In other locations, authorities remain aloof or discouraging of citizen action, yet local residents still find ways to organize themselves around common interests.

In Phuc Tan, a poor neighborhood along the Red River, the club wanted to improve abandoned land into a community garden. This area was filled with weeds and trash, and at night it was occupied by drug users. When the ten women of the first green living team started meeting, they tried composting for their home gardens and it worked well. They then looked for more land to plant vegetables. They came to the riverside and started to clean up a small piece of land for their garden. Then more women from the ward came and started clearing more land. After one year the entire area of ten hectares became vegetable gardens. The local government is happy because the area along the river is now clean and crime has reduced. However, they are worried that people would use the garden as a pretext to live there as squatters or claim usage rights over the land. So far, no disputes have occurred. According to Ms. Le Mai, a green living coach in Phuc Tan quoted in a community-edited publication:

> *The thing that makes me proudest is that I've learned how to make compost successfully and teach this to many other women. Before we started, every family threw out five kilograms of trash a day. Now we separate trash into organic waste for composting and use the compost for ornamental trees and vegetables in our home gardens. This is good for the plants and saves almost two kilograms of trash a day from being dumped into the environment (Action for the City 2012, p. 9).*

In another ward, Ha Dinh, the green living club decided to restore a dilapidated community house for meetings and neighborhood activities. They raised about eight million dong ($400) from the residents in the neighborhood, and Action for the City funded an equal amount. With this, they bought paint to repaint the house, installed new windows and bought tables and chairs. The yard of the community house has also become a favorite public space in the neighborhood. In the words of Mr. Vuong Xuan Hung, a community coach in Ha Dinh, 'Since we finished repairing the cultural center in 2010, it has become a common meeting point ... To boast a little, there aren't many places that have a neighborhood cultural center with as much open space as we do. Now every time we have a green living meeting, a poetry reading or children's cultural performance, all of these events are organized here' (Action for the City, 2012, p. 25). Although some local authorities still propose plans of how the site can instead be rented to earn an income, club members argue that the space belongs to everyone, and therefore should not be used privately.

Partnership principles

In each location, Action for the City works with different local partners, either neighborhood committees set up by local authorities, or local branches of mass organizations such as the Women's Union and Red Cross. These partnerships are established for practical reasons so that green living teams and clubs may use existing venues and structures to implement their activities. Linkage with one or more local partners provides legitimacy for green living activities. However, compared to existing structures, the green living teams and clubs are open in membership and operations, led by community members themselves.

Action for the City supports partner organizations through the four phases described in Box 12.1. Action for the City has also developed media strategies to publicize neighborhood efforts and involved the Vietnam Association of Architects in designing community public spaces.

The response of local authorities is critically important in determining the effect of community projects on local governance. The third and fourth phases of community action are more challenging for citizens, since they require contact with governmental authorities in order to organize public activities. It is often necessary to involve some branch of the local leadership in green living club activities. Having retired officials and leaders as members of clubs is also helpful, as these residents are generally well-educated, already viewed as local leaders, and tend to be listened to by the current leaders. These local leaders can then advocate upwards within their organizations to convince district and city officials that the green living process is positive and non-threatening (Wells-Dang, 2011). If authorities are supportive, a good model of cooperation can develop between government and civil society. If authorities are dismissive of the project, it is very difficult for citizens to organize on their own, yet the example of Phuc Tan shows that some activities are possible independently from local authorities. The gardeners in Phuc Tan are not confronting authorities or breaking laws, but they are operating in a grey area and face an unplanned path to success.

Box 12.1

Four phases of supporting partners

First phase: Adaptation phase at office

This phase aims to support partner organizations by allowing them to test the model and give feedback to Action for the City before adapting to the community. It also helps Action for the City to evaluate the skill and the commitment of partners.

Second phase: Community needs survey

Action for the City works together with partners' staff to clarify the needs of community and select the model that best suited them.

Third phase: Adaptation phase in the community

After clarifying the needs of the community, our partners will implement the adaptation phase in the community at a small scale. In this phase, Action for the City provides techniques and material in order to work more effectively with the community. Also, we build capacity for partners' staff and core people in the community in order to develop resources for the next phase.

Fourth phase: Pilot phase

In this phase, partners expand the model in the community and develop community coaches to facilitate the green living teams. Action for the City will support partners to develop plans for future sustainability through fundraising, capacity building, and other elements.

Effects on local governance

The key factors in determining local governance outcomes appear to be the following (Action for the City & Irish Aid, 2012):

1. Whether local authorities are from the community themselves and are well connected to community concerns
2. The presence of economic pressures and opportunities for rent-seeking
3. The personal character of leaders
4. Whether local authorities have previous experience with large donor-funded projects.

Factor (1) is clearly a positive contributor: the more responsible and accountable leaders are to the community, the better they will understand and support residents' actions for sustainability. Perhaps surprisingly, Action for the City's experience is that factor (4) has a negative impact: authorities who have benefited from donor projects are less receptive to community initiatives, since they have been accustomed to large budgets and big-scale activities. In fact, many environmental changes can be made without much money or technical skills, if there is strong community participation. As a result of green living activities, local residents have gradually become more active in preserving public space and speaking out about their needs. They have started to take part in cleaning and maintaining public space, initiating new actions such as composting, community gardening and organizing events to raise environmental awareness.

In Phuc Tan ward, factors (1), (2) and (4) were the primary determinants in restricting cooperation: authorities who were not representing community interests had strong economic incentives to rent public space out for private use and their own benefit. In Thuong Dinh, factors (3) and (4) were primary. Both wards also have had international projects that brought a lot of money in the past, which resulted in unrealistic expectations of the Action for the City project and a willingness to work only when money was available. These factors resulted in challenges in Action for the City's relations with local authorities and some delays, but this did not impair the developmental value of the project (Action for the City & Irish Aid, 2012).

Action for the City's strategy is to demonstrate models of environmental sustainability that others will adopt without needing external funding and facilitation. The next step in a self-replicating process of community building, which is currently underway, is formation of a network of local communities that is made up of green living teams, community leaders, and representatives of mass organizations. The expectation is that leaders of the existing communities in the green living program will eventually become coaches who can start green living and public space campaigns elsewhere. Depending on governance structures in various cities, it may be easier or more difficult to win public and official support for sustainability efforts.

Lessons for building livable cities

The primary implication of Action for the City's efforts is that community environmental action is possible, even in a challenging setting such as Hanoi. Urban environmental issues often seem enormous and complicated, but a small

NGO can achieve impacts in coordination with multiple partners. Successful community projects can bring about changes at the individual and local levels, then link these examples to the policy level through linkages with government, media and other allies. Work at the grassroots level allows us to document data, facilitate local actions, and research the implications of these actions. These data then can be used by the media and academic researchers for policy advocacy.

The key to work at the local level is winning trust from the community, the local government and other stakeholders. To local people, Action for the City staff have become known as committed and dynamic colleagues who can mobilize resources to support communities. To local authorities, we represent an independent group that is capable in raising funds and delivering results. The process of trust building also leads to more open space for self-organized groups, such as the green living movement, to operate in civil society. Ward-level green living clubs are well structured and equipped to lead community initiatives around environmental issues.

Before building a social movement, however, individuals need to lead through modeling positive, small-scale behaviors. Waiting for government to act simply reinforces a top-down approach to community change. Although activists may be tempted to short-circuit the process of local organizing to carry out direct advocacy with leaders, there is really no alternative to the slow, complex process of growing support organically from the grassroots. In theoretical terms, this is called an agency-centered model (Fay, 1996, p. 242); instead of focusing on structural constraints that affect each individual, the question becomes how each person can affect the situation. Perhaps in many cases local residents' influence is limited, but even small changes can build confidence and lead to larger actions.

This approach to building communities does not mean forgetting about big improvements, such as infrastructure projects. Such changes do indeed require higher-level support and budgets. But they are not empowering, so Action for the City does not emphasize them. Instead, in focusing on local actions, we gain recognition from the media and professionals, such as academics, researchers and technocratic officials, who are looking for positive examples of solutions to environmental issues. Since these people are also city residents, they are well aware of existing problems, but are accustomed to stories of why things don't work: why public space is disappearing and urban improvements are hopeless, and why. Seeing evidence-based work at the local level shows a variety of possible answers as to how these issues might actually have solutions. This gives opinion-makers and professionals hope.

Life in present-day Hanoi and other Vietnamese cities is powerfully mediated by the market and profit motives. These forces both support and complicate the goals of Action for the City. For instance, the riverside vegetable garden initiative in Phuc Tan owes some of its popularity to the opportunity it gave residents to cut costs and grow their own produce. The economic benefits of the project helped to convince local officials to support it, since they are relieved from pressure to find secure income sources for the residents. On public space issues, however, economic incentives often pose a barrier to our work. Land is a scarce resource in the city, and negotiating its use for the common good is always in tension with enclosing it and using it for a profit. The benefits of reclaiming and using public space for health, leisure, exercise, and neighborhood events compete with the motivation of local officials seeking to maximize profits from the public areas they manage.

If trust building is the key at the local level, then networking is the key for increasing impacts. The green living network consists of the local community teams and clubs, including members from different geographical areas and different sectors (such as environmental protection, education, and architecture). The members of this network are green living clubs in Hanoi, several Vietnamese and international NGOs from different parts of Vietnam, the Danang city Women's Union, and individuals from government agencies. The diversity of the groups helps to exchange experience and contacts. In Hue and Ho Chi Minh City, Action for the City is cooperating with other Vietnamese NGOs. At the central level, a project partner from the Ministry of Education and Training introduced the network to an agency in the Ministry of Environment and Natural Resources that is responsible for environmental education. Action for the City's experience shows that there is space to make change to improve the environment, instead of only waiting for the government to make it easy for NGOs to work and attract public support. Like individual members of green living teams, social organizations can and should widen the space for sustainable cities through our own actions, in Vietnam and throughout Southeast Asia.

References

Action for the City (2012). Telling Community Stories: Residents share experiences about green living and improving public spaces. Hanoi.

Action for the City (2007). 'Who Does Hanoi Belong To?', short film, available at vimeo.com/10654732/.

Action for the City and Irish Aid (2012). Project evaluation, Neighborhood Empowerment in Hanoi, Vietnam Civil Society Facility Project 2008.06, January 2009 – December 2011.

Agence France Presse (AFP) (2007). 'Urban growth threatens heritage of Vietnam's capital', 17 September, available at http://afp.google.com/article/ALeqM5jp9Uj3uXczek6uAEVfnhP_fK179A.

Evans, P. (2002). 'Introduction: Looking for Agents of Urban Livability in a Globalized Political Economy', in Evans, P. (ed.), *Livable Cities? Urban Strategies for Livelihood and Sustainability*. Berkeley: University of California Press, pp. 1-30.

Fay, B. (1996). *Contemporary Philosophy of Social Science: A Multicultural Approach*. Cambridge, MA: Blackwell.

General Statistics Office of Vietnam (GSO) (2011). Vietnam Population and Housing Census 2009 Migration and Urbanization in Vietnam: Patterns, Trends and Differentials. Hanoi: Ministry of Planning and Investment.

Indrakesuma, T., and Loh, J. (2012). 'Poverty and public services in rapidly growing Vietnam', in Asian Trends Monitoring Bulletin 18: Empowering Hanoi's Poor. Lee Kuan Yew School of Public Policy, Singapore, pp. 4-11.

McMichael, P. (2012). 'Depeasantization', *The Wiley-Blackwell Encyclopedia of Globalization*, Blackwell Publishing Ltd.

Oxfam and ActionAid Vietnam (2012). Participatory Monitoring of Urban Poverty in Vietnam: Five-Year Synthesis Report (2008-2012). Hanoi, November.

Sen, A. (1999). *Development as Freedom*. Oxford: Oxford University Press.

United Nations Development Program (UNDP) (2010). Urban Poverty Assessment in Hanoi and Ho Chi Minh City.

United Nations Population Fund (UNFPA) (2007). State of the World Population 2007: Unleashing the Potential of Urban Growth.

Wells-Dang, G. (2011). 'Community Environmental Action in Hanoi', paper presented at the 2011 Vietnam Update conference, Australian National University, Canberra, November.

World Bank (2012). Well Begun, Not Yet Done: Vietnam's Remarkable Progress on Poverty Reduction and the Emerging Challenges. Washington.

Yale Center for Environmental Law & Policy and Center for International Earth Science Information Network (2012). Environmental Performance Index and Pilot Trend Environmental Performance Index, released at the World Economic Forum, Davos, Switzerland.

Chapter 13

Sustainable community development in northeastern Thailand

The Inpaeng Network

ISTVAN RADO

ABSTRACT

This chapter discusses the activities of *Inpaeng,* a farmers' network in Northeastern Thailand committed to empower farming households through a mix of homegrown strengths and acquired know-how. Based on on-site findings as well as secondary data the chapter demonstrates innovative strategies to maintain economic, social, and environmental sustainability in the region. The example of Inpaeng moreover shows that the initiative of farmers themselves and their engagement in an ongoing learning process are crucial factors for the long-term success of community development projects.

Introduction

This paper discusses the Inpaeng Network in Northeastern Thailand, which has originated from a collaboration of local scholars and farmers since the mid-1980s in the village of Ban Bua, in the province of Sakon Nakhon. The main objective of the network has been to find ways to improve the lives of farming households in the area. Northeastern Thailand, commonly referred to as 'Isan', is the largest rice producing region among all five regions (Bangkok, Central Region, North, Northeast, and South) of the country. However, the problems faced by Northeastern farmers are characteristic of most rural areas in Thailand: rising household debts, loss of biodiversity, and loss of communal cohesion (UNDP, 2010).

Over the years, Inpaeng has sought various solutions in confronting these problems; these involve upgrading the skills and knowledge of local farmers both in terms of traditional knowledge and modern processing techniques. The network has established enterprises for example, which process local fruits and herbs into value-added products. Another feature of the Inpaeng network is to share acquired knowledge among network members and non-members alike. Today it offers training for interested farmers about integrated farming techniques, herbal medicine, the production of organic fertilizer, shampoo and dish liquid.

From its humble beginnings almost 3 decades ago the network has grown over the years both in terms of membership and in scope (currently 58 community enterprises producing a variety of products). According to the Thai Agricultural Land Reform Office (ALRO), which assists individual farmers and communities in 69 provinces, the Inpaeng Network is by far the largest and most successful farmers' network in Thailand (personal interview on 21 Jan 2012).

The paper demonstrates how past and present activities of the Inpaeng network are intended to maintain economic, social, and environmental sustainability in the region. Each activity referred to in this chapter responds to the vulnerabilities of typical northeastern farmers: reforestation efforts and the emphasis on integrated farming are promoted to maintain sources of local and healthy food. Household items are produced within the network in order to reduce main household expenditures. Current challenges for the network are also explained in the context of rural livelihood strategies in the region.

Together with secondary data about the network, the paper illustrates the above points through primary on-site findings. The data has been collected over a two week period in January 2012, and includes 50 random household interviews in the village of Ban Bua, 11 expert interviews with Inpaeng leaders from four provinces, and participatory observation. This chapter will first give an overview of the situation of Thai small-scale farmers in general with an emphasis on the situation in the Northeastern region. Since the Inpaeng Network operates in five provinces of the remote Northeast - namely Kalasin, Mukdahan, Nakhon Phanom, Sakon Nakhon, and Udonthani - the main focus of this section will be on the situation of the farming households in the sub-region. Most of the data is derived from the household interviews conducted in Ban Bua, Sakon Nakhon. Section 2 will give a short overview of the effects of development strategies of Thai governments on the rural sector in the past fifty years. The main part of this paper (section 3) is about the development initiatives of the Inpaeng Network. In the final part, the challenges that Inpaeng is currently faced with are highlighted.

Contemporary challenges in rural Northeastern Thailand

Agriculture has often been termed the backbone of the Thai economy (Rigg & Nattapoolwat, 2001, p. 953; see also National Economic Development Board, 1964, p. 10): Two thirds of the population qualifies as rural-based with small-scale farms of 2 to 6 hectares dominating the sector (UNDP, 2010, p. 69). Historically, the most important farming activity has consisted of growing rice, which at the same time is the main staple food for Thai people. Thailand is largely self-sufficient in food and annually exports almost half of the domestically produced rice. The production of other crops and fruits, such as cassava, maize and pineapple, likewise outstrips domestic demand and these are for the most part cultivated for exports. Cassava is currently the most important cash crop being cultivated throughout Thailand.

Despite its important role in the Thai economy, the agricultural sector is facing a number of problems (National Statistical Office, 2011): data from 2009 reveals an average monthly net return from farming of 2,028 baht (about US$66) per household. Low agricultural prices, limited access to land (especially in Thailand's Northern region), and increasing rural debt are for many years threatening the viability of small-scale farming. In Thailand's Northeastern region for instance, where the returns from farming are below the national average, around 78 percent of all households are indebted. The same source indicates that most of this debt is used for consumption goods rather than for investments in business, farming, or education. Farmers have adopted a number of strategies in order to raise their income levels and reduce debt. During the past decades they have diversified their sources of income beyond agriculture, e.g. by seeking employment in Bangkok or abroad. Working-age members of many rural households thus take advantage of higher income levels outside the region in order to support their families back home by sending money on a regular basis. Almost ten percent of the total monetary income of rural households consisted of remittances in 2007; in the Northeast, the poorest province, the share was 18 percent (National Statistical Office, 2007). Correspondingly, a 2001 survey found that around a quarter of all 15 to 49-year-olds of the Northeast lived outside the region (UNDP, 2010, p. 70).

A strategy used in many parts of Isan to avoid debt has been to shift away from capital-intensive cash-cropping and to satisfy most subsistence needs by planting rice and vegetables instead (Blake & Pitakthepsombut, 2006, p. 69 and Keyes, 2012, pp. 223/24). A case in point for this development is the farmers in the village of Ban Bua, located about 600 kilometres northeast of Bangkok, near the

Phuphan mountain range in the province of Sakon Nakhon. Most households in Ban Bua had been engaged in the cultivation of government-sponsored cassava since the 1970s. Interviews as well as secondary data (Tosakul *et al.*, 2005, pp. 12-15; UNDP, 2007, pp. 38/39) reveal that for the following decade most farmers devoted most of their land to the production of cash crops. Since forest land was not yet protected by the state, forest cover decreased dramatically due to expanding cash crop cultivation. Chemical fertilizers were used to further increase the yield. At the same time, household expenses rose, partly due to the loss in biodiversity accompanied by diminishing sources of subsistence goods, as well as rising consumption needs, such as TV sets, refrigerators and other visible signs of wealth. Such increased reliance on cash coupled with rapidly declining cassava prices led many farmers into debt. Average household debt in Ban Bua in the early 1980s was reportedly between 30,000 and 40,000 baht (Tosakul *et al.*, 2005, p. 12).[21]

Figure 13.1 Average land use in Ban Bua

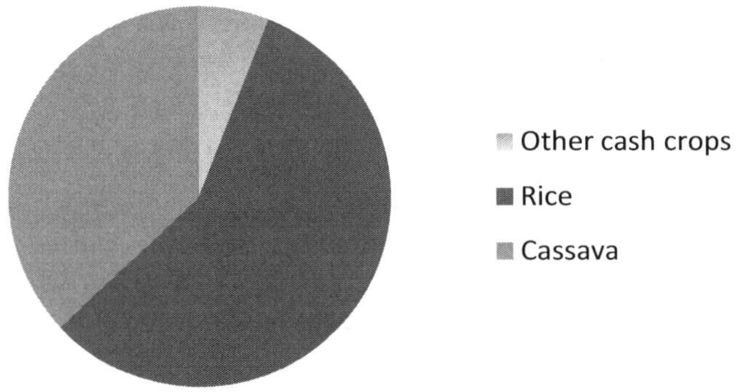

Since the 1990s most farming households in Ban Bua have made a shift away from the cultivation of cassava and have since tried to satisfy their annual rice demand from their own produce: According to the fieldwork data the average farmer in Ban Bua allocates almost 60 percent of his plot for rice, and the rest for cash crops, mainly cassava (see Figure 13.1). Rubber, pumpkin, sugarcane, and eucalyptus, are sometimes planted in addition and in much smaller quantity. Cash crops are sold for the income needed to satisfy household needs beyond food. Cassava is a very undemanding crop, which can be grown and harvested at any time of year. The downside is its low selling price per kilo, as well as daily price fluctuations: farmers can sell a kilo of cassava for a price between 1.4 to more than three baht to the local middleman. According to the fieldwork data 0.48 ha of a median landholding of 1.28 ha are used for cassava, which may yield an estimated annual return of 24,000 baht (about US$780).

---

[21] Calculation based on changes in the consumer price index from January 1980 to January 2011 suggests that the value of these debt figures in 2011 is at least three times as much, approximately 102,000 to 136,500 baht (see the Bank of Thailand website www.indexpr.moc.go.th/price_present/tableIndexCpi_bot.asp). This generally corresponds with current debt levels in Northeastern Thailand.

A third of the households interviewed pursue other, often more rewarding income opportunities in addition. Especially self-employed and contract labor, such as construction, weaving, operating a shop and other forms of occupation, is in these cases, often regarded as the dominant livelihood activity. For the less entrepreneurially-minded farmers, which constitute the majority, income generating options in addition to cash crop cultivation are casual labor on someone else's field for 200 baht (about US$6.50) a day, sale of vegetables from the garden, or outside employment. In almost half of the households interviewed at least one family member has left the village for work in Bangkok or another province, and sends home remittances on a more or less regular basis. Typical jobs in these cases are unskilled labor in factories, construction, or sales. A female respondent indicated that her husband works as a security guard in Bangkok earning 10,000 baht per month, from which he sends 3,000 baht back home (household interview, 20 January 2012).

Figure 13.2 Debt levels of 50 random households (in baht)

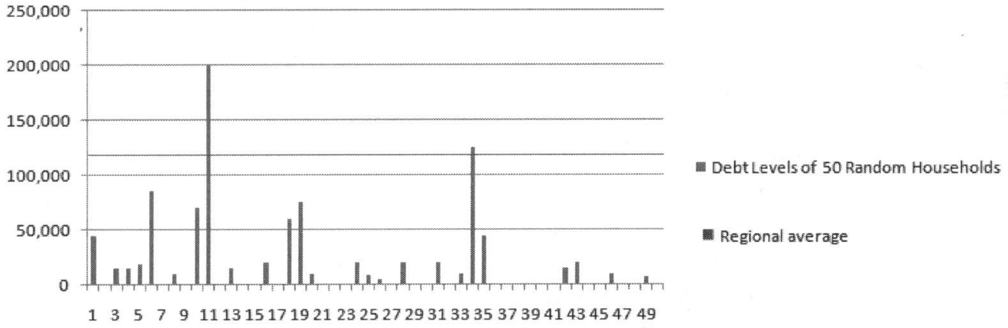

Although relying on low incomes, the debt levels surveyed in Ban Bua are far below the regional average of 118,308 baht (2009) at around 19,175 baht (in 2012; see Figure 13.2). The reason for this is the continued importance of the subsistence sector in this part of Isan. Apart from on-farm produce subsistence goods include fish and frogs from the seasonally inundated rice fields, as well as ants, mushrooms, and vegetables from the forest. Since about 75 percent of the households interviewed produce sufficient rice in at least some years, the purchase of food is therefore often limited to ingredients such as MSG and fish sauce. At the same time existing debt is mostly used to finance farming inputs (fertilizer, gas, hiring labor), and household expenses (mainly clothes and food). Hand tractors have replaced buffaloes for plowing a few years ago and this has since meant an additional financial burden to the villagers. The fact that many households are unable to finance the corresponding costs from agricultural returns shows how vulnerable they are to external financial pressures. Financially the more they rely on the market, the more vulnerable they are. In many cases the returns from the sale of cassava is only sufficient to cover basic living expenses. Too little rainfall in a given year resulting in a bad rice harvest can make a family resort to credit. In some cases households manage to compensate for the risks by relying more on sources of subsistence (fields and forest), by thrift (e.g. foregoing the purchase of fertilizer and hired labor), or by migrating to find employment.

Thailand's development strategy since the 1960s

Since the establishment of the National Economic and Social Development Board (NESDB) in 1959, Thailand puts down its macro-economic development strategy in consecutive five-year plans. Starting with the first plan (1961-66) until the seventh plan (1992-96) Thai governments have pursued an industrialization strategy, in which the rural sector provided primary inputs in the form of cash crops and cheap labor power for the country's emergent industries, including agro-industries (Phongpaichit & Baker, 1995, p. 82). For farmers the focus on the production of cash crops meant rising expenditures for seeds, fertilizer, pesticides, and agricultural machinery. Government policies further squeezed the profitability of farming by keeping food prices artificially low to subsidize wage rates in the industrial sector. These developments made agriculture profitable only for farmers with large landholdings, whereas small-scale farmers have had to supplement their agricultural income with off-farm work as indicated above.

Thai academics and NGO activists have since the 1970s criticized Thai governments for failing to support rural producers so that they could benefit from modernization and economic development. Some of these, such as Seri Phongphit from the 'Village Foundation', have advocated alternative development approaches for rural communities with an emphasis on mobilizing local skills and products (see Phongphit, 2001). The case study described in the following section is in part inspired by the development project of the Village Foundation. Such initiatives have since the late 1990s increasingly gained support from government institutions due to a shift from a growth oriented strategy to a people-centered strategy including communal empowerment and development (see National Economic and Social Development Board, 1997).

The activities of the Inpaeng Network

In 1987 Thawatchai Khunwong from the Village Foundation – an NGO established by the academic Seri Phongphit – came to join the villagers in Ban Bua in order to study communal life and explore possible development alternatives (see Suksudaj, 2010, p. 22; Phongphit, 2001). Together with the village elders Pho Lek and Pho Serm he aimed at identifying unique local products and skills, which could provide a stronger foundation for the local economy in terms of socio-economic and environmental sustainability. They moreover wanted to decrease the strong dependency of the villagers on market relations as was typical at that time. Instead, the group promoted a strong foundation of self-reliance coining the phrase 'grow what we eat, and eat what we grow' (UNDP, 2007, p. 39). Since forest products have constituted an essential part of local food, reforestation has from the beginning been a core activity of Inpaeng.

Initially, they managed to form a community forestry group of thirteen villagers. They undertook excursions to nearby districts in order to collect seeds, and to collect data about the varieties of edible animals and plants in the region. They visited alternative farmers, from whom they learned about the use of tree species for herbal medicine and integrated farm systems. From one of these farmers in a nearby district the group learned about the cultivation of rattan trees, for instance. Rattan can be used both for food and braiding material. They then recreated small forests of rattan trees, which provide a habitat for those plants, animals, and mushrooms, which are typical subsistence goods of communities in the area. Thus, this practice combines environmental rehabilitation with the provision of subsistence goods. The group implemented this and other techniques by joining together working on each others' fields. In addition to putting the acquired integrated farming techniques into practice they exchanged seed varieties and farm animals. They increasingly diversified their products by cultivating a variety of vegetables and fruits, and dug ponds to raise fish and frogs.

The group soon grew in terms of membership. In 1988 they bought up some farmland in Ban Bua and established the first network center, which was meant to serve as a training site and a place for exchanging knowledge (Suksudaj, 2010, p. 23). A few years later the network acquired its current name 'Inpaeng', meaning 'God Indra's creation'; accordingly the center was named 'Inpaeng Center'. Today it is the location of a small herb factory and Makmao processing facility. By processing local fruits into value-added products the network wants to show that locally available resources can successfully be put to commercial use. In addition, the network's aim is for people in the region to regain confidence in their own capabilities, instead of focusing on the things they lack (Pho Lek, personal interview on 17 January 2012). Having such knowledge and confidence, people will be able to distinguish between external know-how, which improves their lives on the one hand, and expertise, which merely reproduces and discounts locally available resources.

Network expansion

From the early 1990s onwards, the Inpaeng Network expanded in terms of membership first to other districts in Sakon Nakhon province, and later to neighboring provinces. Today Inpaeng is present in five northeastern provinces and encompasses around 30,000 members (as of 2009; see Suksudaj, 2010, p. 23). In all cases farmers are drawn to the network by word of mouth, by government projects, or both. One of the first members in Kalasin province for instance had advocated community forest protection before he heard of the network from a relative living in Ban Bua. He later told Sawan, the leader of a farmers' group (Thai-Bru Network) in Mukdahan province, about Inpaeng. The Thai-Bru Network later became part of Inpaeng through a mutual biodiversity project to maintain local tree species. From the government side the Agricultural Land Reform Office (ALRO) supported the project by providing knowledge and tools, including plastic bags for the collection of seeds.

Government organizations promoting sustainable agricultural techniques, such as ALRO, often involve network leaders due to their expertise about the management and use of natural resources. When invited to a certain village, Inpaeng leaders usually conduct a study about the specific weaknesses and strengths in the area. For example, farm use, annual household expenses, and resources available.[22] By doing so possible avenues for development are sought within the local context; e.g. if it is found that households of a community spend large amounts of money on fertilizer, Inpaeng experts may assist the local leaders in producing organic fertilizer from local inputs. If in another case fishing is a dominant livelihood activity, the experts may assist the community in processing fish into value-added products.

Figure 13.3 Seed bank of a network member in Ban Bua

As the network expands to other areas in this manner, the number of new members in a certain district often declines rapidly after a short time: according to Sawan from Mukdahan there were more than forty people in his district joining the network in 2004. Until today membership has decreased to less than half of the original number. Those who left are commercially oriented farmers disinterested in strategies of self-reliance. Thus, in no case does membership extend to all households in a village. Even in Ban Bua, the place of origin, only a minority of people declare themselves Inpaeng members: During the fifty random household interviews seven respondents (14 percent) indicated to be members. Interviews with Inpaeng leaders have moreover revealed that they seek to spread a certain way of life based on self-reliance and integrated farming, more than formal membership.

During the household interviews in January 2012 it turned out that it is hard to make a clear distinction between Inpaeng members and non-members: whereas many formal members follow similar livelihood patterns as others in the village, some of those stating not to be involved in the network exhibited views close to the Inpaeng philosophy or entertain relationships with the network. One

---

22 See the example in Wangsammo district, province of Udonthani in section 'Community enterprises'.

respondent for instance sells Makmao berries to the Inpaeng processing plant. During the interview she declared: 'Are we rich? – We will never be rich, but we have peaceful lives.' Inpaeng leaders frequently make similar statements (Tosakul *et al.*, 2005, p. 28).

Community forestry and integrated farming

Maintaining and increasing forest land has from the beginning been a primary concern for the members of Inpaeng, since it is the source of healthy food and medicinal herbs. Local varieties of forest vegetables, such as phak waan (a leaf-like vegetable) and takhop paa (a plum species), moreover can be sold for a high price in nearby markets. As mentioned above, virtually every household in Ban Bua is to some degree dependent on food from the forest. With the forest disappearing villagers increasingly have to buy food, which in turn increases the cost of living. Apart from deforestation the overexploitation of forest goods for commercial reasons is another factor exacerbating scarcity (household interview on 23 January 2012). According to an Inpaeng leader reforestation efforts near the Phuphan mountain range near Ban Bua have met with little success in the past, which is why some members have created seed banks in their garden (see Figure 13.3), or recreated small forests on their fields.

Figure 13.4 Map showing Praphat's farm divided according to household needs

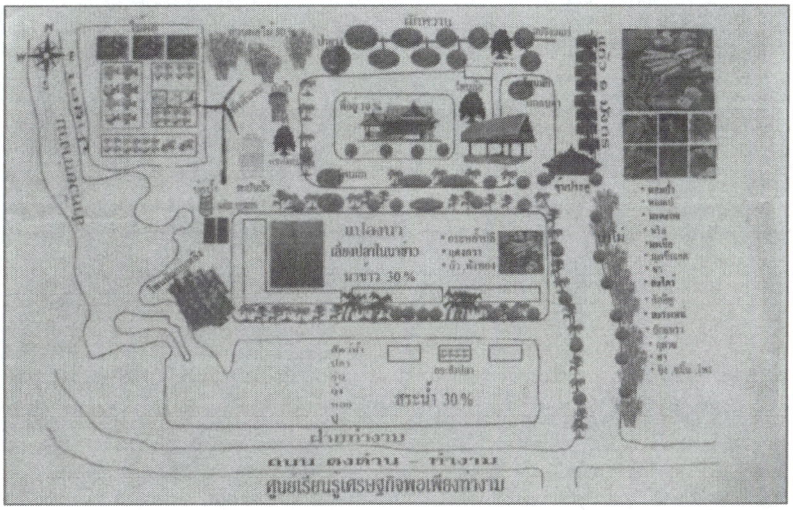

Integrated farming activities include not only the cultivation of fruit trees and herbal trees, but the securing of most consumption needs within the household. In order to manage the farmland to cover household needs farmers must be able to divide the land for the cultivation of rice, other food crops, vegetables and fruits, and farm animals accordingly. This includes taking into account the possibilities and limitations provided by farm size, soil conditions, and weather. A number of Inpaeng members train farmers in land management either on the instructor's field or at a network center. An innovative way of increasing the yields is the use of renewable energy for irrigation purposes. As is the case in Ban Bua, many farming households in Isan rely on sufficient rain for good harvests. Alternative energy experts, such as Mr. Praphat in a northern district of Sakon Nakhon, use wind energy and photovoltaic energy for irrigation and electricity generation. Praphat teaches farmers how to install small-scale windmills used to operate a water pump for irrigation. According to Praphat a turbine can generate 1,000 liters of water per hour when in motion (Praphat, interview on 28 January 2012). When the air is still, the water pumps can also be operated by electricity charged through the solar panels or by hand.

Figure 13.5 Windmill for irrigation, Banmuang District, Sakon Nakhon

Inpaeng encourages farmers to produce for home consumption and to sell only the surplus. Network leaders stress that local vegetables, fruits (such as Makmao berries, which are unique to the Phuphan mountain range) and herbs can yield high prices in outside markets compared to mainstream fruits such as pumpkin, mango and pomelo. Since recently, the Inpaeng Network provides a platform for the circulation of information about the products that can be sold profitably, as well as the buyer markets including restaurants in the region. The information also includes price differentials that particular products yield in different markets. A few years before my research visit in 2012, Inpaeng members in the Phuphan district have started to supply the regional wholesale vegetable market in Kalasin province, supplying rattan, chili, Makmao and other vegetables on a weekly basis.

Community enterprises

Since the mid-1990s Inpaeng has started to set up community enterprises. These either process local resources typical of a region (such as Makmao) into value-added products, or aim at lowering the expenses of local farmers by offering household and farm items (such as fertilizer) more cheaply. Inpaeng members often acquire the skills for product processing from government and research institutes, such as from provincial branches of the Rajamangala University of Technology. The herb and Makmao factories at the Inpaeng Center in Ban Bua were the first such ventures. The first processes herbs into medicine according to traditional knowledge about their effects. Makmao is being processed into juice and wine. The harvesting season for Makmao takes place from July to September each year. According to the manager the factory buys Makmao berries from local farmers and offers seasonal employment for a maximum of 12 staff members, who receive their salary from a government institution. In one season Ban Bua produces around 30,000 bottles of Makmao juice, as well as some wine in addition. These products are sold locally in a small store also located at the Inpaeng Center (personal interview on 17 January 2012).

Figure 13.6 Products of the fruit processing enterprise, Phuphan District, Sakon Nakhon

Whereas the Makmao factory in Ban Bua limits its operations to satisfy local demand, Inpaeng members elsewhere manage community enterprises more commercially. After having acquired the processing techniques from the Inpaeng Center in Ban Bua, members in the neighboring district of Phuphan have themselves successfully produced juice from Makmao, Makkho, and Samo. Since the mountainous area in the district does not support the cultivation of rice, the Phuphan community grows the fruit trees on large self-owned plantations. In contrast to the Ban Bua factory, where the seasonal labor is financed by a government institution, the Phuphan factory is financially viable exporting Makmao juice and wine to outside regions including Bangkok. It produces not only juices from a variety of local fruits, but also a wider range of Makmao products, such as tea made of its leaves and sugar-free Makmao juice. Because of this larger variety of products, the Phuphan factory employs a permanent staff of thirty, as well as three officers, each responsible for accountancy, sales, and security.

In contrast to the above example, the community product in Wangsammo district in the province of Udonthani responds to local vulnerabilities rather than unique resources (Chamnan, interview on 22 January 2012): A study carried out by Inpaeng in one of the sub-districts found that approximately 12 percent of household expenditure is used for fertilizers. The group thus came to the conclusion that by producing organic fertilizer on a non-profit basis they could significantly reduce household expenditures within the sub-district. Out of the 1,700 households in the sub-district 200 families joined together in a cooperative savings group contributing shares for cooperative fertilizer production. In 2002 the group received financial support of one million baht from the provincial governor's fund for the purchase of machines and equipment. The people running the enterprise get no salary apart from fixed returns on their shares. The cost of production is therefore much lower than in commercial enterprises and the product sells for a quarter of the conventional retail price. In field experiments the community organic fertilizer has proven to effect the same quantity of sugarcane - which is the main cash crop in the area - as the use of conventional fertilizer.

Figure 13.7 Herbal mix to replace MSG, from a community enterprise in Phuphan District, Sakon Nakhon

Out of the 58 community enterprises currently operated by the Inpaeng Network about 16 are commercially successful according to Thawatchai[23], such as the two examples cited above. Community enterprises currently produce a wide range of products, including fermented fish, organic rice, shampoo and detergents and herbal medicine. All enterprises are small scale. In some cases they employ less than ten people and in most cases are financed through a share system. Depending on the enterprise only ten to fifty percent of profits is reinvested in the businesses. The rest is divided among the local Inpaeng committee, payments to shareholders, and community welfare activities. In each community enterprise the exact amount for each use is split according to a particular formula, such as 30:30:30:10.

[23] The network leader mentioned this during a presentation for staff of the Agricultural Land Reform Office on 21 January 2012 at the Inpaeng Center in Ban Bua.

Figure 13.8 Logo of an enterprise producing fertilizer in Banmuang District, Sakon Nakhon

Interviews with network members from different communities revealed that the design of the share system also differs from one enterprise to the other; in some cases shareholders may get ten percent per year for their investment, in other cases more. An upper limit on the maximum amount held ensures relative equality among shareholders of an enterprise. At the same time this limit equalizes the maximum return per year from one enterprise to the other: whereas in one case shareholders receive ten percent on a maximum investment of 10,000 baht, shareholders in another case receive 20 percent on a maximum investment of 5,000 baht, for example. Thus, in both cases shareholders receive a maximum annual return of 1,000 baht.

Not all Inpaeng leaders are taken with the share system, however. Sawan, the leader of the Thai-Bru Network in Mukdahan, for instance, fears that the system encourages people to be passive shareholders, not contributing anything within the enterprise but money. The members in his district have not yet set up an enterprise; when they do, Sawan prefers inputs and payments in kind over monetary investments and returns. This would involve stakeholders more actively. They would need to supply raw materials instead of money, process them together, and share part of the output among themselves. At the same time, Sawan does not mean to convince other network leaders about his idea: the share system and his non-monetary model 'should exist side by side' (Sawan, interview on 21 January 2012).

Inpaeng savings group

Savings groups constitute another widespread project among Inpaeng communities; a central aim here is to manage financial risks among the villagers. These groups are open to network members and non-members alike. In Ban Bua, every participant must contribute ten baht per month and receives interest on deposits every year. The interest for loans is one percent according to local respondents. There are no specific requirements for obtaining a loan, except for a debt limit depending on the deposits of the debtor: if one has savings worth a thousand baht, for instance, the maximum loan is set at 3,000 baht. At the end of each year part of the interest payments on debts are divided among the depositors; the interest on deposits thus changes each year. Another part of the funds is used for member welfare expenditures, which cover the costs of hospitalization, and cremation. The interest payments thus stay within the group and benefit the members - including debtors - through welfare payments.

The Inpaeng way: Empowering villagers

As mentioned above, debt levels in Ban Bua are very low compared to those in other parts of the region. This is due to the fact that most farmers rely largely on the subsistence sector with minimal expenses. The more farmers rely on cash crops the greater is their exposure to economic risks. Farmers do not have the know-how to process cassava into animal fodder, or to convert sugarcane into sugar for example. They do not have the bargaining power vis-à-vis middlemen to influence the prices, which are highly volatile in many cases. The measures employed by Inpaeng are each designed to address these vulnerabilities: The network encourages farming households in the region to further reduce cash crop cultivation in favor of self-reliance in foodstuff. By developing appropriate technologies - such as the water-pumping windmill - and efficient farm management techniques Inpaeng aims to increase the capacity of small-scale farms to meet this objective. Reforestation activities are moreover promoted in order to maintain local biodiversity. The forest is the source of additional subsistence goods, without which households would be more dependent on monetary income and thus on cash crops. More than cash crops, which often yield small profits due to a large supply by many individual farmers, surplus products from integrated farming and agro-forestry systems can be profitably sold in regional markets by the farmers themselves. Especially products unique to the area yield higher prices in more remote markets.

The objectives of empowerment and economic self-determination are also expressed in the operations of community enterprises. Most household debt consists either of farm inputs, such as fertilizer and gas, or consumption goods. By manufacturing these goods in community enterprises, Inpaeng creates new income generating opportunities for local farmers. Due to lower prices the enterprises at the same time help to reduce household expenditure and debt. In order to further heighten farmers' self-determination, these enterprises reduce the reliance on middlemen and factory prices by taking over their operations. During our interview, Chamnan from Udonthani province revealed that his community is planning to set up a community rice mill and to take over all operations ranging from buying unmilled rice from farmers to exporting white rice. The profits originally made by intermediaries could be passed on to the farmers (Chamnan, interview on 22 January 2012).

The processing of local products has the additional benefit of revaluing homegrown fruits and herbs, as well as local techniques. The herbal factory at the Inpaeng Center for instance used to sell medicine primarily to outside visitors in the past, since local villagers regarded it as outdated compared to modern medicine, according to the manager (personal interview, 25 January 2012). Nowadays, the majority of customers comes from the village and nearby areas. Yet, herbal medicine is not meant to entirely replace modern health care. In 2010 an observer commented that:

> *From the observations, people could identify the level of healing or health service that matches the severity of the diseases. For minor illness such as rash or food poisoning, people usually use the herbal medicine for first aid treatment. However for a more serious condition such as fever in small children or joint pain, people switch their mode of service into local health centre or community hospital. It can be assumed that, in their perception, there is no categorization of health services. People utilized all available service, either western or traditional ones, according to their severity of illness and their trust to the practitioners (Suksudaj, 2010, p. 42).*

Lastly, the savings group schemes are meant to manage farmers' deposits and debt within the community. Until today the Inpaeng savings group in Ban Bua could only provide a fraction of the loans needed by most households due to limited deposits. The group does not operate like a business venture however, but uses the interest payments for a welfare fund to provide financial security in cases of illness or death. The savings group thus has the potential to utilize the widespread demand for loans in the village for purposes of communal welfare.

Lessons and challenges for the future

The nature of the network activities, as well as the mode of its expansion reveals that its members want to make visible possible and viable alternatives by setting examples. Instead of 'teaching people by using a blackboard' (Pho Lek, 17 January 2012), Inpaeng leaders lead by example and hope to convince others by their own experience and success. Only this way would other farmers be convinced to follow the Inpaeng lifestyle. According to Seri Phongphit, who as an academic has over the years accompanied Inpaeng projects from the beginning, an important underlying condition for such initiatives as the Inpaeng project is that villagers recognize their own capabilities and the value of their knowledge. Modern education and modern medicine have in the past led to a neglect of traditional knowledge (Phongphit, 2001). This has led rural communities to discount their skills as obsolete. To realize their own strengths and to become conscious agents of their development is to him a process of regaining self-confidence.

This attitude directs the attention of farmers towards formerly untapped resources and - as the initiative in Udonthani described by Chamnan shows - even supposed weaknesses as possible sources for self-determined development. The example provided by Inpaeng reveals certain broad elements throughout the process, in which constant learning plays a crucial role, illustrating that development is an ongoing project, never fully complete:

- **Adding to an inventory of local knowledge and resources:** Techniques used - both traditional and acquired - are geared to the specificities of local climatic conditions and to the maintenance of natural resources. These moreover enhance capacities for self-determined development and reduce the need for outside solutions, which perpetuate dependence putting the economic sustainability of the project at risk.
- **The role of model farmers:** Inpaeng members prefer to expose their community to the concept of self-reliance and integrated farming through successful practice. Due to the fact that they share the culture and values of the local community, and face the same economic challenges, they are more likely to influence ways of life within their village. This practice differs from state development initiatives with ready-made solutions, which often fail since they do not respond to local ways of life and needs as perceived by the 'target group'.[24]
- **Free sharing of knowledge:** The community in Ban Bua did not view network members in Phuphan district as competitors, as they acquired their processing techniques. Today, if the Makmao factory in Phuphan produces an oversupply of juice, the Ban Bua community assists in selling the remaining bottles to local villagers (personal interview with the manager of the enterprise in Ban Bua, 17 January 2012). Praphat, who is training villagers in integrated farming techniques in Banmuang district, mentioned that many of his former 'pupils' have since surpassed him in terms of efficient farm use. Sharing knowledge and techniques helps to accelerate learning effects from each other's example. Underlying this practice is an understanding that sustainable development implies recognizing mutual interdependence. This notion does not only encompass people, but also natural resources: the emphasis on subsistence agriculture over commercial interests fosters a sustainable use of natural resources.
- **The supportive role of outside institutions:** Although the involvement of Thawatchai gave a decisive impetus to the development of Inpaeng, he had spent a year learning from the Ban Bua community and then approached the village elders Pho Lek and Pho Serm, who had already aplied integrated farming methods. Ever since, NGOs, as well as state and research institutions have played a supporting role by facilitating existing development dynamics: they have provided processing skills as Inpaeng communities sought to enhance their know-how, provided information on markets, and established linkages between formerly isolated movements. ALRO is moreover using Inpaeng experts on

---

24 This resonates with insights of NGOs following a practice associated with postdevelopment thinking (McKinnon, 2007; see also Matthews, 2009).

integrated farming as resource persons in agricultural training (personal interview, 21 January 2012).

The 25-year history of Inpaeng shows that such community initiatives need time to develop and that setbacks are common along the way. Not all community enterprises are showcases of success: among the 58 enterprises operating in January 2012, 22 are yet considered unsuccessful according to Thawatchai's account. Some activities, such as the supply of agricultural produce to regional markets, have taken place since only recently and network members in Sakon Nakhon yet have to increase their production capacity to meet existing demand in these markets. During the time of research, a group has for the first time left to visit Bangkok's biggest wholesale market in order to explore the possibilities of selling lemongrass there. These activities respond in part to the network philosophy to sell the surplus of the produce of individual farmers. At the same time it also marks a trade-off between Inpaeng objectives and the mentality of younger generation farmers, who are often more commercially oriented.

Network members regard the objective to pass on their way of life to the young as by far the most important challenge of all. According to Thawatchai among the 450 young farmers that have received training from Inpaeng in integrated farming methods, about 50 (ca. 11 percent) are currently putting their knowledge into practice (Thawatchai, 21 January 2012). The Inpaeng community operating the fertilizer manufacture in Udonthani province is currently exclusively run by elders. In order to motivate others to join the community enterprise, they are planning to subcontract the fertilizer production to young farmers, who are allowed to make a profit, but must contribute an annual sum to support Inpaeng.

By accommodating the profit-motive in their operations the network members want to ensure that their sustainable community project will carry on in the future. Their entrepreneurial activities, including the innovative mix of traditional knowledge and acquired know-how, have proved to allow for successful business ventures. The emergence of commercially oriented competitors producing Makmao juice in Sakon Nakhon is indicative of this potential. More crucial for Inpaeng's continuation in the future is a set of cultural priorities: namely the sense of responsibility towards the community, the free sharing of know-how and information, and the protection of local biodiversity.

References

Blake, D. & Pitakthepsombut, R. (2006). Situation Analysis: Lower Songkhram River Basin, Thailand. Mekong Wetlands Biodiversity Conservation and Sustainable Use Programme, Bangkok.

Keyes, C. (2012). The Village Economy: Capitalist AND Sufficiency-based. A Northeastern Thai Case. Proceedings of the Conference *The Meaning of Sufficiency Economy: Theory and Practice in Society, Economy, and Business*, pp. 213-230.

Matthews, S. (2007). What, then, should we do? Insights and Experiences of a Senegalese NGO. In Ziai, A. (ed), *Exploring Post-Development. Theory and Practice, Problems and Perspectives,* 131-144. Routledge, New York.

McKinnon, K. (2007). Postdevelopment, Professionalism, and the Politics of Participation. *Annals of the Association of American Geographers,* 97:4, 772 – 785.

National Economic Development Board. (1964). The First National Economic Development Plan (1961-1966). Office of the Prime Minister, Bangkok, Thailand.

National Economic and Social Development Board. (1997). The Eighth National Economic and Social Development Plan (1997-2001). Office of the Prime Minister, Bangkok, Thailand.

National Statistical Office. (2007). Household Socio-Economic Survey 2007. Ministry of Information and Communication Technology, Bangkok.

National Statistical Office. (2011): Statistical Yearbook Thailand 2011. Ministry of Information and Communication Technology, Bangkok.

Phongpaichit, P. & Baker C. (1995). *Thailand: Economy and Politics*. Oxford University Press, Kuala Lumpur.

Phongphit, S. (2001). People's Development. A Community Governance Tool. UNDP Southeast Asia HIV and Development Project, Bangkok.

Rigg, J. & Nattapoolwat S. (2001). Embracing the Global in Thailand: Activism and Pragmatism in an Era of Deagrarianization. *World Development*, 29, 945-60.

Suksudaj, S. (2010). The Thai Social Capital as a Social Determinant of Oral Health (Doctoral Dissertation). University of Adelaide, Australia. Available from http://hdl.handle.net/2440/65058.

Tosakul, R., Benjasaph, J., Phromduang, P., Wittaporn, S., Juemmi S. & Phaireephinat, S. (2005). Duen thi la kao kin khao thi la kham: phumpanyaa nai kanjadkan khwamru khong chaoban [Walk one step at a time, eat one bite at a time: wisdom in knowledge management of villagers]. Khon Kaen, Thailand.

UNDP. (2007). Thailand Human Development Report 2007. Sufficiency Economy and Human Development. Bangkok, Thailand.

UNDP. (2010). Human Security, Today and Tomorrow. Thailand Human Development Report 2009. Bangkok, Thailand.

Chapter 14

Disaster risk reduction for sustainable development

The case study of Development Workshop France (DWF), Viet Nam

IFTEKHAR AHMED AND ESTHER CHARLESWORTH

OVERVIEW

This chapter is about *Development Workshop France's* (DWF) work in disaster-prone Central Vietnam. Local interviews allowed understanding DWF's efforts for building resilient housing with key stakeholders, highlighting that communities cannot be sustainable without safe housing. Generalisable lessons for agencies in Southeast Asia are thereby offered about building sustainable communities by reducing disaster risk.

Introduction

This chapter discusses a case study of promoting disaster resilient housing in an area highly vulnerable to the effects of natural hazards and climate change in Viet Nam. It focuses on the work of a non-governmental organisation (NGO) called Development Workshop France (DWF).

The contents of this chapter have been derived from two main sources: (a) literature on the work of DWF, particularly from DWF's website and project documents; and (b) interviews of beneficiaries, DWF staff and related stakeholders and partner organisations, supplemented by on-site observations and documentation. Intensive and detailed field investigation was carried out in April 2012 by the authors. The aim of this chapter is to use the case study of DWF to provide lessons for other agencies working in rebuilding houses in disaster-prone regions in Viet Nam and the wider Asia-Pacific region.

Context

It is widely argued that Asia is the continent most affected by natural disasters. This is a trend that has continued to amplify in recent times due to the severe impacts of climate change on many of its coastal cities (EM-DAT, 2012). Southeast Asia is among the most disaster-prone regions on the continent and Viet Nam is one of the most affected countries in the region. With its long coastline, Viet Nam is exposed to a range of climate change impacts and in Southeast Asia, other than the Philippines, Viet Nam is the country most vulnerable to tropical cyclones or 'typhoons'.

The coastal area of the central part of Viet Nam, where Thua Thien Hue province (or Hue as referred to hereafter) is situated and where the case study of this paper is located, is exposed to frequent and severe typhoons. Climate change has led to a situation of continual disasters with increased frequency and intensity of extreme weather events such as typhoons and floods. Typhoon Xansane in 2006 was followed by Typhoon Ketsana in 2009, both causing severe devastation (Minh and Crimmins, 2006; World Vision, 2010). The typhoons were accompanied by 2-metre high storm surges, causing extensive inundation by saline water on settlements, adding to the damage caused by strong wind and heavy rain. Nearly 400 people were killed and many were injured and displaced.

Housing is one of the main infrastructural investment sectors that experiences maximum damage after such typhoons: For example, Ketsana and Xansane together damaged, destroyed or washed away almost 600,000 houses. Achievements in national development through investments of public and private resources can be undone by such disasters, causing critical setbacks to long-term development. In such a context, reducing disaster risk, for example through building resilient housing, is crucial for future sustainable development in the country.

Housing vulnerability

While there are various definitions of 'resilience' (see for example UNISDR, 2009), a key common concept of resilience is the ability of a system (in this case housing) to be able to withstand an external impact (in this case typhoons) and *bounce back* to equilibrium. In this sense, resilient housing has the following two main aspects:

1. It is able to resist and survive through hazard impacts;
2. It does not collapse, requiring minimal repair after a disaster to function adequately.

Building physical and economic resilience in coastal areas is a tremendous challenge in Viet Nam. Despite the huge physical risks, people live in coastal areas because of livelihoods linked to fishing and aquaculture. Poverty is commonly attributed as the main reason why houses are built in such a way that they are vulnerable to hazards (see Figure 14.1), but a number of other factors exacerbate this vulnerability. Since the economic reforms initiated in Viet Nam during the 1980s (the *doi moi* policy), there has been a gradual transition from traditional building materials (bamboo, timber, thatch, etc.) to industrial products such as brick and concrete. However this has not been matched by the production of adequate quality of materials, or by an understanding of how to build properly with the new manufactured materials. For example, very thin walls of 13 centimetres of low quality brick are built with embedded slender reinforced concrete (RC) posts without a tie beam; or roofing is built with framing members running only in one direction. Houses thus built are easily damaged by typhoons.

Figure 14.1 Poverty is often cited as the main reason for vulnerability of such houses in Hue that are made of cheap materials and flimsy construction and easily damaged in typhoons

Additionally there is a lack of skilled professionals and builders in Viet Nam who can support the disaster risk reduction process. Therefore addressing housing vulnerability is not only about improved design and construction, or availability of funds, but also about training and building local capacity – as highlighted in this chapter.

Disaster resilient housing by DWF

Three architectural students in London founded the non-profit NGO called the Development Workshop France (DWF) in 1973. Since then, operating in more than 30 countries, DWF has endeavoured to develop local capacity for improved construction and livelihood development in vulnerable communities. It is one of the only agencies currently operating in Viet Nam with this mandate, despite the huge need for disaster risk reduced housing in coastal areas of the country. DWF employs local building techniques to meet the various challenges facing these communities, including natural disasters, working closely with local people and organisations in developing housing solutions. Its projects aim to reduce vulnerability, improve living conditions and create local jobs. Based in France, DWF is most active in West Africa and Southeast Asia with regional offices in Burkina Faso and Viet Nam respectively.

Since 1989, DWF has been gaining experience in disaster risk reduction and developmental work in coastal areas of central Viet Nam facing the risk of typhoons and has been actively promoting wind-resistant housing. Over a long time DWF houses have demonstrated their resilience to communities and hence gained local acceptance in Hue. Recently after the typhoons Xangsane (2006) and Ketsana (2009), 918 houses were rebuilt or repaired to hazard-resistant standards; with DWF's support (Brouant, 2006; IFRC, UN-Habitat & UNHCR, 2012) (see Figure 14.2).

All these houses incorporate DWF's ten principles of typhoon resistant construction (see www.dwf.org/en/content/ten-key-principles-cyclone-resistant-construction). The main technical concept underpinning the 10 Principles is to ensure that different parts of the building structure are firmly connected to each other to resist strong wind. In places that get flooded or experience storm surges, houses are built on a raised plinth of 1-1.5 metres (see Figure 14.2).

Figure 14.2 A disaster-resilient house built by DWF after Typhoon Xansane

The disaster recovery programs are combined with an ongoing Safer House campaign including training for hundreds of local builders, and it is attempted to disseminate the safer building principles through awareness campaigns animated by songs and folk drama. The campaign is targeted at various levels including mass media (TV, newspapers) and community gatherings, and is aimed at raising awareness and motivating people to build safer houses.

Along with housing, DWF also supports local early warning systems by providing training and equipment such as sirens and megaphones. The housing programs are integrated with livelihood support and implemented in coordination with local authorities. Further integration is achieved through the building of safe community facilities and infrastructure, including schools, harbours and dykes (see Figure 14.3).

Figure 14.3 This dyke built by DWF keeps the community safe in a village in Hue. The fishing boat here was provided by DWF as livelihood support after Typhoon Xansane

Although the main focus of DWF's work in Viet Nam is building and promoting disaster-resilient housing, it also supports wider community development through an integrated approach incorporating livelihoods and skills development, microcredit, school education, etc. Thus, when not helping to build houses, other vulnerabilities within the community are addressed to contribute further to its resilience and sustainability.

DWF's work highlights the impact that can be achieved through such projects that combine practical training and a range of technical and developmental inputs. The organisation has received a number of international and local awards, particularly for its work in central Viet Nam, such as the World Habitat Award (2008), UNISDR Sasakawa Award for Disaster Risk Reduction (2009) and the Hue Province Certificate of Merit (2008).

Identifying success factors

There are many challenges of working in a context such as Viet Nam, not the least poverty, but also widespread lack of awareness, skills and capacity in building disaster resilient housing. Nonetheless, despite such constraints, there are areas of success in DWF's work, which need to be acknowledged with a view to promote wider good practice. A number of factors in combination contribute to the success of DWF's work; some of the keys ones are identified below.

Internal factor: Organisation strengths & expertise

The fact that DWF has been operating in Viet Nam for more than two decades testifies to its organisational success. It is common that after a disaster agencies initiate and implement housing reconstruction projects and fold up their operation soon after project completion. Conversely, DWF has maintained its office and presence in central Viet Nam for an extended period, attempting to gradually consolidate the resilience of local communities. It employs a range of professionals - architects, engineers, social workers, *community animators*[25], etc. - who work together to address the multi-faceted problem of promoting and building safer housing that is integrated with a range of developmental inputs. The development initiative has been a two-way process: DWF's knowledge on typhoon-resistant construction has been derived from the specific hazards confronting central Viet Nam, and shaped from the local building materials and construction, which in turn is transmitted locally.

External factor: Extensive partnership networks

DWF works in close coordination with local government authorities - People's Committees[26] at the provincial and commune or ward levels - facilitating ownership of and consequently support for its developmental initiatives by key local stakeholders. DWF's projects are implemented by an established local construction company, Consultants, Designers and Constructors Corporation (CDC), under the Ministry of Construction, allowing further deepening of its local connection. Additionally, DWF is part of a network of development agencies working in Viet Nam, through which it shares its expertise in building resilient housing and thereby building the capacity of other agencies.

Importantly, DWF has succeeded in serving as a bridge between the international and local domains by gaining credibility and thus funding from a range of key international development agencies such as the European Commission Humanitarian Aid Office (ECHO), International Federation of Red Cross & Red

[25] 'Community animators' are staff members who work at the community level to raise awareness and motivate people to build resilient houses, often using folk drama and songs.
[26] The Vietnamese governmental administrative system consists of a system of tiers beginning with the central government and extending to urban wards and rural communes. At each tier, a People's Committee is nominated by the government to serve as the administrative body for formulating and implementing policy.

Crescent Societies (IFRC), Canadian International Development Aid (CIDA), the French Government and others. In this way it has been able to access international funds and utilise that for facilitating housing resilience and sustainable development at the local level.

Community factor: Consultative approach for local acceptability

A key success factor in DWF's housing work is the extensive consultation undertaken with individual households and builders to develop house designs that are acceptable to beneficiaries. Designs of houses of different sizes and costs incorporating resilient building techniques are produced by DWF architects (see DWF 2011). These are then shown and discussed with beneficiaries, who then consult the architects in choosing or adapting a particular house design that meets their needs. Each design is adapted in consultation with individual beneficiary households so that each house is tailored specifically to the site and the requirements of the household. Although similar strengthening techniques are used, no two houses are the same. Such an approach allows the house designs to be acceptable to the owners by meeting their specific household needs.

Wider impacts

Most of the money in the DWF housing reconstruction and repairing process goes to the local communities as building materials are procured from local shops, and builders and construction workers are local or from neighbouring areas. Along with housing reconstruction and repair, DWF provides support for restoration of livelihoods affected by disasters. For example, funding to buy fishing nets, boats and other equipment were provided to fisherman after the Xansane and Ketsana typhoons; farmers were funded to buy fertilisers and agricultural equipment; craftspersons were provided support to produce handicrafts. Even the suppliers of these materials were local and hence the local economy was supported further in the process.

Additionally, DWF supports the development and construction of community facilities and infrastructure. For example, a school with a teachers' residence was strengthened against typhoons, a safe harbour for fishing boats was improved and dykes to protect villages from flooding were built. In this way, improvement of the wider built environment linked to housing is achieved following an integrated development approach.

Another key impact of DWF's work is the development of skills of local builders in resilient construction methods through *on-the-job* training. This allows replication of these methods beyond the projects, as well as enabling the *know-how* to remain within the communities. The on-going Safer House campaign continues to reinforce this knowledge and experience.

Replication by other agencies

DWF is an active member of a network of development agencies working in Viet Nam and supports them for disaster risk reduction through safer housing. One such agency is Save the Children Fund–UK (SCF). After Typhoon Xansane, SCF adopted DWF's 10 Principles in the reconstruction of 90 houses and repair of 500 houses in Da Nang city, close to Hue (see Figure 14.4).

Figure 14.4 A house built by Save the Children Fund–UK in Da Nang

The architect of this project, Nguyen Thanh Binh, added his innovative ideas to the house design. Three continuous reinforced concrete (RC bands), one each at the top, middle and bottom of walls were included to give lateral strength for resisting typhoons (see Figure 14.5). A loft or RC mezzanine floor slab added more strength; the loft also provides refuge during floods. Concrete rainwater gutters and metal bars were used to secure the roof from lifting off in strong wind. 'My main concern was to design strong wind- resistant houses', emphasised Binh.

The design could be implemented easily in the local context and was affordable (US$1,200-1,500 in 2007). The innovations were based on local construction techniques and locally available materials. Like DWF, SCF provided training to local builders, and some households copied and replicated the resilient designs on their own.

Key stakeholder narratives

Although the key thrust of DWF's work is technical in nature, it should not be viewed only in an impersonal sense. Behind the technical inputs to build resilient housing is a human-interest factor, as became evident from personalised narratives of a range of stakeholders involved in the process, documented by the authors during fieldwork in Hue. These narratives illustrate the intangible but human motivations, experiences, feelings of satisfaction and aspirations that act as a mesh underlying success of the design and construction of resilient housing by DWF.

Figure 14.5 A structural drawing showing the three continuous RC beams (top, middle and bottom of walls) in the Save the Children house design

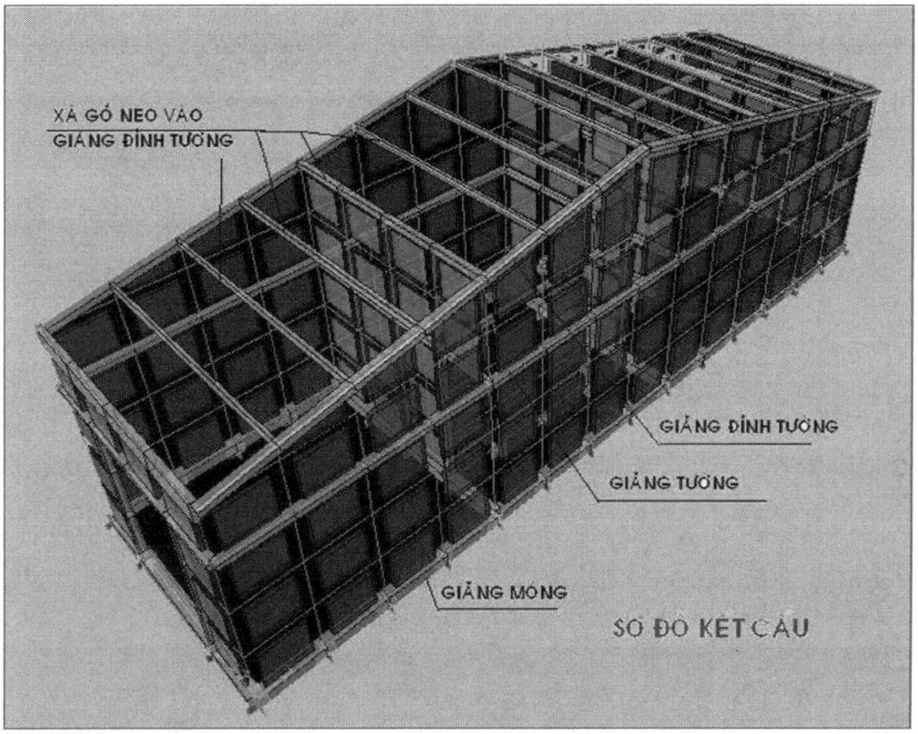

Source: NT Binh, Da Nang.

In a basic sense, there are two main stakeholder groups: (1) Those associated with the delivery process – the organisation itself and its staff, and supporting organisations and individuals (local authorities, partner agencies, builders, etc.); and (2) Those who benefit from the project, that is, local communities and beneficiary households. In the first group, a key stakeholder is the architect (or architects), responsible for conceiving the house designs and acting as a team leader in the implementation process by coordinating the inputs of others with the designs. In the second group, detailed insights can be found at the household level, the unit of the community.

The accounts in the preceding sections have been garnered from various stakeholders, including various individuals and staff members of DWF and associated agencies and a number of beneficiary households. In this section, it has been chosen to focus below on the narratives of the two key stakeholders – architects and beneficiary household – in order to align this chapter to the human aspect so vital to DWF's work.

Narrative 1: Architects

The work of built environment professionals, such as architects, in projects such as DWF's differs from their typical roles in design offices or consulting firms. Therefore the narratives of such local architects are important in understanding how these design and planning professionals contribute to the housing resilience and disaster risk reduction process. During the course of the research fieldwork, Architects Phan Duc Hanh and Pham Thi Thien Tro provided such important accounts, as presented below.

Hanh and Tro had been working at DWF for eight years. Previously they worked at the company that implements DWF's project, Consultants, Designers and Constructors Corporation (CDC). They enjoyed the work at DWF as they often went to the field, and both of them highlighted their interest in the community-based work and the special satisfaction they derived from it, summarised in the comment:

> *We like to visit the communities and meet different people. This work is not like sitting in an office in front of the computer all day. We feel happy to help the people in villages to build stronger homes.*

This indicates that such work appeals to persons with an interest in field-orientated work, but perhaps more importantly, they also tend to be motivated to help vulnerable people. This is underscored by their comments, 'One can learn more each time one goes to the field. For me it was a good opportunity to be able to work in a foreign organisation and learn new things', said Hanh. Tro said:

> *When I was a child I wanted to be a doctor. But my father is an artist and I was influenced by him and studied architecture. Before joining DWF, I used to work at a consulting firm, which is a partner of DWF, so I used to go to villages and meet many people. I began seeing the poverty there and wanted to help the people. That motivated me to work for DWF.*

Hanh and Tro studied architecture at Hanoi University, but their university education did not prepare them directly for this kind of work; they learnt from experience. Tro said:

> *However at university I learnt about design and construction, which helped me in this job. The DWF houses are small and it's not difficult to work on them, but it's more important to be able to understand what people need and how we can help them.*

Hanh added:

> *Like her, I wasn't trained in this field, but could pick up quickly because of my architectural education. Recently in 2010, I completed a master's degree in architecture at Hanoi University and did research on traditional houses in Hue. I realised that the Garden Houses here are protected from typhoons by the trees around them – one of DWF's 10 Principles.*

Both the architects want to continue in the same line of work and help vulnerable communities. 'I want to do more research on traditional architecture as it offers many lessons for my work,' said Hanh. Tro added:

> *I want to work in other places, maybe in another country, and learn from that. DWF has started some projects in the disaster-affected Mekong Delta on which I also work, which I enjoy. It's a different kind of experience there.*

Although there are some gradual changes in architectural education and practice in Viet Nam and there is now growing awareness of socially responsive architecture, Hanh and Tro both suggested a more 'practical' approach to architectural education:

> *It's still too theoretical and can't be applied in reality. A stronger connection to the field is needed; more surveys should be done in villages. Architectural magazines should include articles on this kind of work so that students can read about them.*

These comments highlight an important issue – the training and education of professionals, not only architects, to be able to function in a socially responsive capacity. This is particularly relevant in a country like Viet Nam, where vulnerability and poverty consistently undermine sustainable development goals. Despite the necessity of such education, architectural education in Viet Nam (and more broadly in the Asia-Pacific region) caters largely to the upper end of society and is modelled on curricula in Western industrialised countries. In such a context, organisations such as DWF offer a unique opportunity, for architects to gain experience in projects for vulnerable communities. Hanh summed this up in his comment:

> *DWF has been the bridge for me to connect to the international level on one end and the community level on the other end. I have gained a lot of confidence and skills to communicate with the local people. I now have a chance to do something practical in the communities.*

Because of DWF's other development projects in addition to housing, staff frequently went to the field to monitor, supervise and assess the projects, offering scope to develop special communication skills. DWF had a good relationship with local communities and both Hanh and Tro continued to visit and interact with them. Sometimes Hanh stayed back in the evening, having dinner and drinking beer with the men there. 'It's a good way to communicate,' he said. As Tro narrated, 'This work has improved my communication skills; I can talk to different types of people now. I am more confident. Most importantly, it makes me happy to be able to help the poor.' In addition to developing special professional skills, this type of work also contributes to the personal development of individuals, allowing them to play a more fulfilling role in society.

Thus this narrative of architects indicates on one hand alignment with the success factors behind DWF's work discussed earlier, and on the other hand demonstrates how the organisation has nurtured and built the capacity of a key professional group to contribute to sustainable development. While there are human and personal reasons for the architects to work in this field, it underscores the need for education and training of such professionals, which is largely lacking at the moment in the Southeast Asian region.

Narrative 2: Beneficiary

Mai Thi Yen lives with her husband and two children in a DWF-built house in Le Thai Thien village, Luc Tri commune, Hue (see Figure 14.6). Both Yen and her husband fish for a living in the large lagoon behind their house. Previously they lived in a small temporary type of house built with less durable materials. When Typhoon Xansane hit in 2006, the house collapsed totally. Many houses in this village were affected and most of them lost their roofs. As they lived right next to the lagoon, they were also hit by a storm surge of more than 1.5 metres and everything was washed away. DWF supported them after the storm and helped build this durable and resilient house. Yen also lost her fishing boat in the typhoon, the household's main means of livelihood. DWF gave her a new boat and fishing nets, and thereby enabled her family to recover its livelihood (see Figure 14.3). Yen expressed her gratitude for this: 'Before we didn't have the money to build a strong house and we suffered. DWF has saved us. Because of them, we now also have good conditions for our fishing work.'

Figure 14.6 Mai Thi Yen's house, built by DWF after Typhoon Xansane

In this village, DWF built seven such new houses to replace houses that were totally destroyed, and repaired and strengthened five more houses. Using local building materials and workers allowed supporting the local economy. To avoid floods, the house floors were raised at least a metre above the ground. A dyke was built along the lagoon to protect the village from floods and bank erosion (see Figure 14.3). This was designed carefully with culverts to allow the natural flow of water. In this way, the overall resilience of the community was strengthened. In addition to physical resilience, DWF raised awareness and capacity of the community to deal with disasters. As Yen narrated:

> *Because of this project, we came to know people at the Commune People's Committee. Now my husband is a member of the local Flood & Storm Committee and he has received training on early warning equipment; he goes from door to door to warn people if there is a disaster threat.*

After Yen's new house was built, she added a timber mezzanine floor for a loft to store household belongings. Two years after the house was built, Typhoon Ketsana hit the village in 2009, but this time Yen's house could withstand the strong winds and did not experience any damage. The loft then came in handy; the family took shelter there and escaped from the storm surge from the lagoon. This event strongly demonstrated the resilience of the house, resulting in the community's acceptance of the merit of DWF's work, summarised in Yen's assertion: 'I feel comfortable and safe that I no longer live in a temporary house and don't have to worry about typhoons.'

Households such as Yen's justifiably feel satisfied with receiving a free disaster resilient house of a durable quality that they could perhaps never afford to build on their own. However, in a context such as Viet Nam, the number of such households that live in vulnerable houses and need resilient shelter is colossal; rapid population growth and urbanisation, together with climate change, continues to inflate this number. Thus while households such as Yen's, and even her community to some extent, are safeguarded from future disasters by DWF's intervention, the resources that a small organisation like DWF can access and utilise fall greatly below the mark that is required to make a solid contribution to widespread resilience and sustainable development. Thus it is all the more important that the lessons offered by DWF are shared extensively so that there is wider uptake and replication by a larger cohort of agencies, including the government.

Learning from the case study of DWF: Future recommendations

The work of DWF offers valuable lessons for sustainable development of Viet Nam and the wider disaster-prone Southeast Asia region. Some of Viet Nam's neighbouring countries, for example the Philippines, are also impacted by the same typhoons, such as Xansane and Ketsana. Similar socio-economic and environmental conditions point to the potential for replication of the DWF approach elsewhere in Viet Nam and in the region. Key lessons learnt from DWF's work are:

1. The application of simple, but sound, technical principles (such as DWF's 10 Principles of Typhoon Resistant Construction) can contribute to resilience of housing to disasters and climate change impacts;

2. Working closely over a sustained period in consultation and partnership with local stakeholders and communities on shelter projects enables gaining local acceptance and support of new housing interventions;
3. Operating on multiple levels – international, national and local – allows building fruitful bridges between these levels and leads to a range of productive partnerships;
4. Teamwork between various professionals within a setup that allows gaining capacity in socially responsive professionalism can create an opportunity for such professional development even though such opportunity is largely lacking in mainstream educational institutions;
5. An integrated development approach within which building and promoting resilient housing is positioned offers greater potential for success;
6. Using local building materials and labour allows supporting the local economy and livelihoods, in turn contributing to sustainable development.

DWF is connected to the regional network of the Thailand-based Asian Disaster Preparedness Center (ADPC), which is highly active in Southeast and South Asia on a range of disaster risk reduction projects, so the networks for wider replication are already in place. The work is not new – it has been publicised in prominent publications since more than two decades (see Norton, Chantry & Vien, 1990) and has featured in various international discourses on disaster risk reduction.

Yet there is very little evidence of widespread replication or adaptation of DWF's concepts. DWF has continued to be a largely unique and isolated example. What are the reasons for that? Possibly a complex range of factors are responsible, indicating the need for further exploration with the view of identifying clear avenues and conduits that enable wider replication.

A key issue that perhaps points towards the answer is the small-scale nature of DWF's work. It is a small organisation based in a provincial city and has been operating to a large extent locally. The number of houses it has built is small compared to the vast numbers that are devastated by disasters: 918 houses repaired or built where nearly 600,000 were destroyed by Xansane and Ketsana. Admittedly DWF's Safer House campaign, training of builders and uptake by local communities over a long course of time has spread the impact, but yet, essentially, the work remains small in scale. But then, perhaps that is the reason for the success. Would DWF be able to retain its community outreach and local relevance if it grew into a large organisation? Would it then distance itself from the communities with which it now has such a strong connection?

Another critical concern is regarding the long-term: Although DWF has continued to work in Viet Nam for more than two decades, it cannot be assumed that DWF's presence in Viet Nam would be permanent. In the event of DWF leaving the area, how are the locals going to continue with DWF's initiative? To some extent, the training by DWF of a large number of local builders, householders and partner organisations ensures that the knowledge and skills would remain in the local context. However mobilising and harnessing the know-how through a global network of links requires an organisational set-up, such as that of DWF. Perhaps it is the time that DWF begins to consider developing local organisations alongside its current community development agenda to achieve greater sustainability such that others are able to hold the leadership reins even if DWF is not there.

Thus although the work of DWF represents a well-tested model for genuine sustainable development, it is also a stepping stone to a larger domain of development inquiry as embodied in the questions posed above. Analysis of the Viet Nam case study presented here has opened new windows for research that could further knowledge and building practices, on how disaster risk reduction and consequently sustainable development can be achieved on a wider scale in Viet Nam and elsewhere in Southeast Asia.

References

Brouant, O. (2006). *Rebuilding a safer future for families affected by cyclone N6 Xansane in central Vietnam* (project appraisal worksheet). Brussels: ECHO (European Commission for Humanitarian Aid Office).

DWF (2011). *Atlas of house vulnerability and strengthening*. Hue: DWF (Development Workshop France).

EM-DAT (2012). *The international disaster database*. Louvain (Belgium): Centre for Research on Epidemiology of Disasters (CRED). Online (accessed 5 September, 2012): http://www.emdat.be/natural-disasters-trends.

IFRC, UN-Habitat & UNHCR (2012). *Shelter projects 2010*. Geneva: IFRC (International Federation of Red Cross & Red Crescent Societies), UN-Habitat and UNHCR (United Nations High Commissioner for Refugees).

Minh, H.B. & Crimmins, C. (2006). Typhoon Xansane, flood toll reaches 169. Reuters on Reliefweb. Online (accessed 5 September, 2012): http://reliefweb.int/report/viet-nam/typhoon-xangsane-flood-toll-reaches-169.

Norton, J., Chantry, G. & Vien, N.S. (1990). Typhoon resistant building in Vietnam. *Mimar, 37*, 70-77.

UNISDR (2007). *Building disaster resilient communities: Good practices and lessons learned*. Geneva: UNISDR (United Nations International Strategy for Disaster Reduction).

UNISDR (2009). *Terminology on DRR*. Geneva: UNISDR (United Nations International Strategy for Disaster Reduction). Online (accessed 01 December 2012): www.unisdr.org/we/inform/terminology.

World Vision (2010). *Typhoon Ketsana: One year anniversary*. Hanoi: World Vision Vietnam.

Chapter 15

Capacity, sustainability and accountability in the face of modern development

Lessons from Oxfam Australia's development model in Cambodia

RUTH BOTTOMLEY

OVERVIEW

Oxfam Australia has worked in Cambodian villages for almost 20 years, delivering integrated community development that aimed to meet basic livelihood needs while encouraging community ownership and self-reliance. In the face of rapid economic development, this work could be undermined as communities are negatively impacted by economic concessions or major infrastructure projects. Based on qualitative research in two villages, this chapter considers how well the Oxfam Australia approach has assisted villagers to become engaged as citizens in shaping and defining their own development and demanding accountability from government officials

Introduction

Oxfam Australia has a long history of engagement in Cambodia, beginning in 1982 with an emergency humanitarian response, and then moving to a longer-term approach, bringing integrated community development to some of the poorest communities living in remote areas in the northeast and east of Cambodia (Barter, 2012). In recent years, this development work has taken place in a rapidly changing environment as Cambodia, like much of Southeast Asia, embarks on economic development, with large-scale infrastructure projects and land and forest concessions which frequently threaten the livelihoods of rural communities.

This chapter considers the effectiveness and sustainability of the Oxfam Australia integrated community development (ICD) approach in Cambodia from the perspective of citizenship. As a result of the long-term community development work of Oxfam Australia in their communities, to what extent have the poor and marginalised villagers become engaged as citizens in terms of participating in decisions about their own development and being able to hold the government to account? To what extent might these communities be able to have their voices heard in the future on issues that will impact their livelihoods as a result of the rapid economic development? The chapter concludes that while Oxfam Australia has laid the foundations for active citizenship through increased participation in development processes and by facilitating links to the local authorities, less success has been achieved in supporting communities to actually claim their rights and to ensure that there is institutional and organisational responsiveness from the government, particularly concerning development projects that may impact them negatively.

Background and context

The Oxfam Australia development approach

Since 1993 Oxfam Australia has implemented an integrated community development (ICD) programme in Cambodia, an approach originally developed to address the basic needs of rural communities who had experienced years of conflict, trauma and displacement. The ICD approach integrated a range of development activities, recognising that communities required a diverse range of livelihood and social interventions to assist them to re-establish their lives (Barter, 2012). The ICD approach combined the construction of basic infrastructure, food security, health, clean water and sanitation projects together with capacity development and community organising support. The first ICD project was set up in Takeo province, close to Phnom Penh in 1993, at a time when civil society was weak and insecurity prevalent. As security improved, the programme expanded to remote areas in the northeast of the country, to Kratie province in 1995, Stung Treng in 1997, and finally to Mondolkiri in 2009. These areas had little access to government services, NGOs and livelihood opportunities (Barter, 2012).

The ICD programme adopted what Oxfam Australia refers to as a tripartite system of programme implementation, in which the projects and activities are designed, developed and implemented by communities in partnership with Oxfam Australia and government counterparts at district level. Oxfam Australia believes that the approach has been beneficial in terms of facilitating interaction between the local authorities and communities, thereby strengthening community access to government services and decision-makers and enabling the local government to have an improved understanding of the needs of rural communities. It was also hoped that through this approach Oxfam Australia would be able to influence local government by promoting and modelling 'best practice' for development, for example ensuring transparency and accountability at all stages of the project design and implementation (Barter, 2012).

A bottom-up participatory approach was employed, with community members involved in identifying and explaining their specific needs through participatory rural appraisal (PRA) activities. Initial activities in the early years of programme implementation often included building schools and establishing health and literacy programmes. Oxfam Australia also facilitated the establishment of community committees to manage and oversee the development activities. Rice banks, buffalo banks, savings groups, livestock associations, community fisheries, village health support groups and women's self-help groups were established in many of the villages and local people were trained to manage and run the committees and project activities, encouraging community ownership and self-reliance, while building skills in project management and decision-making. Village development committees, part of the government structure in each village, were strengthened and supported to oversee the preparation and implementation of the village development plans.

Sustainability in the context of the ICD programme is founded on a desire for the activities to be set up in a way that will enable them to continue in the future beyond the time frame of the actual Oxfam Australia intervention (Oxfam Australia, 2009; Rounce, 2010; Crossroads to Development, 2010). Developing a sense of ownership and self-governance of the activities by both the communities and government partners appears to be a key aspect of the strategy to achieve sustainability (Oxfam Australia, 2009; Rounce, 2010). Participatory approaches, capacity building, primarily through training and experiential project management and implementation, and the development of local committees and management systems have been fundamental to efforts to ensure sustainability in this regard (Rounce, 2011; Barter, 2012). Latterly the concern for sustainability has taken on new dimensions as rapid, large-scale economic development has the potential to undermine years of work to improve livelihoods. In this context, Oxfam Australia is also considering how much their work has equipped poor communities to understand these threats and to advocate for their rights and needs.

Oxfam Australia is phasing out of its community development programme in Cambodia and moving to a regional programme on Mekong water governance. The ICD programme officially closed in mid-2012, although Oxfam Australia is continuing to monitor the situation in the target areas and will also involve some of the communities in the broader Mekong governance work.

The concept of citizenship in a changing environment

In recent years the focus of much participatory development has turned towards a concern for increasing the ability of poor and marginalised people to influence the decision-making processes that affect their lives (Cornwall and Gaventa, 2001; Gaventa, 2004). This shift to citizen engagement in policy and governance is very much in line with the adoption of a rights-based approach in development contexts, recasting participation as a right rather than simply an invitation to beneficiaries of development (Gaventa, 2004). While the original aim of the Oxfam Australia programme was to meet the immediate food security and livelihood needs of the communities and to provide access to essential services, over the years there has been an increasing focus on rights and building the skills, capacities and knowledge of the community members and leaders so that they have a better command of their own development.

Today the concept of citizenship is an important one for Oxfam Australia, which has a commitment to support poor and marginalised people to become active citizens and to hold their governments to account (Oxfam Australia, n.d.). By active citizenship, Oxfam refers to the rights and obligations that link individuals to the state (Clarke and Missingham, 2009). It implies that active citizens can use their rights to improve the quality of their life through involvement with the state agencies that are responsible for the provision of services. It refers to ordinary people developing self-confidence and becoming 'empowered', individually or as a group, so that they have the ability to negotiate and influence decisions and confront poverty and injustice (Clarke and Missingham, 2009).

The need for vulnerable people living in poverty to be able to claim their rights and to work to change the policies and practices of governments, corporations and international organisations and to hold them to account for their responsibilities is becoming increasingly important in Cambodia as economic development widens the gap between rich and poor, urban and rural. Over the last decade, Oxfam Australia's community development work has been taking place in a rapidly changing environment, in which communities are faced with major national and trans-boundary economic development projects encroaching on their land and way of life (Ransley *et al.*, 2008). Infrastructure projects, hydro-power and mining, logging and economic land concessions all have a high potential for serious negative impacts for some of the poorest communities, threatening the landscape and way of life for many of the people Oxfam Australia has been working with (Barter, 2012).

Rural communities are frequently not informed or consulted in the process of these developments and are disempowered through a lack of information about the projects and possible options for recourse. Rural families tend to focus on individual household livelihood needs and lack opportunities for sharing information within communities. Ethnicity, poor public education, illiteracy and a lack of access to media and decision-making structures often isolates them from any dialogue processes that may happen around these projects. Their vulnerability is further increased by insecure tenure and control over the land, river and forest resources on which their livelihoods depend.

With the phasing out of the Oxfam ICD programme and the looming potential threats from economic development projects, Oxfam Australia was keen to review how much their programme had been effective in assisting communities to have their voices heard, particularly when confronted by major development projects that may impact negatively on their livelihoods. The following sections consider how the ICD programme, through its focus on participation and the tripartite approach, has encouraged active citizenship and improved the villagers' understanding of and ability to assert their basic rights.

The research project

The findings are drawn from empirical research that was conducted in April and May 2012 as part of a broader study undertaken under the Monash University-Oxfam Australia Partnership. The study aims to examine community understandings of and accessibility to accountability mechanisms in the context of infrastructure and development projects that are impacting on their lives and livelihoods. The study examines three case studies of communities in different geographic locations in Cambodia, each affected by different projects or challenges to their way of life and each with different levels of engagement with local and international NGOs. This chapter draws on findings from the first case study, focusing on two remote, rural villages in the northeast of Cambodia where Oxfam Australia has been working. While the study was not an evaluation of the Oxfam Australia ICD programme, the findings outlined in this chapter contribute to the reflections currently being conducted by Oxfam Australia following their long engagement in Cambodia.

The field research was conducted in Sre Kresaing village in Stung Treng province and in Kampong Roteh village in Kratie province. Sre Kresaing is situated along the Mekong river and Kampong Roteh is located on the Mekong island of Koh Tnoth. Both communities are poor and rely on the natural resources of the river for their livelihoods and cultural practices. The 120 families in Kampong Roteh are predominantly Khmer with some Kuoy indigenous people. The main livelihood activities are rice and vegetable farming, animal raising and fishing. The village will need to be re-located if the proposed Sambor dam goes ahead. Sre Kresaing village comprises a population of ethnic Khmer and Lao, with a total of 339 families. The main livelihood activities are rice and *chamkar*[27] farming, fish raising, small business and labouring. While the village will not be displaced by the proposed Lower Sesan II dam, there could be some substantial downstream impacts on fishery resources.

The research team comprised an expatriate research coordinator and two Cambodian research officers recruited specifically for the project. Four research assistants, seconded from local universities, also joined the team in the field. The

[27] *Chamkar* refers to cultivation of crops other than paddy rice.

research tools were developed collaboratively by the in-country research team and academic staff from Monash University in line with a broader set of questions guiding the overall study. Detailed semi-structured interviews were used to interview community members, committee members, government counterparts, local authorities and Oxfam Australia staff to ascertain their views on the Oxfam Australia activities, village and commune decision-making processes, dispute resolution, community mobilisation, interaction with the government, and any perspectives they had on the potential large-scale development projects. Key informants at community level were initially identified by both Oxfam Australia staff and community gatekeepers such as the village chief. While it is recognised that this perhaps introduced a certain amount of bias into the selection of informants, the research team developed criteria for the selection of participants to ensure that a broad-cross section of the community was reached. The criteria included demographics such as ethnicity, gender, age, income/wealth, source of livelihood, length of time in the community and physical location in the community. If identified informants were not available the team randomly selected other informants, either referred by existing informants or identified by the team during their stay in the village. Participatory mapping exercises such as time lines, venn diagrams and force field analysis, were facilitated with groups of five to six participants selected according to the criteria developed by the research team. All interviews and mapping exercises were conducted in Khmer language, with transcripts from the recorded interviews and field notes later being translated into English. Interviews were also conducted with Oxfam Australia staff in Phnom Penh, and a literature review of relevant reports and evaluations was carried out.

Investigation outcomes

Enhanced participation

The concept of participation is familiar in development discourse, and is increasingly being connected to citizenship and democratic governance. Participation is the first key step in citizenship, and citizen engagement can be linked positively to achieving development and democratic outcomes (Gaventa and Barrett, 2010). The core of the Oxfam Australia programme revolved around participatory techniques that enabled local communities to determine their development needs and to be involved in the actual implementation of the activities and monitoring of the results. People were organised around committees responsible for overseeing and implementing the activities. The involvement in the committees allowed for strengthened participation and agency, and by seeing themselves as actors, rather than simple, passive beneficiaries, there is evidence that both individuals and groups were better able to assert their citizenship and seek greater accountability within the framework of the project.

Many of the committee members interviewed spoke of how they had improved their own skills and obtained some level of individual empowerment through their participation in the committees and development activities. During the interview process the research team found that committee members were confident to express their opinions and had a good knowledge about village meetings and development processes. Interviewees mentioned training that they had received both in technical skills and also in management, leadership, facilitation skills and report writing. It was often mentioned that their participation in the Oxfam activities and on the committees had helped them to increase their knowledge and confidence so that they felt they had more ability to speak out at meetings. A male village health worker explained, 'Yes I have changed myself. I dare to speak, educate and share ideas. Before I was so shy.' A female member of a village savings committee noted, 'There have been a lot of changes for me. For instance, during meetings I have become braver since I have experienced various training courses, so I have some understanding and can get my voice heard on any plan discussed.' The ability of women to speak out and be more involved in discussions was something that was also mentioned by local authorities and leaders. A traditional leader in Kratie said, 'In the past, when we asked the women, they knew nothing, but now they can answer quickly.'

Oxfam Australia staff members feel that community members have become more empowered through the activities. As one provincial staff member reflected, 'Normally they did not understand why it is important to make decisions and how important their opinion is. But as time goes by, I noticed they have more understanding and expressed more opinions on women's involvement, village development and communication ... Later they were prepared to be involved in the district council, or as deputy chief of the village and so on. As such they started to feel proud and understood their value.' It was found that several committee members from both the villages had been elected to take up positions in the local authorities or commune council, which was mainly attributed to their pro-activeness and decision-making ability in the committees.

As groups, the strengthening of community structures such as the village development committees and the establishment of the other sub-committees, provided people with the experience of how being organised can have an impact.[28] The organising of the committees provided people with the experience of electing representatives, receiving training on roles and responsibilities, and in preparing village development plans. The value of getting things done as part of a committee or group was expressed by many of the interviewees. The government officials recognised that the groups brought people together to help themselves, but also contributed to the ability of people to participate in decision-making. As one government official noted, 'They are braver when they work in a group. If they do not work in a group they dare not to express their ideas in a meeting.'

Another benefit of working in committees or groups that was noted by the interviewees was the fact that it allowed for the sharing and dissemination of information among the group members. The setting up of the committees also

[28] Personal communication with Oxfam Australia staff members, 24th September 2012.

created a space for allowing people to meet, to discuss and make decisions, something that had been limited before when households had remained relatively isolated from each other with little chance to meet to discuss issues. A community leader explained, 'When we are in groups we can understand a lot because we can gather the villagers to create a group to unite with each other and exchange ideas.'

While there is evidence that the participatory approach employed by Oxfam both empowered individuals and increased the dialogue and consultation between people in the village, participation also comes with its own issues of power (Nelson & Wright, 1995). Communities are not holistic entities but are comprised of individuals with differing ideas, needs, capacities and motivations. Citizen participation is not something that can be achieved universally and much depends on how citizens take up the opportunities presented and also the conditions under which the poorest and most marginalised are able to participate. As Gaventa and Valderrama (1999) point out, 'citizen participation is about power and its exercise by different social actors in the spaces created for the interaction between citizens and local authorities.' During the research it was noted that there was a clear difference in knowledge between those community members who held senior positions in the committees and those who were just members. This was also noticed by government staff, as one commented, 'Usually there are 15 members in each group, and there are only two to three members who are intelligent decision makers.' Villagers who were interviewed who were not members of committees had far less understanding of village development processes and also had less access to information. The research found that non-committee members, especially women, were more likely to give a summary, deferential answer, such as 'I don't know'. It appears that there was little transferral of skills, knowledge and information to non-committee members. If they knew about the development activities, they were more likely to list the tangible assets, such as buildings, latrines, water filters and buffalo, rather than building skills and community cohesion. As one respondent stated, 'Like I told you, I have no idea regarding what they are doing in this village. So far I have never been informed about any information from my village or commune chief.'

Certain villagers were members of several of the committees and had obviously gained a lot from the experience, both in terms of personal development and material benefits. However, other groups and individuals in the communities were excluded or absent from the activities, suggesting that there are still significant barriers to encouraging the engagement of less vocal and powerful members of communities. Interviewees speculated that this was perhaps due to lower levels of knowledge, a lack of literacy skills and a lack of time to participate. While Oxfam made every effort to work at times of the day and times of the year when workloads are lighter, participatory approaches are time consuming and for those struggling to earn a living on a day to day basis, the time to participate in meetings is limited. Many of the villagers who did not participate mentioned lack of time as the main constraint to their participation, and even those who were members of committees noted how it meant they were now always busy and had less time than before. Rounce (2011) also noted that the capacity of the poorest for investment to join a group that required initial capital investment also tended to exclude them from participating.

Participation in relation to citizenship refers to the shift from the participation of 'beneficiaries' in projects to the more political and rights-based definitions of participation by citizens who become the 'makers and shapers' of their own development (Cornwall and Gaventa, 2001). While it seems clear that the participatory approach of Oxfam did help to empower people and build skills and confidence which they previously lacked, there is less evidence that they have been able to employ these skills to influence the broader decision-making and policy environment outside of projects. Participation in the Oxfam Australia ICD programme was around a frame of reference of development projects, such as rice banks, buffalo banks and savings groups. Thus it is often difficult for people to have the agency to make choices or influence decisions outside these frames of reference. Davis (2010) also found that the participation in the programme had not resulted in a broader conceptualisation of Oxfam Australia and its position in relation to the government and other local and international development agencies.

With low levels of education, rural villagers in particular often feel inferior to those in higher positions who are more educated and self confident. A local government official, when talking about the community perceptions of the impacts of large-scale development projects noted, 'They dare not talk about these issues in the face of high-rank officials. They just talk with their peers.' This does raise the question as to whether participatory engagement around projects is in itself enough to build the knowledge and agency required to challenge or participate in the decision-making around the larger, macro-level policy issues.

Linking citizens to the state

A key aspect or challenge of citizenship is linking ordinary people to the institutions, especially those of the state, that affect their lives. Often state institutions are remote and neither responsive nor accountable to the poor. Closing the distance between the state and the people and building relationships is an important goal to achieve. As Gaventa (2004) explains, 'as participatory approaches are scaled up from projects to policies, they inevitably enter the arena of government, and find that participation can become effective only as it engages with issues of institutional change.'

The Oxfam Australia projects helped to develop relationships between the community members and the local authorities charged with the task of working with the community. The government counterparts remained government employees but worked for up to 15 days per month as community facilitators and technical advisors. They were involved in the operational planning and delivery of projects and provided technical support to the various committees and activities. They also attended bi-monthly coordination meetings held in the villages.

The fact that local government officials worked on a regular basis in the villages meant that they were much more aware of the issues faced by the communities and could understand the practical needs of the local people. Several of the government counterpart staff had worked in the role for nearly 10 years and so had built up a comprehensive understanding of their areas of responsibility. Government officials interviewed during the course of the research stated that due to their knowledge of the field, they were able to pass on information to their department about the situation at local level. As one district official noted, 'Working with Oxfam Australia, I can visit villages and know the situation there, the situation in the village ... I can know more. In turn, in regard to work at the district office, I have learnt a lot, such as sharing information. For example, er ... the officials in the district office have no idea about the situation because they do not visit the villages.' The enhanced knowledge of local livelihoods also meant that they were able to reflect on the potential impacts of the large-scale hydropower projects. One official, noting fewer fish, extremes of weather and increased weed in the river commented, 'Thus I just wonder why they still carry out the dam project if there are so many impacts.'

However, the ability of the local district officials to raise concerns to higher levels appears questionable, and it seems there is a further gulf between the lower level district and provincial officials and central government. As one district staff member noted, 'We cannot change the project because it is the government project. Large projects are not easy to change like the small projects, ones which only spend only one or two million.' Another district administrator mentioned that there had been a meeting about a planned hydropower dam with more senior government officials, but because 'they had planned things already, they told us about the positive impacts more than the negative ones.' It was also apparent that the local authorities at commune and district level often had little information about the large scale development projects. A study by Kim and Öjendal (2007) also found that local authorities at commune and district level are often 'kept in the dark' by higher authorities and lack influence in the political hierarchy, which can result in a lack of responsiveness or willingness to take responsibility.

Because the Oxfam Australia staff worked closely with the communities and developed strong relationships of trust, the government counterparts were also accepted by the communities despite the fact that, due to the numerous regime changes of recent history, rural Cambodian villagers often have little trust or confidence in the local authorities (ANSA-EAP, 2010). However, the communities were often found not to differentiate between the Oxfam Australia staff and the government counterparts. While this indicates the level of trust that Oxfam was able to bring, it does also raise the question of the ability of the people to validly identify the government agents. Throughout the course of the project, some local government staff members were recruited as Oxfam staff, which further diffused the lines between government officials and NGO facilitators.

Many local communities in Cambodia have lacked any effective government services for many years and are used to international and local NGOs filling this gap. The research found that the communities did not see the activities as led by the government at all, despite the involvement of the government counterparts. Instead, the activities were always referred to as part of the Oxfam Australia project. Davis (2010) had similar findings, and also found that despite the work of the government counterparts, the communities he interviewed said that they still mistrusted the government. This also leads us on to the question as to whether government counterparts perceived they were conducting government work, or whether they felt they were simply seconded to an NGO project, which could have implications for future sustainability and continuation of the work between the district level government and the communities. The research found that there was a lot of uncertainty on the behalf of the government officials as to how they would be able to continue the work in the future without the Oxfam Australia budget and support, a finding also reported by Rounce (2011). A member of the Department of Women's Affairs noted that future work would probably be done through their networks of focal points, but that it would not be as easy as doing the actual practical work and meeting people in person. Some counterparts even drew a distinction between the work of Oxfam and the way the government works, noting that while NGO work is coordinated, government work is directed from the top down. As one official explained, 'To be honest, if we work with the government, we will not observe directly without any support. This is the weakness of the government. So if we want to visit [the village] we may wait for the order from the upper level on how to do it ... the upper level orders to observe or visit, not coordinate, but order.'

Despite this, during the course of the project there have been some positive developments which suggest that, at least between the village and commune level, activities and coordination may continue to take place. The establishment of the commune councils in 2002, as part of the government programme for decentralisation, provided a local level governance unit which enabled the Oxfam Australia programme to link village development planning with local level government planning. In the two villages visited, the commune councils hold monthly meetings with the village authorities and committee members to provide for updates on activities. There were also signs of bottom-up linkages to the authorities, where members of the village development committees or other committees had moved up to take official positions as village leaders or within the commune council. As one commune council member explained, 'There were savings group leaders and they attended much training with Oxfam. Therefore they improved their awareness and dared to express their ideas in meetings. Seeing this, the commune chief knows that they are qualified and dared to express ideas. Finally they can work as village chief or commune council members.'

The programme has also tried to ensure that the village development plans are fed into the commune investment plans, thus ensuring that villagers are voicing their development needs and influencing the development plans of the commune. While Oxfam Australia staff are able to cite cases where this has been effectively achieved, there is still uncertainty as to how the local development planning process will continue once Oxfam Australia withdraws and there are less donor funds available.

Oxfam Australia hoped that by working closely with the local level authorities, best development practice could be shared and instilled. In its programme work, Oxfam Australia made a serious attempt to be transparent about is goals and practices and established two-way channels of communication around planning and implementation. Information shared with the communities and local government counterparts included project budgets, operational plans, time lines, labour requirements and the respective contributions of the communities, the counterparts and Oxfam Australia. As an Oxfam Australia staff member explained, 'We are open. Our project is open, written and presented to the villagers on which activity is approved to be implemented in the village and how much [the cost] of the activity.' Oxfam Australia staff believe this openness did reduce the risk of corruption.[29] Government counterparts were also aware of the need for transparency and accountability in the Oxfam programme and were able to explain the process: 'We need to tell people the amount of money that we received from Oxfam to carry out the project. We also need to tell them the amount of money that we give them for food, transportation and so on.' However, as yet there is no clear indication as to whether the government officials viewed these procedures as only relevant to the work with Oxfam Australia or whether they could see the applicability of them to their own work with the government.

Implications for the field

When the Oxfam Australia ICD programme began, Cambodia was emerging from more than 30 years of civil war and turmoil which had left the population traumatised and poor. The approach taken by Oxfam was initially a needs-based approach which continued throughout the life of the programme. However, overtime the programme began to introduce a stronger focus on rights and building the participants' skills, capacities and knowledge, so that they were better able to lead and shape their own development. The second approach reflects more the aspects of citizenship and theoretical debates regarding 'rights-based programming', which now form a central part of the Oxfam regional programme. However, how much did this combined approach of needs and rights enable the communities that Oxfam Australia worked with engage as active citizens around the large-scale development issues that concern them?

Oxfam Australia continued to keep the programme grounded in the livelihood needs of the communities. According to the Cambodia-based Oxfam staff, this was based on the premise that poor people cannot participate effectively or meaningfully if they are not meeting basic food needs.[30] The buffalo banks, rice banks, community fisheries and improved agricultural techniques all supported the aim to improve and stabilise livelihoods. Improved health care and literacy also created an enabling environment for people to be better able to participate. Evaluations of the Oxfam Australia programme show that food security in the target areas did improve (Rounce, 2011; Crossroads to Development, 2010).

---

[29] Email correspondence with Oxfam Australia staff 24th October 2012.

[30] Personal communication with Oxfam Australia staff 24th September 2012

SPARC[31] (quoted in Cornwall and Gaventa, 2001), note that the poor will not be taken seriously if the level of engagement with the state is only confrontational or ideological. 'No doubt advocacy is important, but it must be rooted in the practical difficulties that the poor face daily: poverty, homelessness, lack of access to services, education and health.' The Oxfam Australia approach ensured that all activities were firmly rooted in dealing with the practical difficulties faced by the poor, rural communities with which they worked. The ICD projects also created spaces for citizens to exercise their voice and to make decisions about development projects to meet their needs. Livelihoods have improved and communities developed skills in technical areas of expertise, such as agriculture and health, and also in community organising and managing and running their own development committees. However, the speed of economic development in Cambodia has been extremely rapid and in many ways was counter to the development approach of Oxfam Australia, which invested in communities for a long period of time to allow for greater community ownership over activities, thus presenting a substantial challenge to the programme in terms of how to respond to the external pressures of economic development and 'skill up' the communities and facilitators in the time required.

From projects to issues

While Oxfam Australia set up good structures for committees around need-based development activities, it appears that these may have constrained the ability to address broader issues outside of the immediate micro-level development projects. The programme focus was largely on the village projects, with the information flow being mainly on project issues and processes such as reporting, budgeting, implementation, and monitoring. In more recent years Oxfam Australia began to engage some of the community and committee leaders, particularly the community fisheries groups, and government counterparts in national-level workshops to talk about the macro-issues, such as the hydropower dams, but this engagement appears to have been intermittent and was not incorporated more broadly in to the programme. As one government official explained, they were involved in distributing leaflets about the hydropower dam construction and asking whether people agreed, and what they felt the impacts would be. 'After people put their signature, we collected the leaflets and sent to advocacy groups in Phnom Penh, but I do not know what the advocacy groups in Phnom Penh will do with the leaflets. We just disseminated and distributed the leaflets to the people.' Interviewees mentioned that they had attended workshops and training carried out by Oxfam in collaboration with other NGOs on the possible affected areas and were able to share the information with other villagers through the committees. However, there was less engagement and follow-up on the issues at a local level. In hindsight, Oxfam Australia believes more should have been done to facilitate increased dialogue between the people and the authorities on these macro-issues, and to support the development of advocacy

[31] An association of slum dwellers in Bombay

plans and strategies to include within the village development plans, although this was never an explicit goal of the ICD programme.[32] The communities would have benefited from more knowledge in terms of mobilising and organising to address issues beyond the project activities and in finding out how to access relevant information. Tools such as action research and exposure visits to other communities impacted by dams and mega-infrastructure could have increased awareness of potential impacts, initiated alliances and networks, and provided more of a context for the rights training provided by the programme.

Spaces of interaction

The Oxfam Australia programme worked closely with local level government and some modest gains were made in bringing the state closer to the citizens by collaborating with the counterparts from the district authorities and ensuring the integration of village development plans into commune level plans. However, while it seems that work with the government helped to develop the skills, capacities and understanding of individuals, there was less focus on influencing the government departments beyond the individuals in terms of work practice and accountability. Counterparts clearly increased their knowledge about the local areas and the potential negative impacts of large scale infrastructure, but at the bottom of the government hierarchy, they also had little ability to influence and thus were constrained in their responsiveness to issues outside of the project mandate. This also raises the question as to how effectively communities can demand accountability through the conventional, local government structures when it often appears that decision-making concerning large-scale national and trans-boundary economic development projects bypasses these levels of authority.

Despite this, increased citizen participation in government dialogue and processes and greater responsiveness of the state institutions to the people, could have been facilitated by focusing more attention on the interaction and spaces between the government and the people. As Gaventa (2004) argues, closing the gap between the citizens and the state requires working on both sides of the equation, 'going beyond 'civil society' or 'state-based' approaches, to focus on their intersection, through new forms of participation, responsiveness and accountability'. Of course, this also has to be considered within the political context of the country and in Cambodia at this present time the avenues for decision-making and participation remain extremely limited and there is little real decentralization of power. However, the Oxfam Australia programme could have engaged more with the local authorities at an institutional level and focused on the mechanisms and learning obtained from bringing the communities and the authorities together. Valuable lessons could be drawn from the initiatives where there was successful cooperation with and response from government departments. The community fisheries project, for example, did have some success in terms of establishing fishing zones and conservation areas and registering these with the support of the district department of fisheries. Analysing and documenting the

---

[32] Email correspondence with Oxfam Australia staff 24th October 2012.

lessons learned on the processes and conditions that enable models based on local actions to be scaled up and supported through the broader policy mechanisms will in the future enable stronger cooperation between communities and local authorities and ensure that there is better institutional and organisational responsiveness from the government.

Conclusion

This chapter has examined at a broad level the integrated community development programme of Oxfam Australia in rural areas of Cambodia and has considered the extent to which the programme assisted the communities to become engaged as citizens in shaping and defining their own development and demanding accountability from government officials. It is clear that over the years Oxfam Australia has had a tangible impact on the communities in terms of improving food security and livelihood needs and in laying the foundations for active citizenship through participation in the development process and facilitating links to local authorities. However, there is less evidence from the research that the villagers of Kampong Roteh and Sre Kresaing are able to participate in dialogue around economic development projects which will likely impact quite severely on their livelihoods, nor that a level of engagement has been achieved with the local authorities, which could create new spaces for policy level dialogue between state actors and communities. Despite this, the analysis provides some clear indications of how development organizations can continue to work towards the goals of active citizenship by shifting beyond project based participation and dialogue to widen engagement with policy level issues and by focusing on enhancing the mechanisms and processes for interaction between state and citizens.

References

ANSA_EAP. (January 2010). *The Evolving Meaning of Social Accountability in Cambodia*. Manila: Affiliated Network for Social Accountability in East Asia and the Pacific (ANSA-EAP).

Barter, D. (2012). *Our Cambodian Legacy: Oxfam Australia*. Oxfam Australia.

Clarke, M. & Missingham, B. (2009). Guest Editors' Introduction: Active Citizenship and Social Accountability. *Development in Practice,* volume 19, issue 8, pages 955-963.

Cornwall, A. & Gaventa, J. (2001). *From users and choosers to makers and shapers: repositioning participation in social policy*. Sussex: Institute of Development Studies.

Crossroads to Development, (2010). *Integrated community development project: Final Evaluation report*. Phnom Penh: Oxfam Australia.

Davis, T. (2010). *Oxfam Australia Accountability and Cohesion Review: Cambodia.* Melbourne: Oxfam Australia and the University of Melbourne.

Gaventa, J. (2004). Towards Participatory Local Governance: Assessing the Transformative Possibilities. In Hickey S. and Mohan G. (eds.), *Participation: From Tyranny to Transformation.* London: Zed Books, pp.25-41.

Gaventa, J. & Barrett, G. (2010). *So What Difference Does it Make? Mapping the Outcomes of Citizen Engagement: IDS Working Paper 347*. Sussex: Institute of Development Studies.

Gaventa, J. & Valderrama, C. (1999). *Participation, citizenship and local governance: Background note prepared for a workshop on 'strengthening participation in local governance'*. Sussex: Institute of Development Studies.

Kim S. & Öjendal, J. (2007). *Where Decentralisation meets Democracy: Civil Society, Local Government, and Accountability in Cambodia.* Phnom Penh: Cambodia Development Resource Institute.

Nelson, N. & Wright, S. (1995). Participation and Power. In N. Nelson and S. Wright (eds) (1995), *Power and Participatory Development: Theory and Practice.* London: IT Publications.

Oxfam Australia. (2009). *Final Report on Integrated Community Development: Stung Treng Program 2010-11.* Phnom Penh: Oxfam Australia

Oxfam Australia. (n.d.). Central Commitments: Active citizenship and accountability. Retrieved from www.oxfam.org.au/about-us/assessing-our-performance/what-we-plan-to-achieve/central-commitments.

Ransley, C., Cornford, J. & Rosien, J. (2008). *A Citizen's Guide to the Greater Mekong Subregion: Understanding the GMS program and the role of the Asian Development Bank.* Melbourne: Oxfam Australia.

Rounce, T. (2011). *Final Evaluation: Integrated Community Development ICD, Kratie 2008-2011.* Phnom Penh: Oxfam Australia.

Chapter 16

Cultural traditions, sustainable livelihoods and community-based ecotourism

Alternative development paths for tourism on Bali

CHRISTIAN BYCZEK

OVERVIEW

Tourism development has created substantial sustainability challenges for Bali in Indonesia. This chapter shows that community-based ecotourism initiative, *Jaringan Ekowisata Desa,* promoting traditional ecological knowledge and resource management practices can empower local communities with the ability to help mitigate effects of a rapid shift from an agriculture-based economy to a service-based economy.

The beginnings of applied psychology

This chapter describes the links between cultural traditions and the sustainable development of community-based ecotourism in Bali, Indonesia. Balinese farmers and fishermen have created unique experiences by accommodating visitors in home-stays and letting them participate in their daily activities. This case study is within the Jaringan Ekowisata Desa (JED) ecotourism village network, which is assisted by Yayasan Wisnu, an environmental NGO.

The communities seek to meet criteria such as minimizing negative impacts on the ecology, creating environmental awareness, enhancing financial benefits for conservation and community development, generating incomes for community members as well as fostering intercultural exchange and understanding. Owned and managed by the communities themselves, the network aims at empowering its stakeholders, enabling their political participation and ensuring their entitlements in natural resource management on the local level. The network has established the venture in reaction to several conflicts that have arisen with massive tourism development on the island over the past decades. According to the network's website, JED is 'a strong statement from four communities who want to decide for themselves the future of their people, their culture and their environment'. (JED, 2007) Conflict has long existed between property developers and the tourism industry in opposition with farmers and local communities as well as representatives of religious associations. Media and advocates of the traditional culture as well as members of the Balinese intelligentsia often support the latter group. There are also frictions between modern and traditional spheres as well as between localizing and globalizing forces.

The stakeholders of JED have utilized their model of society and their farming and resource management practices as a pioneering model to be adapted in their educational approach to tourism. Traditional knowledge and local forms of wisdom such as the Hindu-Brahman Tri Hita Karana (THK) philosophy are important foundations on which their livelihoods are based. The THK concept aims at human well-being through regulating the relationships between human and divine beings and the natural environment. With a religion that regards every plant as of divine nature, it is not difficult to comprehend that the environment is treated with great respect. Furthermore, the THK concept holds that subsistence farmers and even commercial farmers do not overwork their gardens and plantations.

JED incorporates a decision-making process that includes a consideration of agricultural as well as tourism-related activities. Also, the decision-making process is conducted within community organizations on a local level, where JED integrates official government structures as well as customary organizations and farming associations. JED is currently growing a larger island-spanning network and is a model for sustainable development through community-based tourism activities in an increasing number of villages on Bali.

Tourism-led development as sustainability challenge for an island destination

A century ago the Balinese society was mainly agricultural and its economy was based on subsistence farming. Even today the majority of the Balinese work in agriculture. However, tourism has taken hold of the island's economy as one of the strongest contributor to Indonesia's gross domestic product. Since the early years of tourism-led development the 'island of gods' has over the course of time acquired its iconic status as one of the 'last paradises' on earth (Vickers, 1989). After the archipelago's independence and the birth of the Republic of Indonesia in 1950, both the governments of President Sukarno under the so called 'Guided Democracy' as well as under President Suharto's 'New Order' regime (*Orde Baru*) from 1967 to 1998 had chosen tourism as development path for the island and several other destinations within the country. The technocratic approach of 'New Order' Indonesia was aided by authoritarian and military power and aimed at the modernization of the nation with a gradual transformation from an agrarian to a service-based economy (Rubinstein & Connor, 1999; Suasta & Connor, 1999). As such, the Nusa Dua complex in the south of Bali, a prototype for a luxury resort destination was established. Throughout the following decades resort facilities and tourism infrastructure grew excessively all over the island. Rising arrival figures were only interrupted by a few violent events such as the anti-communist persecution in 1965 and the 2002 and 2005 Bali bombings. In recent years Bali faces another tourism construction boom as a result of the change in government policies since 1998. These changes have led to greater levels of decentralization, described as the *Reformasi* era.

In accordance with new regional autonomy laws, tax income is allocated on regency-level (principalities under the former Balinese kingdom). This has fostered competition among Bali's eight regencies and acted against an understanding of the tourism sector as a shared asset of the province of Bali (Koch, 2007; Picard, 2003; UNDP, 2003). Currently there are many tourism related construction sites fringing the southern coastlines of the island. Bali ranges among Southeast Asia's major destinations with more than 2.8 million international arrivals in 2011.

The shifts from a farming economy to tourism infrastructure and the massive influx of foreign visitors have put pressure on the carrying capacity of the densely populated island of more than 4-million inhabitants. Environmental degradation appears into the depletion of ground water reserves, mangrove forests salt-intrusion, insufficient waste water treatment, destruction of coral reefs and massive waste pollution. Local NGOs and media reports increasingly voice the destructive effects of unchecked mass tourism development and insufficient spatial planning (Nurhayati & Kertaraharja, 2012). It is not a new phenomenon that advocacy groups demonstrate against overdevelopment and the so-called 'mega-projects'. There is strong criticism of national and provincial government bodies, investors and property developers (Howe, 2005; Picard, 2003). Socio-cultural impacts, such as questions around the commoditization of culture and cultural survival, have also been major themes in the Balinese discourse on tourism development (Picard, 1996).

Economically, the island is wealthier than other regions in the country, and this can be linked directly to tourism income (Cukier-Snow & Wall, 1993, p.196). However, there are increasing inequalities in wealth distribution (Suasta & Connor, 1999, p.115). The presence of the tourism industry has led to an increase in living costs and land prices as well as higher taxes, as infrastructure development to support tourism is hard on the local budget. Consequently, the gaps between high-income and low-income earners are increasing (Radetzki-Stenner, 1989; Picard, 2009; Yamashita, 2003). It is a recurrent theme that impoverished farmers are selling their land to property developers (Forbes, 2007; Hobart, Ramseyer & Leeman, 2001). For them this is often just a temporary solution, although loss of land for a farmer goes along with the loss of their livelihood. Due to the strong spiritual connection among the Balinese people with their land, this results in consequences in view of the islanders' social capital.

Reactions from the grassroots: A community-based Village Ecotourism Network

There are two distinct threads of criticism towards tourism development in Bali. The first is that property development confers benefits only to entrepreneurs and investors and not the traditional landowners. The second is that the social and environmental costs of tourism development remain unresolved and are borne by the wider society (cf. Telfer & Sharpley, 2008). In reaction to such conflicts, four village communities in remote areas of Bali have, in 2002, officially established Jaringan Ekowisata Desa (JED), translated as the Village Ecotourism Network. This grassroots organization offers community-based ecotourism experiences.

JED aims to be a strong statement from four communities who want to decide for themselves the future of their people, their culture and their environment (Jaringan Ekowisata Desa, 2007). Assisted by Yayasan Wisnu, an environmental NGO, local farmers and fishermen have created unique tourism products by accommodating visitors in home-stays and by letting the tourists participate in the farmer's daily activities. In Kiadan Pelaga village, visitors experience the production of organic coffee in mixed crop gardens. In Dukuh Sibetan, the cultivation of snake fruit and the distillation of snake fruit wine are showcased. Tenganan Pegringsingan is well known for *Gringsing*, which is cloth interwoven in a sophisticated double *Ikat* technology. The village is also known for its *Lontar*: this writing on dried palm leaves has for centuries been a medium for Hindu epics and other texts. Nusa Ceningan, a small islet 12 kilometers off the coast of Bali, consists of seaweed farmers and fishermen. Their visitors learn the process of seaweed cultivation and processing. All villages, except for the self-contained and isolated community of Tenganan Pegringsingan, which is exclusively inhabited by the autochthonous *Bali Aga* people, offer home-stay accommodation. In each village, a local tour guide accompanies visitors, meals are home-cooked, and several stakeholders and families from each village community are involved.

JED is organized around agricultural cooperatives, which consist of associations of landowners, mortgagees, tenant farmers and sharecroppers, the so-called *Subak*. These organizations fulfill functions such as the irrigation of wet rice land and resource management. Instead of establishing new organizations for the purpose of community based tourism (CBT) development, the decision-making process regarding the implementation and activities of JED has been placed within traditional institutions of social organization of the Balinese society – the *Banjar*. These most important reference groups of the Balinese commoners (non-aristocracy) have to be understood as subdivisions of the village (*Desa*), in which all married men of a village community assemble, with legal, fiscal and ceremonial obligations. Decisions are ideally based on consensus and after hearing all parties declared as mandatory by the *Banjar* head (Leemann, 1993; Picard, 1996; Wälty, 1997).

The village communities are located in relatively remote areas of the Balinese island and have only basic infrastructure. Major incomes are drawn from agriculture; only some families receive income through trade or employment as workers, craftsmen or officials. By providing tourism services at grassroots level, JED seeks to minimize negative impacts on the ecology through the creation of environmental awareness among hosts and guests. This will hopefully lead to financial benefits for conservation and community development in the villages. The JED system will help to provide a sustainable income source for the villagers in addition to fostering intercultural exchange and understanding. Owned and managed by the respective communities, JED aims at empowering its stakeholders, enabling their political participation and ensuring their entitlements in natural resource management on a local level.

The aim of this research was to verify whether an approach such as that of JED qualifies as model for alternative development to mass tourism in Bali. The UNEP and WTO define sustainable tourism as taking 'full account of its current and future economic, social and environmental impacts, addressing the needs of visitors, the industry, the environment and the communities' (2005, p.12). The aim was to investigate tourism development based on the local *Tri Hita Karana* philosophy as a central foundation of the way of life of the Balinese Hindu-Brahman population. As mentioned, the island's culture strives to live in conformity with the principles of *Tri Hita Karana*, that is, in harmony with each other and with their natural and supernatural environment (Hauser-Schäublin, 2000: Krishna, 2008).

Research design

Primary research took place in January and February 2010. Three research instruments were applied in four project communities: 1. Participant observation, as a first approach to the field; 2. qualitative community survey was undertaken; 3. analysis of existing survey data and questionnaires (Byczek, 2011). Capturing the state of implementation of the JED initiative from different perspectives, the surveys provided a comprehensive picture against the backdrop of general definitions of sustainable tourism from the viewpoint of different stakeholders

Participant observation

Initial participant observation aimed at a better understanding of the initiative within the context and allowed for comparison between the offers communicated by JED and the actual products offered. Analysis of the information communicated through JED's website, leaflets and literature and newspaper articles was undertaken with a view to seeing whether what was communicated was veracious.

The community survey

The community survey sample consisted of 16 participants (n=16) from communities who were involved in the initiative in different ways. This corresponds to an average of four participants per community. In each community between 16 and 21 persons are involved and receive recurring income from the initiative. Thus, the sample size equals to about one sixth of the overall number of stakeholders. Performance was measured against internationally recognized principles for sustainable development of ecotourism (Honey, 2008) and community-based tourism (CBT) (Suansri, 2003).

CBT reflects the aspect of ownership and control of the community rather than on that of the private sector. The community survey was performed in form of explorative-guided interviews with an interview guideline comprising 18 open questions. Questions included: 'Do you teach the tourists about your natural environment? If yes, what and why?', or 'Did the villagers learn anything from the tourists since JED was initiated?' The interviews aimed to explore how and why environmental protection and conservation activities are performed and whether there are learning and awareness creation elements connected to such activities. There were also questions aiming at understanding employment and income generation as well as income distribution strategies. In addition, gender issues and village decision-making process among JED stakeholders were explored. Within the *Banjar* community, institutional and organizational aspects of the initiative, and changes in the village induced through JED were asked, such as for example: 'Is there anything that has changed in the village since the JED project has been initiated, for example, the way of thinking or quality of life?' Finally, more general questions on the personal understanding and history of involvement as well as perceptions on what is being done and ideas of what could be improved were included in the interviews.

The visitor survey

In order to ensure that visitors' viewpoints were accounted for, an appraisal of visitor satisfaction and information on the fulfillment of visitor needs was undertaken. To this end, 165 questionnaires was analyzed. This sample size corresponded to almost two fifth of the visitors that had visited any of the JED village communities throughout the year 2009. In that year, 449 visitors had booked a trip with JED. Between 2007 and 2011 a total of 1597 visitors stayed in the four communities - averaging at about 319 visitors per year.

The research results

Participation as a prerequisite for the expression of human needs is a key element in CBT (Beyer, Häusler & Strasdas, 2007). Participants reported that the facilitation of CBT development and its localization within the *Banjar* communities provided a consensus-based decision-making process at a local level. Participants also reported a high degree of participation (measured by the community-involvement typologies of Pretty (1995) or Palm (2000)). One of the participants even mentioned the concept of 'light democracy', which may suggest that support of democratic movements is important for ecotourism developments (Honey, 2008; cf. Byczek, 2011). However, in the *Banjar* and *Subak* communities only men take part in gatherings (Ariani & Kindon, 1995). Thus, the communities are not truly inclusive in democratic terms. In the JED communities, women do participate in the meetings of the JED committee, and they also actively take part in the delivery of tourism services. However, specific roles differ among men and women as a result of cultural conditions (Byczek, 2011).

Fostering exchange and respect between the cultures are important aspects in both CBT and ecotourism (Honey, 2008; Suansri, 2003). This is especially the case in Bali, where there has been a broad discourse about whether increasing commodification leads to the Balinese losing their 'Balineseness' (Picard, 1996; 2009; 2008). The participants differentiate between insiders (Balinese or members of their respective community) and outsiders (not only tourists but also immigrants or the local urban population). Participants described the culture of the guests and their behaviour generally as positive, however, with one participant commenting negatively on modes of dress. Generally, there is a good understanding among the communities with regard to foreign cultures and cultural differences. In order to foster intercultural understanding and mutual exchange, intense interaction is important. The participant observation showed that there are certain limitations to interaction, mainly due to language constraints. Also, one of the participants commented that the length of stay is not sufficient to foster such understanding - an issue also addressed by Suansri (2003). Tourism is generally welcomed; its cultural impact is not perceived as intrusive. Certain activities are always subject to availability, and on several days, traveling to a village may not be possible due to the people being busy with ceremonial preparations. Thus, the potential conflict between permanent employment and religious and community obligations, which is observed in modern Balinese life and especially in connection with tourism, is solved in the way that JED operates (cf. Cukier-Snow & Wall, 1993). Despite these constraints, open interaction is given and intercultural understanding is enhanced. One participant commented: 'We do not only teach but also learn' (cf. Byczek, 2011, p.117).

The interviews and participant observation demonstrate that negative environmental impacts are minimized; the communities control the number of visitors and no additional facilities have been built in order to serve guests. However, the participants mentioned few active measures for environmental protection. Financial benefits for conservation are generated, but they are rather small. Major arguments among the participants indicating conservation practices were related to traditional livelihoods and respective farming practices in conformity with *Tri Hita Karana* principles. The coffee plantations in the *Banjar* of Kiadan Pelaga for example are cultivated as mixed-crop gardens, which in opposition to monocultures maintain tropical forest features. A farmer commented that these practices are the result of an '[...] interrelationship between tradition, custom and culture'.

This research process did not identify whether all agricultural practices in the JED villages are indeed sustainable. Nevertheless, these land uses have been in practice for centuries, and they are likely to be more preserving than mass tourism facilities which threaten to over-consume natural resources on the island. Picard (1990) claims the Balinese human-ecology system is based on and related to agriculture, and that for this reason religious and cultural practices as well as ecologic concerns have to be understood in connection with each other, and cannot be considered separately. The *Tri Hita Karana* philosophy was repeatedly mentioned in the interviews as the basic conservation ethics of the stakeholders and as a concept of life that also matches with the principles of JED.

Local empowerment

In all four project communities, farmers perceived a threat from investors whose aim was to acquire land for the purpose of resort-style tourism facilities. Loss of land and consequently natural resource management entitlements would negatively impact the farmers' livelihoods (cf. Byczek, 2011). Many participants revealed a strong relationship with their land and perceive themselves to be an integral part of the environment and their use of the land is in accordance with these ancestral traditions.

The sale of land was mentioned as not desirable and not even socially sanctioned by traditional communities. A participant commented: '[...] we have chosen ecotourism as an activity, despite it is not our main income. According to some people tourism means money. They sell their land. We still need to improve local awareness, for our heritage, which is a sustainable way of life' (cf. Byczek, 2011, p. 106).

The *Awig Awig* regulations promote the practice of remaining in possession of land among the villagers. According to Berkes (1999), such codes could be understood as ideological and the ethical basis of the management systems. Land conflicts have been described in more detail by participants from Nusa Ceningan, where local seaweed farmers were threatened by a loss of their land, their access to the coral reefs and consequently of their livelihoods through a resort project.

Income generation

Individual incomes generated by the participants turned out to be relatively low. Incomes generated by tourism activities are a supplement to the income from agricultural activities or other occupations. The importance of local guides was emphasized repeatedly. That way, the tourism income stays in the community, rather than 'leaking' to external guides and tour operators. Mass tourism, usually with higher likelihood for leakage, is perceived as a threat to local communities, whereas stakeholders see CBT as more equitable in character.

The visitor perspective

The visitor profile generated from the existing questionnaires shows that the majority of guests are from the typical ecotourism markets - Europe and North America (cf. Weaver, 2001) whereas Indonesians account for only four percent of the clientele. Fifty-eight percent of the guests were female and the majority were of middle to senior age. Two thirds were first-time visitors, and the average length of stay in Bali was 13 days. Guests were mainly interested in local culture and life, flora and fauna, and some specifically in ecotourism. The visitor satisfaction with JED was high, with the majority of guests rating quality either 'very good' (77%) or 'good' (23%). The most satisfaction was perceived in the areas of local cuisine and the guides. Visitors expressed the view that the environment at the villages seems to be unharmed and intact. Some negative statements were made, for example about garbage in some of the natural areas as well as about the basic condition of the facilities. Overall, it can be concluded that JED meets the needs of its visitors and from this perspective an important criterion for its sustainability is fulfilled.

Implications for the field: Recommendations and best practices

The JED communities demonstrate that it has minimal negative impacts of tourism. Activities are community-based, which means that they are owned and managed by the people, thereby helping to keep the number of visitors to the sensitive areas in check. The limited number of guests, however, goes along with limitations to the economic benefits generated by the initiative. CBT and ecotourism are often criticized as having low potential for poverty reduction, involving small areas, having few people, and showing weak links between biodiversity gains and commercial success (Lengefeld, 2007; Kiss, 2004).

JED works for its stakeholders in harmonizing tourism activities with traditional livelihoods. It was not intended as a project that would shift the community economy towards traditional tourism activities. The aim was rather to diversify economic activities between the participating stakeholders and their livelihoods. New dependencies on mono-structural and crisis-prone income sources are avoided. Rather than selling their land and becoming employees of privately owned tourism or hospitality ventures, farmers remain in possession of their traditional livelihoods, a sustainable way of life and their cultural heritage.

Development, according to Suansri (2003) should be embedded in local culture. Placing the decision-making process regarding JED activities within existing institutions of social organization has proven advantageous. It helps not only to gain acceptance within the wider village communities (on *Banjar* and *Desa* level), but enables stakeholders to take ownership of the venture. With the organization of tourism activities around the *Bajnar*, the interests of local communities as a whole are being represented and a basis for empowerment is created. In establishing community-based ecotourism through traditional local institutions, the potential for traditional ecological - and one could add 'social' and 'economic' - knowledge to contribute to a higher degree of sustainability is tapped. As a society that still carries much of this knowledge, the *Banjar* function as institution that concentrates traditional wisdom and through the JED initiative links it with the modern world of international tourism. In this way local interests are communicated to a wider and global public.

A major factor in sustainable tourism development is the attribution of decision-making power (Telfer & Sharpley, 2008). There are many positive as well as negative examples for the development of sustainable tourism around the world. Conflicts usually appear in connection with ownership and control. Indigenous Balinese lack bargaining power when it comes to mass tourism projects. Foreign experts implement projects that neglect the principles of sustainable development due to a lack of understanding of the fact that tourism is a social system itself and that tourism development needs to be carefully aligned to the respective host societies' social systems (Nash, 2001). JED may be understood as an alternative where private sector models fail to solve the tragedy of the commons (cf. Berkes 1999, p. 142).

References

Allon, F. (2004). Bali as Icon: Tourism, Death and the Pleasure Periphery. In: *Humanities Research*, 11, 1, pp. 24-41, Retrieved 9th April 2010 from: www.anu.edu.au/HRC/publications/hr/issue1_2004/3_Allon-HRC11.pdf.

Ariani, I. G. A. A. & Kindon S. L. (1995). Women, Gender & Sustainable Development in Bali. In: *Department of Geography Publication Series*, 44, pp. 507-519.

Bateson, G. (1972). *Steps to an Ecology of Mind*. New York: Ballantine.

Barnett, Patricia (2011, July). Speech on *The Non-Governmental Organizations Perspective*, Session 2, Tourism Ethics for Better Tourism Products and Services Assurance, UNWTO Seminar on Tourism Ethics for Asia and the Pacific, Responsible Tourism and its Socio-Economic Impact on Local Communities, Nusa Dua, Bali, Indonesia.

Berkes, F. (1999). *Sacred Ecology. Traditional Ecological Knowledge and Resource Management*. Philadelphia: Taylor & Francis.

Beyer, M., Häusler N. & Strasdas, W. (2007). *Tourismus als Handlungsfeld der deutschen Entwicklungszusammenarbeit – Grundlagen, Handlungsbedarf und Strategieempfehlungen*. Eschborn: Deutsche Gesellschaft für Technische Zusammenarbeit (GTZ).

Byczek, C. (2011). *Community-Based Ecotourism for a Tropical Island Destination. The Case of Jaringan Ekowisata Desa - a Village Ecotourism Network on Bali.* Saarbrücken, Germany: VDM Verlag.

Cohen, E. (1972). Toward a Sociology of International Tourism, *Social Research*, Vol. 39, No. 1, pp. 164-182.

Cukier-Snow, J. & Wall, G. (1993). Tourism Employment. Perspectives from Bali, In: *Tourism Management*, 14, pp. 195-201.

Fariborz, A., Sarjit, S. G. & Farshid, A. (2010): Tourism Development in Local Communities: As a Community Development Approach. In: *Journal of American Science*, 6, 2, pp.155-161.

Forbes, C. (2007): *Under the Volcano, The Story of Bali*. Melbourne: Black Inc.

Hauser-Schäublin, B. (2000): Dynamik zwischen Dissonanz und Harmonie: Kulturelle Ord-nungssysteme unter dem Eindruck der Tourismusentwicklung, in: Hauser-Schäublin, B. & Rieländer, K. (eds.). *Kultur - Tourismus - Umwelt, Die indonesische Ferieninsel im Schnittpunkt lokaler, nationaler und globaler Interessen*. Hamburg: Abera Verlag, pp. 142-158.

Higham J. & Lück, M. (2007): Ecotourism: pondering the paradoxes, in: Higham, J. (ed.). *Critical Issues in Ecotourism: Understanding a complex tourism phenomenon*. Oxford: Elsevier, pp. 117-135.

Hitchcock, M. & Putra, I N. D. (2007): *Tourism, Development and Terrorism in Bali.* Voices in Development Management. Hampshire: Ashgate.

Hobart, A., Ramseyer, U. & Leeann, A. (2001). *The People of Bali, (Peoples of Southeast Asia and the Pacific)*. Oxford: Blackwell Publishers.

Honey, M. (2008). *Ecotourism and Sustainable Development. Who Owns Paradise?* Washington DC: Island Press (2nd ed., first published in 1999).

Howe, L. (2005). *The Changing World of Bali: Religion, society and tourism*. London & New York: Routledge-Curzon.

JED, Jaringan Ekowisata Desa (2007). Retrieved 30th September 2012 from: www.jed.or.id/EN/background.php.

JED, Jaringan Ekowisata Desa (2012). *Laporan Perkembangan Pengelolaan JED Jaringan Ekowisata Desa Periode 2011*. Kerobokan: Jaringan Ekowisata Desa.

Johnson, V. & Cottingham, M. (2008). *Plane Truths: Do the economic arguments for aviation growth really fly?* London: New Economics Foundation (NEF).

Kiss, A. (2004). Is community-based ecotourism a good use of biodiversity conservation funds? In: *Trends in Ecology and Evolution*, 19, 5, pp. 232-237.

Koch, M. (2007). Bali im indonesischen Nationalstaat. Die Bedeutung ethnischer Identitätskon-struktionen. In: Hermann, S. & Holst, F. (eds.). *Gesellschaft und Politik in Südostasien. Eine studentische Festzeitschrift zu Ehren von Prof. Dr. Ingrid Wessel.* Südostasien Working Papers No. 31. Berlin: Institut für Asien und Afrikawissenschaften, pp. 85-94.

Krishna, A. (2008). *Tri Hita Karana. Ancient Balinese Wisdom for Neo Humans*. Jakarta: Anand Krishna Global Co-Operation.

Leemann, A. (1993). Organisationsformen der Balinesischen Gesellschaft. In: *Geographica Helvetica. Schweizerische Zeitschrift für Geographie und Völkerkunde*, 48, 1, pp. 6-18.

Lengefeld, K. (2007). Masse und Klasse – Welchen Tourismus brauchen die Entwicklungsländer. In: *Eins Entwicklungspolitik*, 2-3-2007, pp. 26-30.

McRae, G. (2005). Growing Rice after the Bomb: Where is Balinese Agriculture Going? In: *Critical Asian Studies*, 37, 2, pp. 209-232.

Nash, D. (2001). *Anthropology of Tourism*. Oxford: Pergamon (first edited in 1996).

Nurhayati, D. & Kertaraharja, A. (2012, June 6). Activists sound environmental alarm. *The Jakarta Post.* Retrieved 30th September 2012 from www.thejakartapost.com/bali-daily/2012-06-06/activists-sound-environmental-alarm.html.

Ostrom, R. (2000). Bali's Tourism Interests: Local Responses to Suharto's Globalization Policies. In: *Southeast Asian Journal of Social Science*, 28, 2, pp. 111-130.

Palm, P. (2000). *Community Based Tourism als eine Form des nachhaltigen Tourismus in kom-munalen Gebieten Namibias*. Eschborn: Deutsche Gesellschaft für Technische Zusammenarbeit (GTZ).

Picard, M. (2009). From 'Kebalian' to Ajeg Bali': Tourism and Balinese Identity in the Aftermath of the Kuta Bombings. In: Hitchcock, Michael, King,Victor T & Parnwell, Michael (eds.). *Tourism in Southeast Asia. Challenges and New Directions*. Copenhagen: NIAS Press, pp. 99-131.

Picard, M. (2008). Balinese Identity as tourist attraction: From 'cultural tourism' (pariwisata budaya) to 'Bali erect' (ajeg Bali). In: *Tourist Studies*, 8, 2, pp. 155-173.

Picard, M. (2003). Touristification and Balinization in a Time of Reformasi. In: *Indonesia and the Malay World*, 31, 89, pp. 108-118.

Picard, M. (1996). *Bali, Cultural Tourism and Touristic Culture*. Singapore: Archipelago Press.

Picard, M. (1990). Kebalian Orang Bali: Tourism and the Uses of 'Balinese Culture' in New Order Indonesia. In: *Review of Indonesian and Malaysian Affairs*, 24, pp. 1-38.

Pretty, J. N. (1995). Participatory Learning for Sustainable Agriculture. *World Development*, 23(8), pp. 1247-1263.

Radetzki-Stenner, M. (1989): *Internationaler Tourismus und Entwicklungsländer: die Auswirkungen des Einfach-Tourismus auf eine ländliche Region der indonesischen Insel Bali*. Mün-ster: Lit Verlag

Roth, Dik (2012, July). *Reframing Balinese Water Scarcity: From 'Culture' to the Politics of Water?* Unpublished paper presented at the conference 'Bali in Global Asia - Between Modernization and Heritage Formation', Denpasar, Bali, Indonesia.

Rubinstein, R. & Connor, L. (1999). *Staying local in the global village: Bali in the twentieth century*. Honolulu: University of Hawaii Press.

Ryan, C. (2005). Introduction: tourist-hist-nexus – research considerations. In: Ryan, C. & Aicken, M. (eds.). *Indigenous Tourism: The Commodification and Management of Culture. London*: Elsevier pp. 1-11.

Suansri, P. (2003). *Community Based Tourism Handbook*. Bangkok: The Responsible Ecological Social Tours Project (REST).

Suasta, P. & Connor, L. H. (1999). Democratic Mobilization and Political Authoritarianism: Tour-ism Developments in Bali, in: Rubinstein, R. & Connor, L. H. (eds.). *Staying local in the global village: Bali in the twentieth century*. Honolulu: University of Hawaii Press, pp. 91-122.

Tambunan, T. (2007). Importance of Agricultural Growth for Poverty Reduction: The Indonesian Case, In: *Asia-Pacific Journal of Rural Development*, 17, 2, pp. 1-26.

Telfer, D. J. & Sharpley, R. (2008). Tourism and Development in the Developing World. London and New York: Routledge.

TIES, The International Ecotourism Society (2006). Fact Sheet: Global Ecotourism. Retrieved 22nd July 2008 from: www.ecotourism.org/webmodules/webarticlesnet/templates/eco_template.aspx?articleid=351.

UNDP, United Nations Development Programme / WB, World Bank (2003). *Bali beyond the tragedy: Impact and Challenge for Tourism-led Development in Indonesia*. Consultative Group Indonesia, Denpasar: United Nations Development Programme / World Bank.

UNWTO, United Nations World Tourism Organization / UNEP, United Nations Environmental Programme (2005). *Making Tourism Mote Sustainable. A Guide for Policy Makers*. Madrid.

Vickers, A. (1989). *Bali: A Paradise Created*. Hong Kong: Periplus.

Wälty, S. (1997). *Kintamani. Dorf, Land, Rituale: Entwicklung und insitutioneller Wandel in einer Bergregion auf Bali*. Münster: Lit Verlag.

Warren, C. (2005). Community mapping, local planning, and alternative land use strategies in Bali. In: *Geografisk Tidsskrift, Danish Journal of Geography*, 105, 1, pp. 29-41.

Weaver, D. B. (2001). *The Encyclopedia of Ecotourism*. New York: Cabi Publishing.

Yamashita, S. (2003). *Bali and beyond: explorations in the anthropology of tourism*. New York & Oxford: Berghahn Books.

Chapter 17

Personal hygiene, environmental sanitation

A case of social marketing in the Mekong Delta

LUKAS PARKER

ABSTRACT

This chapter presents a case of using social marketing to improve personal hygiene and environmental sanitation within schools throughout the Mekong Delta in Southern Viet Nam. The campaign incorporated appeals to the social benefits of good hygiene behaviour alongside a conventional health education campaign. The *Cuu Long Rural Water Supply and Sanitation Project* was demonstrably successful in improving these behaviours, which can lead to a reduction in incidences of waterborne disease. Recommendations are made for how to ensure sustainable outcomes for similar projects.

Introduction

The fundamentals of social marketing have been used successfully in community development and public health campaigns throughout the world (e.g. Grier & Bryant, 2005; O'Reilly, Freeman, Ravani, Migele *et al.*, 2008). Social marketing uses the fundamentals of commercial marketing and modifies them for the purpose of social change (Kotler & Zaltman, 1971). Target marketing, positioning, product, price, place and promotion, traditionally commercial marketing concepts are repurposed to create positive behaviour change instead of merely selling products (Leo, 2013). This case study focuses on a personal hygiene and sanitation project from five rural provinces in the Mekong Delta in the south of Vietnam. It is an example of social marketing in practice in a rural context, providing the results of the intervention and finally shows the lessons learned which are applicable for those considering similar interventions in the greater Mekong region.

The Vietnamese context

The Cuu Long Delta Rural Water Supply and Sanitation project was initiated by the Australian Agency for International Development (AusAID) which is the official Australian government agency for dispensing aid. The project centred in five rural Vietnamese provinces in the Mekong Delta: Bạc Liêu, Bến Tre, Kiên Giang, Long An and Vĩnh Long. The project was complex and had a heavy focus on capacity development with various levels and portfolios of Vietnamese government, including national ministries, provincial departments and district level government entities, from the agriculture and rural development, education and training, and health portfolios in all five provinces. The provincial people's committees of each province (executive arm of provincial governments, and are responsible for formulation and implementation of policy) and also were the key Vietnamese local counterparts who were to manage the infrastructure and any further communication and education programs beyond the completion of the project. The key consideration of this intervention was to ensure that any response was sustainable beyond the completion of the project.

The goal of the project was, 'to reduce poverty and improve overall living standards and health of between 384,000 and 400,000 rural poor living in the Cuu Long Delta by assisting them gain sustained access to improved water and sanitation services' (Shanks, O'Shea & Cheong, 2008, p.vi). The main components of the project related to infrastructure development for water supply and sanitation, and an information, education, and communication component, which was designed to maximize the benefits of the infrastructure built.

One of the key health outcomes sought was the reduction of water-related illness. Diarrhoea from inadequate hygiene and water supply has been cited by the Asian Development Bank (2012) as one of the top two causes of death amongst the poorest fifth the world's population. Washing hands with soap and water is considered one of the easiest and most effective means of reducing the risk of diarrhoeal disease (Curtis & Cairncross, 2003; Langford & Panter-Brick, 2013). A downside to this solution is that hand-washing has been found in some studies to be not as cost-effective as other solutions (Curtis & Cairncross, 2003; Luby, Agboatwalla, Painter, Billhimer, Hoekstra *et al.*, 2004). Children are particularly vulnerable to the health consequences of poor hygiene, because they come into contact with contaminants that can cause diarrhoea on a daily basis. Furthermore, children are generally only in the early learning stages of the personal hygiene by the time they are beginning school (Le & Luu, 2013). This means that they are often not certain of good hygiene practice at a time that they become somewhat independent to their parents.

Winblad and Dudley (1997) identified four key priorities for maintaining students' health: keeping school grounds clear of faecal matter and other waste, providing and maintaining clean toilets, providing convenient and clean hand washing facilities and encouraging their use, and providing safe drinking water. The focus of this case study is the *Healthy School* campaign which ran in 118 schools and was run concurrently with the construction of toilet, hand-washing and waste-disposal facilities at project schools as part of the Cuu Long Delta Rural Water Supply and Sanitation project. Its purpose was to maximise the benefits of the new infrastructure and enable sustainable personal hygiene and environmental sanitation benefits to the communities.

The provinces where the intervention was staged are farming provinces with the main crops being rice, fruit, and aquaculture. This area is particularly fertile given the alluvial soils and ideal climate conditions mean high and multiple harvests of rice. The Mekong Delta has been identified as an area particularly at risk of sea rise as a result of global warming (Asian Development Bank, 2012). Furthermore, the water of the Mekong River is of particular importance as it is a key mode of transport, irrigation, fish, and shrimp farming (Asian Development Bank, 2012). In many cases the water of the river in these provinces has also been used for drinking, cleaning, for defecation and other refuse disposal (Asian Development Bank, 2012; Few, Lake, Hunter & Tran, 2013). This is problematic, as the water used for defecation and refuse-disposal often contaminates drinking, washing and irrigation water (Few, Lake, Hunter & Tran, 2013).

In Vietnam, government involvement in projects of this type is a necessity. The Vietnamese government has a comparatively well-functioning bureaucracy. Therefore, projects must have processes in place to ensure that the relevant Vietnamese government departments are informed and also included where necessary. Approval processes are important and often complex, sometimes involving multiple government departments and at multiple levels of government. Hierarchy is important, and possibly indicative of a high power-distance society (Hofstede & Hofstede, 2004). Whilst this is the case, Vietnamese governing groups are very much standardised, centralised, and structurally organised from hamlet, commune, district, provincial, and national levels (Nachuk, 2000) - meaning that navigation is reasonably clear.

Vietnamese society has a Confucian heritage (Jamieson, 1995) and is often regarded as collectivistic (Hofer, Fries, Helmke, Kilian *et al.*, 2010; Hofstede & Hofstede, 2004). This is true of the people in the Mekong Delta. Moreover, inhabitants of the Mekong delta are renowned to be hospitable, friendly, and open people. Teachers and education, in Vietnamese society, are highly prized and revered (Nguyen, 2010). Teachers are also respected by students and their families' and teachers' knowledge and authority are often relied upon (Nguyen, 2010). As an information source, teachers and schools are trusted and are an effective means to transmit social marketing message (Gordon, McDermott, Stead & Angus, 2006).

From an economic perspective, although considered developing economies, compared to many other rural provinces in Vietnam the provinces of the Mekong Delta are reasonably prosperous partly due to the reliable food harvests. However, compared to the major cities of Vietnam, living standards, wages and education are generally not as high, and infrastructure in these rural provinces are not as well developed (General Statistics Office, 2009; Asian Development Bank, 2012). Technical and other water infrastructure in the rural and remote areas of these provinces is generally poor. Land travel in the provinces is slow due to high levels of traffic (Asian Development Bank, 2012), partly due to overcapacity and under-maintained roads. Many of the hamlets part of this project were only reachable using combinations of motorcycles, bicycles and small boats. This made the distribution of social marketing materials and on-going supply and maintenance the project-built facilities slower and more complex.

Background to social marketing

Whilst the main focus of the projects was the provision of much-needed water and sanitation infrastructure, social marketing principles were one of the means used to help ensure sustainable change as an outcome of the project. Ever since Kotler and Zaltman (1971, p. 5) defined social marketing as the 'design, implementation and control of programs calculated to influence the acceptability of social ideas', social marketing has undergone some transformation and adaptation. However the central tenets of marketing have remained largely intact in social marketing principles. Social marketing principles have been used in hand-washing, personal hygiene and environmental sanitation projects throughout the developing world (e.g. Curtis, Kanki, Cousens, Sanou *et al.*, 1997; O'Reilly, Freeman, Ravani, Migele *et al.*, 2008; Scott, Schmidt, Aunger, Garbrah-Aidoo & Animashaun, 2008). These have had varying levels of success; however the principles are increasingly being used in behaviour change interventions.

Andreasen (2002) devised social marketing interventions as having six main benchmarks, 1) behaviour change, 2) consumer research, 3) segmentation and targeting, 4) marketing mix, 5) exchange, and 6) completion. Although this case embraced all six benchmarks, the more innovative components were related to segmentation and targeting, and marketing mix. For this reason the case is analysed with a focus on these two core elements.

Case study

Market segmentation involves the breaking down all the potential audiences for the social marketing inventions into groups with similar characteristics. In this case the key segments were school children, householders (usually mothers), money-earners (usually fathers) and teachers. Targeting, on the other hand, involves selecting suitable groups and aiming social marketing activities and promotion activities around those groups. In this intervention, the primary target was school children. The tools that social marketers use to reach and influence the target market are those traditionally used by marketers - the marketing mix: product, price, place and promotion. The intervention in this case was consistent with the social marketing four P's marketing mix framework:

- Product - the notion of personal hygiene and environmental sanitation.
- Price - the inconvenience or immediate financial costs associated with the desired behaviour.
- Place (distribution) - availability of the means and facilities for personal hygiene and environmental sanitation such as toilet blocks, soap and waste disposal facilities.
- Promotion - communication and education activities to entice the target market to take on the desirable hygiene and sanitation behaviours.

With these principles in mind the intervention is discussed in terms of its key social marketing elements: target audience, product, price, place and promotion.

Target audience

The purpose of the social marketing campaign was to maximise the benefits of the newly built toilets, hand-washing facilities and waste disposal facilities built at the 118 project schools. The primary target audience were students at these schools, with the parents of these students as secondary target audiences. Given the nature of the intervention, teachers were also a target audience as they needed to be mentored and trained in such a way to become advocates. Given that the teachers were the key transmitters of the information it was important for them to have a sense of ownership and control over the activities (Parker, 2009), and their engagement with the activities meant that they were able to lend their credibility to the messages.

The targeted school children were mostly between the ages of five and twelve. The reasons for this were threefold. Firstly, correct hygiene messages could be used for the students at a time that they are often learning to undertake these behaviours at home and independently. Secondly, it was, in some cases, the first time the school children had actually used these types of facilities, therefore they could be taught the correct behaviours from the beginning. Thirdly, given the high respect for schools and teachers in Vietnamese society, we believed that the messages would make the greatest impact in families if they were delivered by the school but particularly by teachers. In turn it was hoped that students would become initiators and influencers (Chang, Chen & Somerville, 2003; Douglas,

1983; Hempel, 1975; O'Reilly, Freeman, Ravani, Migele *et al.*, 2008) when they went back to their homes. In interviews undertaken on householders in the project's rural hamlets, we were told of numerous instances where parents had taken on the ideas and advice of the children. These ideas and advice generally came from what the children had learned in the classroom and related to concepts of personal hygiene, treating potential drinking water and in some cases agriculture. Parents were often willing to take on these new ideas, because they had come from the teachers in the school and their knowledge was considered important and reliable.

In order to get the teachers to become advocates for the personal hygiene and environmental sanitation project, we needed to overcome a number of hurdles to having this program being allowed to run in project schools. These processes and hurdles included: 1) getting approval from the national ministry of education and training and the provincial departments of education and training to have our extra-curricular materials run in the schools, 2) training the teachers in current best-practice in personal hygiene and environmental sanitation, and 3) motivating already busy teachers to want to run these extra-curricular activities at their school.

After approvals were given, we were able to begin the training programs for the school teachers to introduce them to our proposed school activities and refresh them in basic personal hygiene. In all provinces, day-long and multiple-day training workshops were held for teachers in project schools. In most provinces, senior education department officials led the training with the support project staff. Because the proposed school activities were extra-curricular they could not be made compulsory in the schools. Therefore, it was important for the teachers to want to run them in their classrooms and schools. With this in mind, the school activities taught were designed so that they would be fun for teachers and students. Also they were designed to be easy to facilitate and using everyday objects available around the school. Each school activity was aligned to the ministry-approved curriculum so that these activities could be potentially run by teachers in parallel to existing classes. It was critical that all activities were easy to set up and run, otherwise there was little incentive to run these extra-curricular activities within their already jam-packed class schedules.

Product

The key *products* or ideas that needed to be *sold* or transferred to the target audiences were specific personal hygiene and environmental sanitation behaviours. These behaviours included: operating the toilets and urinals correctly, keeping the toilets clean and sanitary, washing hands with soap after going to the toilet and before eating, and disposal of other waste at the school correctly. The key enabling factors for these behaviours to occur included availability of sanitary toilet facilities, the provision of hand-washing facilities with soap and facilities to dry hands, availability of rubbish bins, and systems for the disposal of solid and liquid waste. The key disabling factors were the lack of school budget allocated to the ongoing cleaning, supplying, and maintenance of the newly built infrastructure, and the inconvenience and lack of immediate gratification for good hygiene behaviour.

The complexity of advocating these personal hygiene and environmental sanitation behaviours was the lack of direct immediate benefit to the target audience. Improved personal hygiene and a sanitary environment would mean that students would be less susceptible to illnesses including diarrhoea, and the school would become a more pleasant and attractive learning environment. Also, provision and maintenance of hygienic separate sex toilets have been found to improve attendance and learning, particularly for female students (Birdthistle, Dickson, Freeman & Javidi, 2011). However none these benefits are particularly attractive to students especially given that there is no immediate direct benefit or reward to students. We needed a new angle to make all of these time-consuming activities more desirable.

With this in mind, the social marketing intervention concentrated its efforts on social desirability as a means to make these ideas more palatable to the students. Appeals to children need to focus more on the immediate and obvious benefits to them (Evans, 2008). Before deciding upon this appeal, a number of appeals were considered, but the two most popular in the test focus groups were, 1) *the soap makes my hands smell nice and my friends will like to play with me*, and 2) *my teacher will be pleased with me if I wash my hands*. Both of these were largely social appeals (Evans, 2008); however we elected to go with the first option because we wanted this behaviour to translate both on and off the school grounds. Furthermore, the teacher is not always visible at school for approval on the school ground meaning that this appeal may not be so strong.

Place

Apart from *product*, *place* was the most important consideration for this intervention. We needed to ensure that the students received the messages about personal hygiene when and where it was most needed. This was particularly salient when students may not directly recognise this need. Distribution was critical in terms of both delivery and maintenance of facilities such as toilets and rubbish bins, the provision and use of soap. Most of the new facilities were in predetermined locations, so therefore our efforts focused on making the process of washing hands quicker and ensuring the availability of rubbish bins in locations where students ate. Also social marketing messages were put in places nearby where the hygienic behaviour were sought to occur and where *slip-ups* were likely to occur. Laminated posters were located on the insides of toilet cubical doors, above urinals, near toilet block exits, near or in classrooms, and near formal and informal eating areas.

Price

The biggest price or cost, of this intervention was co-related to distribution, which was the inconvenience of students performing the desired behaviour. For example, for children hand-washing takes immediate time away from their leisure, sporting activities, and eating. All positive behaviours advocated by this campaign faced this same issue. At a higher level the costs of maintenance and provision of toilet facilities were also an issue for the intervention. These costs not accounted for in already tight school budgets, were also something that had to be dealt with in the campaign albeit with a different target audience, parents.

In terms of dealing with the *social* inconvenience for children, we needed to provide students with efficient means to wash their hands. Facilities including rubbish bins had to be conveniently located in places where students likely to need to dispose of waste. Fixed facilities such as toilet blocks could not be changed or moved to provide convenience, however we needed to show children techniques on how to quickly, but correctly wash and dry hands. These were addressed in extra-curricular education materials provided to schools.

In terms of dealing with the running costs, different solutions were agreed to at different schools. Some schools charged a small levy to parents to cover the running costs of these new facilities and, in some cases, to pay for a school cleaner. Other schools elected to reduce financial costs by making classes take turns in taking responsibility for the cleaning and maintaining the new facilities on a rotational basis. This cost was more difficult to cover because the school had to work with the parents to come up with a solution that was mutually acceptable. Also, these costs were harder to justify to the parents because the services were largely invisible to non-users.

Promotion

Whilst the desired behaviours had the aim of improving the health of students and the environment, this as a message was not particularly attractive to students. Children are less likely to deal with an appeal to their health, especially when they are healthy. Also, children are less likely to be able to draw linkages between their actions and their long-term consequences. Also, given that in the majority of cases when students do not perform the desired behaviours they do not get sick, this health message is unlikely to be successful. Consistent with the product, our message was that clean hands would not only feel and smell good, but make their friends want to play with them. This idea was also extended to other personal hygiene and environmental sanitation behaviours; friends' approval and social desirability were linked to performing the desired behaviours.

Whilst this was by and large a social marketing program, there had to be an educational element. In order for our communication and marketing materials to be accepted by the various levels of the provincial departments and national ministry of education, our program had to have an educational component in order for them to be approved to be extra-curricular resource materials. While the materials had a strong educational core there was also social appeal thread through the materials of the potential approval from friends. Materials at the school included a music compact disc which had children singing songs about personal hygiene and environmental sanitation, class activity books for teachers with fun, but educational activities about hygiene and sanitation - with links to the national curriculum shown throughout. Overall the social marketing messages were delivered in two events, posters in key locations and solidified in the education campaign delivered by teachers.

Two events, a Healthy School activity day and a Healthy School festival were held to coincide with the opening of the new school facilities. The activity days were led by the teachers with the assistance of the project team. Personal hygiene and environmental sanitation activities were selected from Healthy Schools class activity books. Activities included hand-washing relays, quizzes, demonstrations, role-plays, and other highly interactive and educational activities. The activities were about generating excitement about the new facilities, generating interest about the concepts being demonstrated, getting the teachers to practice facilitating the new activities, and about launching the Healthy School campaign in the school. In tandem to this event, a second festival was held usually within two months of the original activity day. The festivals were more formally organised; and local government officials, leaders from the local women's union, parents and often the media were invited to attend. These events included some activities from the school resource materials, student performances, and competitions. Healthy School festival supporters, the Unilever Vietnam Foundation, also gave out free bars of soap to students as prizes for their participation. This broader event was partly to launch the facilities, but also to generate interest and awareness in the local community. It was hoped that this could help initiate the discussion of personal hygiene and environmental sanitation within the school children's households.

Apart from the educational messages delivered by teachers, the communications campaign also comprised of other conventional advertising paraphernalia including posters, brochures, and music compact discs containing songs about personal hygiene and environmental sanitation sung by children. The copy, word choice, and some of the visuals used in many of these promotional materials were based on student input and feedback from focus groups of students.

Implications for the field

After the completion of the project, over one hundred schools had participated in the full social marketing program. In terms of hand-washing, the instances of school students with clean hands had increased by over twenty percent (Parker, 2009). Structured observations of schools three and six months after the opening of facilities found that around 95 percent of toilet and hand-washing facilities had been cleaned recently (Parker, 2007). There had been a marked improvement on the previously high levels of litter in school grounds as well. Whilst it was not possible to measure changes to levels of sickness, some schools reported that there was a reduction in the numbers of students absent due to sickness.

In total, 33,193 students were direct participants in the Healthy School program (Parker, 2007). The core elements of this campaign: focus on students, using social acceptance as an appeal, relying on the teachers as change agents and provision highly interactive educational activities were all to varying degrees successful. In an independent completion report for the project it was noted that materials were well adapted to southern Vietnamese behaviours and expressions (Shanks, O'Shea & Cheong, 2008) and also realistically and honestly depicted the typical living environments. It was also noted that the materials and innovative social messages were well received by the teachers and education departments.

It was identified that the main issues with the intervention were related to timing and coordination of the roll-out of the program and cross-sector coordination (Shanks, O'Shea & Cheong, 2008). School toilets were being built across a wide geographic area and were opening at a fluctuating rate meaning the social marketing programs were not always in-sync with the construction completion. In some schools the social marketing program would begin weeks or months after the completion of the toilet facilities. Conversely, in other schools the social marketing program had begun, and often completed, before the toilet facilities were open. The problems with this lack of coordination were twofold. Firstly, when social marketing campaign had begun after the toilets had been open then incorrect behaviours had been adopted and meant that these behaviours had to be corrected. Secondly, if the program began too late in that hamlet or commune, then the initial community interest in the project had diminished and teachers, student and parents were less interested in the program of school activities. In all cases the events were run, however future projects where possible should take into consideration the greater likelihood of *unforeseen events* in this type of rural context.

Upon reflection to have further maximised the effect of the intervention, we believe that more sustainable results could have been achieved by including householders, usually mothers, more in the school learning activities. In the intervention, school teachers were the agents of change in the community, in turn these ideas were introduced into the students. However, we believe that broader awareness and greater inclusion of the mothers would have helped ensure sustainability of these behaviours within the home. Moreover, that way the children would have been more likely to have seen consistent, and potentially more sustainable, behaviours in both the school and at home. Lastly, it may have made parents more open to the need to further fund the supply, cleaning and maintenance of unbudgeted school facilities.

One year after the completion of the project, most the facilities had remained reasonably well maintained according to project evaluation reports (Parker, 2007). Beyond the project, the long-term level of success of the project is a little less certain. Whilst the project was successful at the time when the community members were receiving new school toilets and other in-home water facilities, the momentum beyond the project has not been as pronounced (Shanks, O'Shea & Cheong, 2008). Earlier and more inclusive collaboration with the various provincial departments of education and training, throughout the full process may have resulted in more institutional *clout* in the running of the programs within schools. This could have potentially led to greater levels of sustainability and the possibility of institutional funding for the upkeep of the new facilities.

This case demonstrates that the fundamentals of marketing and social marketing can work in a rural context. Segmentation, target market and audience, and the four Ps can be used effectively to initiate change. However greater consideration needs to be given to what happens after an intervention, particularly given the unique characteristics of the region. Bigger picture issues of economic and social sustainability, such as how to ensure that communities remain motivated and financial wherewithal to stay committed to any sustainable behaviour deserve further deliberation. Also the aforementioned political cooperation is essential and has a major influence on likelihood of the sustainability of this type of intervention. This project was able to respond to the unique dynamics at play in this region and successfully improved the environment and hygiene of the participating schools and communities.

References

Andreasen, A. R. (2002). Marketing social marketing in the social change marketplace. *Journal of Public Policy and Marketing*, 21(1), 3-13.

Asian Development Bank. (2012). *Greater Mekong Subregion Atlas of the Environment (2nd ed.)*. Manila: Asian Development Bank.

Birdthistle, I., Dickson, K., Freeman, M. & Javidi, L. (2011), *What impact does the provision of separate toilets for girls at schools have on their primary and secondary school enrolment, attendance and completion?: A systematic review of the evidence.* London: EPPI-Centre, Social Science Research Unit, Institute of Education, University of London.

Chang, C.-O., Chen, S.-M. & Somerville, T. (2003). Economic and Social Status in Household Decision-making: Evidence Relating to Extended Family Mobility. *Urban Studies*, 40(4), 733-746.

Curtis, V. & Cairncross, S. (2003). Effect of washing hands with soap on diarrhoea risk in the community: A systematic review. *The Lancet Infectious Diseases*, 3(5), 275-28.

Curtis, V., Kanki, B., Cousens, S., Sanou, A., Diallo, I. & Mertens, T. (1997). Dirt and diarrhea: formative research in hygiene promotion programs. *Health Policy and Planning*, 12(2), 122-131.

Douglas, S. P. (1983). Examining family decision-making processes. *Advances in Consumer Research*, 10(1), 451-453.

Evans, W. D. (2008). Social Marketing Campaigns and Children's Media Use. *The Future of Children*, 18(1), 181-203.

Few, R., Lake, I., Hunter, P. R. & Tran, P. G. (2013). Seasonality, disease and behavior: Using multiple methods to explore socio-environmental health risks in the Mekong Delta. *Social Science & Medicine*, *80*, 1-9.

General Statistics Office. (2009). Tổng điều tra dân số và nhà ở Việt Nam năm 2009: Kết quả toàn bộ (The 2009 Vietnam population and housing census: Completed results). Ha Noi: Ban Chỉ Đạo Tổng Điều Tra Dân Số và Nhà ở Trung Ương, Tổng Cục Thống Kê (Central Population and Housing Census Steering Committee, General Statistics Office).

Gordon, R., McDermott, L., Stead, M. & Angus, K. (2006). The effectiveness of social marketing interventions for health improvement: what's the evidence? *Public Health*, 120(12), 1133–1139.

Grier, S. & Bryant, C. A. (2005). Social Marketing in Public Heath. *Annual Review of Public Health*, 26, 319-339.

Hempel, D. (1975). Family Role Structure and Housing Decisions. In M. J. Schlinger (Ed.), *Advances in Consumer Research* (pp. 71-80). Chicago: Association for Consumer Research.

Hofer, M., Fries, S., Helmke, A., Kilian, B., Kuhnle, C., Živković, I., Goelineer, R. & Helmke, T. (2010). Value orientations and motivational interference in school-leisure conflict: The case of Vietnam. *Learning and Instruction*, 20(3), 239-249.

Hofstede, G. & Hofstede, G. J. (2004). *Cultures and organizations: Software of the mind: Intercultural cooperation and its importance for survival* (2nd ed.). New York: McGraw-Hill.

Jamieson, N. L. (1995). *Understanding Vietnam*. Berkeley, CA USA: University of California Press.

Kotler, P. & Zaltman, G. (1971). Social marketing: An approach to planned social change. *Journal of Marketing*, 35(July), 3-12.

Langford, R. & Panter-Brick, C. (2013). A health equity critique of social marketing: Where interventions have impact but insufficient reach. *Social Science & Medicine*, 2013.

Le, T. T. X. & Luu, N. H. (2013). Handwashing among schoolchildren in an ethnically diverse population in northern rural Vietnam, *Global Health Action*, 6, 1-8.

Leo, C. (2013). Social marketing customer orientation: A conceptualization, typology, and conceptual framework. *Journal of Nonprofit & Public Sector Marketing*, 25(1), 56-8.

Luby, S. P., Agboatwalla, M., Painter, J., Altaf, A., Billhimer, W. L. & Hoekstra, R. M. (2004). Effect of intensive handwashing promotion on childhood diarrhea in high-risk communities in pakistan. *JAMA: The Journal of the American Medical Association, 291*(21), 2547-2554.

Nachuk, S. (2000). Competition, service delivery, and poverty alleviation in Viet Nam: The role of the Ministry of Education and the Vietnam Bank of Agriculture. London: Oxfam Great Britain and Novib. Retrieved from http://unpan1.un.org/intradoc/groups/public/documents/apcity/unpan030260.pdf.

Nguyen, T. T. L. (2010). Commercialising higher education: lessons from Vietnam. *Journal of the Pacific Circle Consortium for Education*, 22(1), 45-56.

O'Reilly, C. E., Freeman, M. C., Ravani, M., Migele, J., Mwaki, A., Ayalo, M., Ombeki, S., Hoekstra, R. M. & Quick, R. (2008). The impact of a school-based safe water and hygiene programme on knowledge and practices of students and their parents: Nyanza province, western Kenya, 2006. *Epidemiology and Infection*, 136(1), 80-91.

Parker, L. (2007). Healthy schools in rural areas of the Mekong River Delta in Vietnam. In *The Second Annual WEPA (Water Partnership in Asia) Forum: International Forum on Water Environment Governance in Asia* (pp. 158-163). Beppu, Oita: Ministry of the Environment, Japan.

Parker, L. (2009). The challenges of social marketing in practice: hand-washing in rural and remote Vietnam. In *International Nonprofit and Social Marketing Conference 2009 - Proceedings*. Melbourne, Victoria: Victoria University and Swinburne University of Technology.

Scott, B. E., Schmidt, W. P., Aunger, R., Garbrah-Aidoo, N. and Animashaun, R. (2008). Marketing hygiene behaviours: the impact of different channels on reported handwashing behavior of women in Ghana. *Health Education Research*, 23(3), 392-401.

Shanks, E., Shea, P. & Cheong, G. (2008). Cuu Long Delta Rural Water Supply and Sanitation Project: Independent completion report. Canberra, Australia: AusAID. Retrieved from http://www.ausaid.gov.au/Publications/Documents/Vietnam-CLDRWSSP-ICR-Apri-2008.pdf.

Winblad, U. & Dudley, E. (1997). Primary school physical environment and health: WHO global school health initiative. Geneva, Switzerland: World Health Organization SIDA.

Chapter 18

Where to from here?

Lessons for sustainable community development

LINDA BRENNAN AND JOHN FIEN

As long ago as 1992, The Rio Declaration outlined some principles for the environment and development. The Rio+20 Summit in 2012 reaffirmed the common vision which was a …

> *commitment to sustainable development and to ensuring the promotion of an economically, socially and environmentally sustainable future for our planet and for present and future generations.*

However, it would appear that, despite 20 years of good will and commitment, the challenge remains for many lesser developed countries; that is, developing the nation at the same time as reducing poverty and conserving the natural resource base upon which all development depends is proving to be an enormous challenge. While this book focuses on Southeast Asia, issues such as climate change, poverty, food, energy and water security are affecting the globe and the lessons from this book may be applicable to other regions. The principles outlined in Agenda 21 at the Rio+20 Summit in 2012 fall into the categories of environmental, economic and social elements; sustainability actions have to combine these dimensions to be truly sustainable.

Potentially the greatest risk faced by Earth in dealing with sustainability is the requirement for global action, when there are inequities in the nation states that make up the globe. The 'tragedy of the commons' still exists and there is as yet no global treaty on many substantive environmental concerns. There have been moves to develop global laws for dealing with environmental issues although with varying levels of success. Attempts at drafting 'universally negotiated agreements' (Agenda 21) tend to fall on the dual complications of having to sacrifice living standards and economic well-being in order to sustain the biosphere. Thus, the three platforms for sustainability are not easily achieved. For example, Australia refused to sign the 1992 Kyoto Protocol until 2007, and its carbon emissions remain high at more than 24 tonnes per person in 2012, despite being one of the first countries to introduce a carbon pricing scheme in June 2012. These would seem to be, on the face of it, contradictory outcomes. However, they illustrate the nature of the complex problem that is sustainability. These complexities are magnified in lesser developed countries where the trade-offs between elements in the model are likely to have greater impacts overall.

Figure 18.1 Dimensions of sustainability

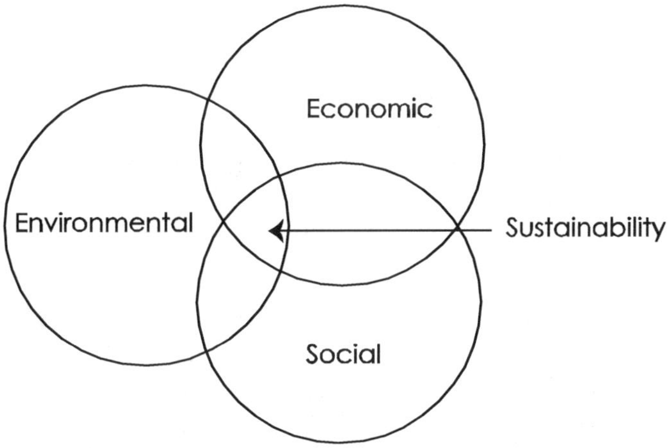

There are some powerful lessons from this book, however. The case studies provide examples of peoples rich in tradition and culture whose material well-being in some cases is 'enough' to be truly sustainable without being excessive. This is not a matter of settling for less, it would appear that some of the case study participants are undertaking a close examination of their material needs in relation to their environment and opting for modest solutions that do not stress the biosphere.

Lesson 1

Do not underestimate the importance of the 'collective' in decision-making

A majority of research in the area of environment is about how individuals respond to environmental issues. However, as these chapters show, collective decision-making is required for sustainability to be achieved. People must be informed, empowered and organised. One person does not make much of a difference but the village and the city together can make serious inroads into solving the problems. Previte (Chapter 10) provides insight into how partnerships can, by their very nature, resolve the intractability problem that exists in many environmental situations. Such coalitions of interests and resources can address problems at a much higher level than individuals or organisations can on their own. An example of this is the establishment of the Greater Mekong Sub-Region, a cooperative network of six countries connected by the Mekong River whose activities are closely intervolved with each other and where there is significant risk to downstream lifestyles as a result of upstream activities such as dams and industrial waste disposal.

Another collective approach that presents itself is the prospect for global information sources to be made available to all and in an accessible form. In the current era data democracy is increasingly possible. However, the ensuring the veracity of the data requires global cooperation beyond that which currently exists. NGOs can collaborate in the development of metrics and monitors that will enable not only researchers but also others, to track progress against some tangible measures. At present there are a number of disparate and contradictory environmental risk measures that are only small fragments of the picture that needs to be told. In addition to data being available for research and benchmarking, veracious public data can also provide motivation for change in macro level practices. When it comes to environmental risk factors, if nations can hide their performance behind inaccurate and unverifiable figures, then there is no incentive to make positive improvements. Shame is a powerful motivator, even for governments.

In addition to these macro level opportunities, there is a strong message about the role of the community and the collective in connection with sustainability. Thus, human beings are at the centre of sustainability issues and harmony with nature is both healthy and productive (Agenda 21). However, many of the cases in this book demonstrate that groups of people can be mobilised and these groups can take specific and constructive action that results in positive outcomes both for the community and the environment. In this way it becomes evident that even community-led micro level actions can result in meso- and macro-level change. Bottomley's chapter (Chapter 15) applied a grass roots, bottom up participatory approach incorporating micro-meso and macro level partners and constituents over many years, resulting in sustainable outcomes for their communities.

Lesson 2

Harmony with the environment is respectful of past and present: The future is a gift from the past

The ancient and often culturally bound traditions included in the pages of this book are indicative of how important 'harmony' is to a healthy environment. Harmony with nature is inextricably wrapped up in the intimate connection of action and outcome. In the communities whose stories are told here, *every* 'thing' matters. Every action from planting crops to hosting visitors in your home has an outcome which is earnestly considered in terms of the health and well-being of earth, nature and humanity; one does not benefit at the expense of the other; all have rights to share in the bounty that is provided.

A long and rich cultural history, duly respectful of the past can appear on the surface to be unchanging and unresponsive to global trends. This can be interpreted as a lack of development; an unwillingness to modernise. However, these chapters show that this is not necessarily the case. The sustainable past has some promising examples to offer the future. Traditional owners know how to work in harmony with their lands and their communities to ensure that nothing is wasted, and further that poverty is lessened in the process. Thus, understanding and extending indigenous knowledges can potentially find new ways forward that others can not.

Importantly, for much of Southeast Asia there is still a way to go in responding to the long lasting, sometimes negative, effects of colonisation. The period of independence seeking and war has left a legacy of damage that will require some generations to fully recover from. There is still much work to be done to find harmonious relationships between the economic, social and environmental dimensions of sustainability. This recent history is more salient than the ancient, indigenous history and some reminders of the value of a more sustainable past may be needed. However, with the race to modernisation, there is a need for balance. As cogently pointed out by Savengseuksa and Perényi and Donovan (Chapters 6 and 2), there is a need to assist with overcoming the disempowerment of the nations that came about as a result of long periods of colonisation and recurrent wars. This will require generational change and a long-term view of the future as indigenous peoples learn to be independent creators of their own solutions.

Lesson 3

Protecting the environment is not serendipitous; it requires active participation and leadership

Fien and Brennan's chapter (see Chapter 1) indicated a series of steps that involved a need to take concrete actions – at all levels – and gave an example of how this was done within the Thailand context. The necessity of taking action that might be useful in turning around the impact of people on the environment and the impact of the changing environment on the people most affected is a key theme of the book overall. Each of the case studies illustrated, to a certain extent, the need to build resilient communities through proactive participation in environmental concerns at a grass roots level. Ahmed and Charlesworth's project (Chapter 14) is an exemplar of how to develop community resilience through building and rebuilding; assisting their communities to be in control of their environment and to tackle the consequences of climate change at a local level.

Importantly these case studies demonstrate that 'someone' has to take the lead and it does not actually matter who it is, as long as the momentum in the right direction is established. Individuals, community, INGO, NGO or government, if someone takes the first necessary step then others will follow if it is the right thing to do. The principle lesson is that initiatives matter and that sometimes these initiatives involve taking risks. Taking leadership in these cases sometimes meant going against accepted wisdom and taking the bold steps that might prove to be 'wrong' – a big risk to take in collectivist traditions. However, despite the risks, starting something new also allowed communities to start afresh and adopt new ways of moving forward that were more inclusive of their needs and wants. A fresh start combined with skills development puts these communities in control of their destiny in very actionable and sustainable ways. That is, doing things; not simply planning them. Ware's Myanmar case study (Chapter 9) is a cogent reminder that people can and will work together given the 'right' circumstances, as this quote from the chapter demonstrates:

> *With minimal government assistance, few civil society organisations beyond religious institutions, and little by way of international assistance, people apparently learned to depend on themselves and one another.*

Wells-Dang and Wells-Dang's case study (Chapter 12) also provides some useful background to how these initiatives can develop into long-term sustainable change. This change is fostered through partnerships that aid communities to do things for themselves and provide the requisite tools for developing environmentally sustainable communities with sufficient well-being in the other dimensions of sustainability. The key lesson from their case is that it is essential to find the 'right' people on the ground to assist and to develop grass roots advocacy that affords respect and dignity to the local community members. Another case that provides insight here is that of Byczek (Chapter 16) who demonstrates that working *within* the local culture is critical to success and that externally applied solutions to environmental solutions are difficult to embed. It is important to start with an understanding of what has already been done and to include elders and community leaders in framing activities if you want them to be sustained over time.

Lesson 4

Mobilise the disempowered to change the world – Women and children first, Gentlemen

It is easy to forget in a debate dominated by politics and science, areas that are indisputably led by men, that women and children have a significant role to play in developing sustainable communities. However, social change starts with the family and women, especially in Southeast Asia, are at the core of 'family' and therefore their respective communities. While the title of this lesson is a somewhat tongue in cheek play on an old metaphor of what should happen in case of a sinking ship, it is also a reminder that the world consists of both sexes and that children are the ones who will be affected by climate change to a greater extent than the 'men' who are at the centre of the debate.

Agenda 21 allocated billions of dollars to the science and technology issues related to climate change and only millions, not even tens of millions, to considering the issues of vulnerable communities and the impact of climate change. The case studies here have clear examples of why more investment in engaging women and children in sustainability issues is likely to result in greater returns. Watne *et al.* (Chapter 4) illustrate that adolescent children are active negotiators with their families and are potential leaders of environmental sustainability at home. Goodwin and Parker's case studies (Chapters 11 and 17) both show the importance of women in leading sustainable development activities. A ripple effect of action starting with the family unit and spreading outward might be a more effective method of embedding sustainability than government led 'top down' directives that have limited capacity to be enforced. It only takes one child, one family and one community to change the future for that community thereafter.

These case studies also show that disadvantaged groups also have a role to play in developing sustainable communities. Indigenous ways of knowing are not all lost (yet); there are communities that still know how to be sustainable. Ethnic minorities across the region are in decline in some ways due to enculturation by their more urbanized neighbors. Some investment in understanding what these communities have to offer before their languages are lost forever is necessary. Alleviating poverty in these groups should not be about forcing them into urbanized areas so that they can be 'looked after'. There is potential for disadvantaged groups to participate in creating sustainable futures for themselves and their communities. Wares' case study (Chapter 9), in particular, is a hope filled example of what can happen when disadvantaged groups are empowered through collective action at a local level.

Lesson 5

Connection to land and spirit is important for people; farmers need support and land security

Agenda 21 stated that a key platform for sustainability was land security for farmers and disadvantaged. The concept is not new news for people engaged in understanding the connection between poverty, sovereign rights to land, and other dimensions of sustainability (see Figure 18.2). However, while there remains a significant degree of angst about what this means for those people and governments currently holding on to vast tracts of land, this goal is unlikely to be achieved in the medium to long term. Notwithstanding the political anxiety surrounding the UN goal, the issue remains that a farmer's connection with the land is deeply spiritual in some regions.

Several case studies pointed out the relationship between farmers' right to use and develop their own resources and successful strategies for building sustainable lifestyles. Wood's case study in Thailand (Chapter 8) indicated that when given the choice, farmers will choose to adopt practices that are both healthier and more sustainable and whereby they benefit not only themselves but the wider society in which they are embedded. Fly and Vu's fishing communities were also exemplars of how such communities, given the tools and techniques required can develop into more modern and sustainable communities at the same time (Chapter 3). However, they also provide a cautionary tale of where these actions can lead to unacceptable burdens of debt and concomitant unsustainable lifestyles. The erosion of indigenous farming communities through externally applied and primarily economic forces is an example of how fragile is the nexus between land use and social and environmental development. Lamballe's case, also set in Vietnam, is another instance of developing sustainable practice against the prevailing political and social pressure (Chapter 7). This case illustrates again that given the opportunity and the tools, sustainable practices are feasible.

These cases also point out the need for provision of support that goes beyond subsidies. Promoting cash crops that are not sustainable only builds dependence and not independence when it comes to financial and social sustainability. Indigenous crops that are less environmentally damaging can be used to create sustainable communities if supply chains and markets can be established and 'marketing' research and education can be provided. Rado's chapter (Chapter 13) is an excellent example of where this has been achieved.

Figure 18.2 Environmental links to poverty

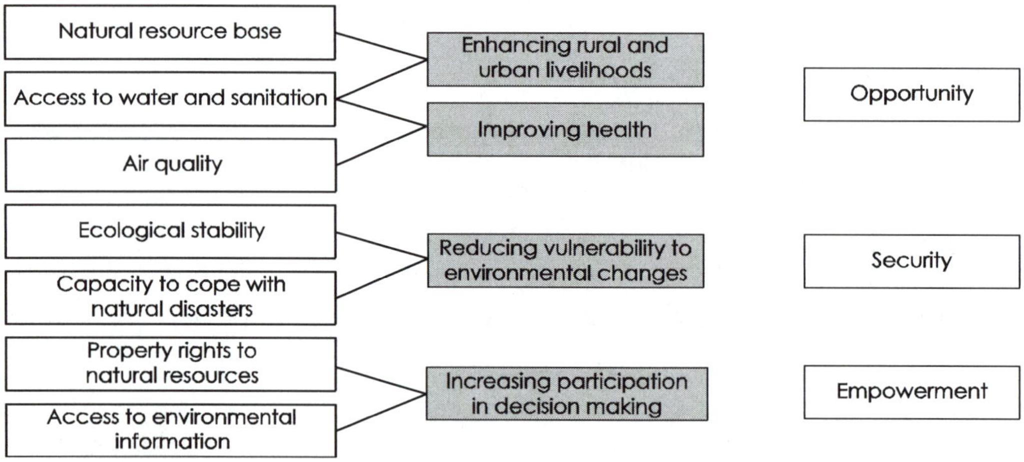

Source: Greater Mekong Sub-Region Atlas of the Environment, *2nd Ed p 66, Asian Development Bank (2012).*

There are also lessons for how a 'fair trade' market orientation can provide added value in agricultural products and lift output from being simply a commodity to being something that is desirable and more sustainable as it is providing farmers with a fair price for the product. Market research combined with cooperation between partners in the supply chain provides more access to markets but also fairly distributes the benefits. In addition, environmentally sustainable agricultural production has provided an increase in health and well-being that comes about as a result of the shift to organic, low chemical interference in production. In these cases, environmental action is also saving money through use and reuse of waste and byproducts. However, how to do these things still requires education into developing sustainable agricultural practice.

Lesson 6

Address the root cause of the issue not its manifestations

As a result of the 'wicked problems' and complex nature of the issues that surround debates about the environment there are many potential solutions that present themselves at any one time. A lesson from this book is that it is important to address the cause not the manifestations of the problem. For example, urban flooding is as a result of rising sea levels. While building new flood-resistant homes is necessary now, some alleviation of the root cause is also needed if the issue is to be dealt with in the longer term. Furthermore, rural and regional flooding is measured in metres, not centimetres, and therefore a greater effort should be placed on ameliorating the effects for those who will suffer the most.

Walsh and Chintratruck's chapter (Chapter 5) makes an important contribution to consideration of water management, marketization and the transboundary challenges that face communities in Southeast Asia. While they demonstrate how difficult it is to get to the root cause of issues that affect many people, they also provide some insight into what is being done to address constituents' concerns while protecting the environment. Some of the tensions described in their chapter are as a result of urbanization and lack of available water sources as a result of economic conditions. In such circumstances, addressing poverty is an important priority. The people most at risk of feeling the effects of climate change are those who are least able to deal with the consequences. Poverty is the root cause of many of the issues described in this book. However as this book also shows, alleviating poverty does not necessarily mean that people become materialistic consumers of modern lifestyles; they can and do seek other outcomes such as health and well-being, better and more comprehensive nutrition, sanitation, improved water and education for their children.

Lesson 7

People are at the nexus of the sustainability 'problem' and the catalyst for the solutions

It should not be a surprise that people are at the nexus of the sustainability 'problem' as it exists today. Importantly, however, they are also the core of the myriad of potential solutions. They are also the catalyst for change. The cases in this book show that it is possible to harness community level expertise and to develop strategies based on people's experiences within their local contexts. A number of chapters showed what is possible when you draw on people's own potential to find solutions to their own problems.

The capacity to generate solutions to micro level problems with meso- and macro-level partners offers genuine promise for the environment. Thus, the co-creation of value by community members, their partners and their wider societies goes beyond concepts of coproduction which have been established as being useful elsewhere. The co-production metaphor is not a useful one here as it includes market based concepts of consumption. That is, something is produced and then subsequently consumed – and therefore is destroyed in the process. The co-creation concept comprises the building of something new and generative, something that adds value to the system, not something which subtracts value. What is valued and valuable is not able to be determined externally to the system which is why it is critical to engage with the communities most affected by the issues. Increasingly citizens are demanding new forms of dialogue with government and policy makers. Participation in decision-making is no longer 'enough' - the need is now for active co-creation in solving the problems faced and jointly producing the delivery of service outcomes. Such co-creation results in more sustainable outcomes by engaging the people at the core of the problem area with the solution, thus building social capital.

The challenges and opportunities presented in this book shift the debate about environmental sustainability away from science and pseudo-science and back to the human factors that are at the core of the situation. This focus on people is likely to lead to better solutions overall, as there is nothing like a little 'personal relevance' to motivate people to change their behaviours more rapidly than they might do if they think it is someone else's problem.

Lesson 8

Cultural context is important when it comes to finding solutions to environmental issues.

Integral to the challenges, opportunities and interventions described in this book is the cultural context in which they occur. It is clear that Western solutions won't solve Eastern problems. 'Cookie cutter' responses and interventions brought in from the West don't take into account the uniqueness and diversity of the region. The recipe for success has been to work with the constituents to develop homemade solutions. That is, working *with* and not *for* the communities in question.

Southeast Asia represents a rich tapestry of cultures, histories and languages and solutions must be adaptive to the context and take into account local variations, both across and within the various countries. While there are eleven nations in the region denominated as Southeast Asia, such regionalization is potentially a matter of modern cartography and there is an overlapping and interchange of cultures and conditions connecting the people throughout the region. However, while closely interconnected, there are still significant differences between the various language groups, sub-cultures and local histories. In addition, throughout the region, there are many traditions that could have a significant role to play in helping us to sustain the environment if a stage for them can be found and an audience gathered who want to learn from other's experiences.

Furthermore, as demonstrated by many in this book, cultural context can be both a barrier and a facilitator for effective strategies for sustainable development. The chapters of this book illustrate the variety of approaches to issues being addressed across the region. They also show how important it is to deeply understand the community in relation to their ethos and belief systems before designing sustainable strategies.

Lesson 9

Persistence is important and we should never give up

The final lesson is a short one. Sometimes it takes a long time to make a difference. In the words of the Dalai Lama:

> *Because we all share this planet earth, we have to learn to live in harmony and peace with each other and with nature. This is not just a dream, but a necessity.*

And:

> *Human use, population, and technology have reached that certain stage where mother Earth no longer accepts our presence with silence.*

So, the lesson is – do not give up. Earth needs your support.

Index

F

G

H

I

J

L

M

N

O

P

R

S

T

U

V

W